Todd,

Give Longe &

Stay in touch!

The Redouins

Oct. 4, 2011

Encinitas, California

7 H.

A PEDOUIN LIFE

A Pedouin Life
Stop and Smell the Artichokes

Bill and Amarins Harrison
with
Cheyenne, Jasmine and Robin

www.Pedouins.org
www.aPedouinLife.com

THE PEDOUINS
FAIRBANKS, ALASKA

Self-published in Fairbanks, Alaska, by The Pedouins.
www.Pedouins.org
www.aPedouinLife.com

ISBN-13: 978-0-98321-040-5
ISBN-10: 0-98321-040-3

Printed in the United States of America

In memory of
Callie Thomas
A true Alaskan

1922 – 2007

We may not make her larger than life, but without her
we might not have found a life larger than we could ever fathom.

CONTENTS

FOREWORD
Emmett Finch, The Malibu Poet

THIS IS AN INCREDIBLE BUT true story that stretches the envelope of our thinking for the courage, daring and fulfillment, of the first family to cross the North American Continent; pedaling on a quint bicycle. Their planning, travels, and moving experiences, during their 13 months of travels for 6,439 miles, reveals so much about themselves, and their amazing, challenging journey. Proving that the seemingly impossible can happen, and the thrill and call of adventure can be answered and fulfilled.

Like the Pioneers who helped build our Nation, so has this lovely family built a legacy for those of us who can share and experience in their adventures and travails. And we can see this great Nation first hand, as they describe it, and the grand people they met along the way. We too can encounter the

Divine Nature and natural beauty of North America, as revealed during this hard to believe journey and adventure.

I highly recommend this true story and account, by a courageous family that fulfilled their dreams, overcoming obstacles and difficulties, having Faith in The Power that makes all things possible.

– EMMETT FINCH, The Malibu Poet

In my 90 years of adventuring, experiencing the incredible, the vast changes and happenings during this time, I am deeply impressed by the accomplishments of the Pedouins: Bill, Amarins, Cheyenne, Jasmine, and Robin. May their successful journey and adventures be a moving inspiration for others in our new and changing future.

PREFACE

LIFE IS FULL OF UNEXPECTED surprises. One such surprise came our way just before San Francisco, California. Fertile fields surrounded us in every direction. Mixed in with a fabulous yellow ground cover of flowers were acres and acres of thistles. Even the girls noticed them. A fellow rider for the day informed us that they were artichokes. We were truly surprised and fascinated to learn that they are in the same family as the thistles that grow in our Kentucky fields. We consider them a weed, but in this form they are a delicacy. We pulled to a stop to experience these plants from up close while perched high atop our five person bicycle.

THE MORE TIMES WE MAKE it around the sun, the coarser life seems to get. We become jaded to life's surprises because we think we have seen it all. It takes the refreshing views of life of a child or a beautiful natural experience to snap us out of these dark recesses of our mind's lies.

THE SURPRISE OF THE ARTICHOKE seemed to capsulate our whole venture from conception to conclusion. Though one cannot truly smell an artichoke's aroma on the plant, we can still smell the California valley's earthy scent that accompanied our first encounter with her prickly leaves and mysterious fruits.

Acknowledgements

Fᴵʀꜱᴛ ᴏꜰ ᴀʟʟ ᴛʜɪꜱ ᴊᴏᴜʀɴᴇʏ would not have happened if it had not been for our three daughters, Cheyenne, Jasmine, and Robin, who all joined in the effort to get ready for it and to travel so bravely across the continent. For their openness to life, their endurance to proceed, and their unconditional love and devotion, we give thanks.

To all of you who shook your heads at our plans, but supported us nonetheless, knowing that our spirit would lead us to where we are today.

To Larry Burdette, whose entrepreneurial spirit went ahead of us across the country via his internet radio and his media contacts, garnering us much attention.

Sᴇᴄᴏɴᴅ, ᴀꜱ ᴛᴏ ᴛʜᴇ ᴡʀɪᴛɪɴɢ of this book, we could not have done it without Kevin McClave, who devoted so much of his free time to help us on the journey of writing. If it had not been for him, we would still be rewriting chapter one.

To Carolyn Webster, for editing and helping us fill in the gaps we left in the text.

To Barbara Prairie and Glenda White, for giving us their time to proofread each chapter.

Tʜɪʀᴅ, ᴛᴏ ᴀʟʟ ᴏꜰ ʏᴏᴜ who generously helped us across the country with your hospitality, love, encouragement, tangible gifts, and friendship. We've done our best to name each and every one of you in the back of the book.

Aɴᴅ ʟᴀꜱᴛ, ʙᴜᴛ ᴅᴇꜰɪɴɪᴛᴇʟʏ ɴᴏᴛ least, to RHT and KONG for lending us the money to pay for the first print of this book.

A Pedouin Life

Stop and Smell the Artichokes

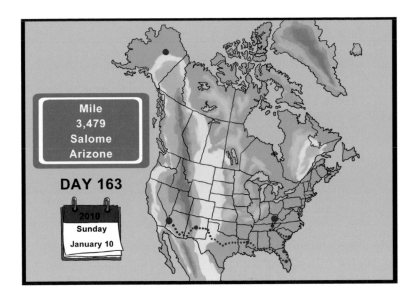

Mile
3,479
Salome
Arizone

DAY 163

2010
Sunday
January 10

CHAPTER 1

THIS MORNING WE LEFT SALOME, Arizona, under a clear blue sky. Our fourteen-foot, five-person bicycle is riding smoother than it has done in a long time. The gears appreciate the desert's low humidity and higher temperatures. They shift smoothly into the higher speeds as we glide over the black asphalt. Our family of five is pedaling strong and in sync. Moments like this when we move like one organism are high points of the journey.

For lunch we stop at a wide spot next to the roadway on the eastbound shoulder. We are in the middle of the desert. There are no trees; only sand and sparsely scattered tumble weed type plants spread out into the horizon. In the distance are the Castle Dome Mountains. Closer, over an old rusted barbed wire fence, are some abandoned farm sites. Cheyenne, Jasmine, and I climb the fence to look for hidden treasures. We hope to find some old western cork type

Robin enjoys the rocks and sand to play with.
January of 2010

bottles or early tin cans at the old house site. Robin enjoys digging holes in the sand for pretend fire pits. Amarins takes this moment to soak up the surroundings with her camera.

THE LONG BREAK OF FOOD, sun, and play does us well. We're ready to hit the road again. I straddle the bike and waddle it to the edge of the road, our traditional starting ritual. I hold the bike and wait as my girls pile on. Amarins makes sure that their feet are secured in the foot cages and that their helmets are on correctly. I watch for traffic, trying to gauge each driver's speed and habits. There is an occasional eighteen wheeler with a string of cars behind it, alternated with a lone car or truck.

When we're all set to go, I spy a semi truck about a mile away, heading toward us from the direction of California. The mid afternoon sun is behind him so I know he can see us if he is alert. The rest of the road is clear. Assuming the truck is going sixty miles per hour, we have one minute to get across the road into our westbound lane. "Plenty of time," I say to myself. Then I call out the cadence: "Three, two, one… Go!" We press down on the left pedal, all at the same time, and ease onto the pavement.

We're halfway across the lane when the rear wheel locks up. I know by the sudden thud and the feel of the bike that it is serious. I holler to Ama, "Hold the bike up!" In an instant, I hop off and see that the chain is locked between the hub and the sprocket. There is no going forward or backward. There is no time to get the girls off or to disconnect our fully loaded trailer.

Our damn bike is stuck halfway across the eastbound lane of state road 72 in western Arizona. The semi truck barrels out of the sun straight for us and is showing no signs of slowing or getting into the westbound lane, which is empty for miles. Silhouetted against the afternoon sun, smoke billowing from its stacks and warped by the atmosphere, the semi looks like some demon come to take us.

My mind flashes to an image of Amarins and the girls in a bloody pile at the side of the road, the bike blown to pieces down the highway. Dad instinct kicks in and I bark at Ama to grab the rear of the bike and pull with all her might. Veins bulging, muscles straining, we drag the five hundred pounds of bike, girls, and gear off the road. We've barely cleared the yellow line when the truck speeds past us like we're not even there. Sand and gravel flick from under its wheels against us, the girls, and Yeller. I notice his California tags as I watch him scream away to the east.

We stand on the sandy roadside, our hearts beating like Masai drums. We try to calm our three girls: Cheyenne (six), Jasmine (four), and Robin (three). They cry and want off the bike "NOW!" Ama and I are upset and yell. It transfers directly to the girls; they reflect our feelings exactly.

We're almost 3,500 miles into our cross country journey from Kentucky to Alaska and this is by far the scariest moment we've experienced. What are we doing here anyway?

As WE REGAIN OUR WITS, my thoughts drift back to the fall of 2008. Back to our fresco yellow house with earth red trim that sits in the woods atop Pongo Ridge in the mountains of Eastern Kentucky. The undergrowth has already turned crimson red. The oaks, hickories, and maples show us their amber, orange, and red colors. Another winter looms. Besides the change of the seasons I sense another change in us.

My Frisian wife, Amarins, and I have felt unsettled lately. Fryslân is one of twelve provinces in the Netherlands. They have their own language and are a very hardy and proud folk, kind of like hillbillies from Kentucky (but without the hills). Amarins likes to say she descends from the Vikings, with the wanderlust and attitude to match.

Amarins has been a sojourner since she left her parental home at nineteen. She was born in the front room of that house, home births in the Netherlands being as common as hospital births in the States. Life there is fairly predictable and planned out from cradle to grave, and Ama is a natural rebel against societal conformity. Her way of living creates its share of problems and concerns for her family. Since she struck out on her own, she has been drifting, in search of a place where it is okay to be different.

In 2001, the wind took Amarins to the Western United States. Inspired by the cowboy novels she read as a child, she finally decided to follow her dream to see what was awaiting her in the Wild West. I'm glad she did, or else we'd never have met at the bottom of the Grand Canyon one afternoon in July of that year. It was there where two drifters, off to see the world on their own, decided to see it all together.

I believe that when I was conceived, I instantly got all of the gypsy blood from my mother's side and the die-hard energy from my dad. I was fourteen when my family disintegrated; I was on my own. These early teen years were a mixture of exhilaration and loneliness—new experiences minus the daily family dysfunctions. I was missing people I could trust and be nurtured by, such as my Grandpa Byers who lived with us. I was his favorite and he lavished me with affirmation and taught me many life lessons. Leaving home at such an early age, my focus was on surviving. It involved a lot of moving around for work and educational opportunities.

It is a struggle for Amarins and I to stay put. We often talked about how two free spirits keep from imploding with the desire to sell everything and head out.

THIS PARTICULAR FALL AFTERNOON IN 2008, our restless souls play off each other. Amarins says, "I am tired of doing the same dishes and sweeping the same floors. It's the same old thing every day. I need a change of scenery."

I respond, "I am sick of earning a living with my back—new jobs but same old boring procedures. It doesn't feel like we're making any progress. What are we aiming for anyway?"

A conversation that is common between any young couple. Where most would leave it at that, our words, once spoken, only agitate our restlessness.

We earn money by working hard, like the vast majority of Americans do, at skilled and semi-skilled jobs. Amarins prepares taxes in a small eastern Kentucky town. She loves the educational part of it. I am self-employed; which is a blessing and a curse. Once I have mastered something, I am ready to move on. Routine kills me. I have two degrees and have mastered spoken Arabic.

At this moment I am an overeducated handyman. To offset the rigors of routine, I find delight in the diverse relationships that are formed with my customers. We choose jobs for what we can learn from it and take pride in doing it well, not for the size of its paycheck. Money is not necessarily the sole motive.

Our ridge top home in Kentucky.
October of 2008

We watch the sun set over our mountain top as it turns the forest and our house a butterscotch gold. We have attained the American dream of home ownership. It's paid for too. We custom built it piece by piece as we could afford it.

In the spring of 2002, we started by putting up a sixteen by ten foot shed with an enclosure for the porch made from recycled glass. A year later Amarins, our (then infant) daughter Cheyenne, and I lived in it for several years without electricity or indoor plumbing. We did without so we could build the house and not have a thirty year mortgage hanging over our heads. My sisters and I laid the floor joists and center beam in pouring rain that same year. Over the following years, friends like Hal and Tonya from South Carolina, Harding and David both from North Carolina, Fletcher from New Mexico, and my brothers from Florida and Illinois would all share in our house raising. In time, Ama and I painted the finished siding one board at a time with a fresco yellow color off the palette of Louisville's Porter Paint company. After six years, with our home complete, what more could a blue collar couple want?

Our house is for pleasure and refuge, a place to return to after a journey. We call it our home. Society says, "A stable place is needed to raise children." But does stable mean a fixed earthly spot? Just over a hundred years ago, families crossed the Rockies in wagons, and Gypsies roamed Romania with their broods.

We've decided that home is where we're all together, surrounded by each other's love, pitfalls, encouragement, and individuality, no matter the type of shelter. As modern people, we have forgotten what it is to wander.

IN THE FINAL MONTHS OF 2008, as our house neared completion, we realize how long we have been fixed to this one piece of earth. Despite all its joys and the satisfaction of land ownership, we feel the need to stretch our legs again. We want to see the world, see what else there is to experience, to travel while we're still young and share these experiences with our girls. Too many people use their children as reasons not to venture out, no matter the journey. We say that our children should be the reason we live a life of abundant experiences rather than hide from them.

That evening, after the girls are in bed, Amarins informs me we are headed to Alaska. After experiencing Kentucky, she is ready to see everything between here and the Last Frontier. I would have been happy with just the lower forty-eight states, but being Frisian, Ama paints with broader strokes. Somehow I missed this one coming.

She tells me, "I want to pack up and explore North America." Cheeks flushed, she adds, "I want to experience Alaska, it sounds so wild and rugged!"

Over the last seven years, I've filled her with stories of the interior and it has only re-birthed the spirit of the girl who read those Western novels so long ago.

I reply under my breath, "I don't mind an adventure, but my gosh, a cross continent one?" I ask her, "How do you plan for us to get there, Mrs. Harrison?"

Hands on hips she goes on, "Billy, we're going by bicycle."

I suppose this is what one should expect of one from the Netherlands. Immediately, my tail end felt sore.

Amarins had scoured the internet and stumbled onto the quint concept; not just a bicycle, but a bicycle built for five.

I begin to protest, asking about the route and costs, but all I get is, "It will work out." Sometimes, as a dutiful husband, one has no choice but to answer, "Yes, ma'am."

OUR HOME SITS IN A chronically depressed part of the country. Change has been slow in Kentucky since Virginia cut us away and we became a state in 1792. I could see the next ten years here rolling by without us being any further ahead. As members of the media wring their hands and look for whom to blame, I recall our ancestors, most with nothing but the possessions on their backs, who left the coastal states for places like Kentucky. They became the buffer between the fat cats of the colonies and the Indians of the western areas. What seemed to some as a raw deal was instead an opportunity. Not all stayed in Kentucky. The likes of Tom Joad are what this country is really about. He piled his family into the jalopy to head for mystical California, with only rumors of work and the promise of new hope echoing in his ear. If we are indeed facing the greatest downturn since *Grapes of Wrath*, why not head out on a journey? Who knows what opportunities might arise?

Over the following months, I thought long and hard about what my wife was proposing. How could we head out with our three girls on a cross continent journey? How could we make it from the top of Pongo Ridge all the way to Fairbanks, Alaska? How would I feed my family without a job? Being dreamers and risk takers, can we step out on faith in humanity's charge and go that far? Can we do this journey for the pure pleasure of it?

The more I think about the idea, the more I like it. There will be advantages to traveling by bicycle. All five of us can share in its workings. The slow pace will enable us to soak up our surroundings and see things you miss when traveling by train, plane, or automobile. We won't even have to buy gasoline.

The angle of (re)discovering America also intrigues me. In a politically divided and depressed economic climate, it is a perfect time for a blue collar family to prove that America is still a place of unbridled optimism and opportunity, without someone telling you what to do and how or why to do it. With the cyclical downturn in full swing and with millions losing their jobs, striking out on such an improbable journey might bring levity to the situation. At the least, we can bring some laughter. At the most, hope—hope that life is bigger and vastly greater than this little blip in American history. This country is still the one place where anyone can think and act without fear of political or social encumbrances. We can still dream dreams and take steps to fulfill them. Well, let's prove the theory!

IN JANUARY OF 2009, WE make the decision. Along our way, we will show our girls the greatness of this country, the beauty of her people, and the vastness of

Robin, Amarins, Cheyenne and Jasmine in the woods behind our home in Kentucky.
October of 2008

our continent as we use our five senses to explore it. We will remind the world and teach our girls that anything is possible.

We'll put ourselves into the flow of great possibilities! They say the definition of insanity is doing the same thing repeatedly but expecting different results. Well, we're no longer doing the insanity plot. We are doing something that has never been done before.

Robin enjoys walking in the rain.
October of 2008

Jasmine loves to help in the kitchen.
December of 2008

Cheyenne, Robin, Jasmine and Bill explore the rocks.
October of 2008

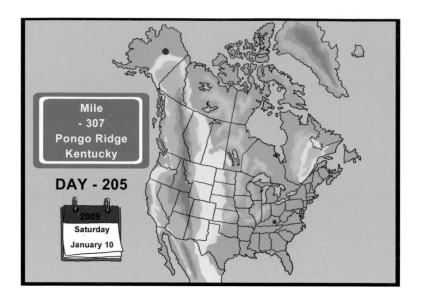

CHAPTER 2

A MARINS' OFFICE IS HER SANCTUARY. Located in the northwest corner of our home, it contains the only interior keyed doorway. Before it was our command and control center for this expedition, it served as her getaway, as any mother can appreciate. One of my duties is to shield this space when she's locked inside her confines.

On the south wall opposite the entryway is her desk, made from a narrow piece of oak veneer plywood. The tools of her trade—maps, calculators, office supplies, and a computer—are waiting. A faint sound of the girls' voices comes from upstairs in the house. It seems to be choreographed with the slight wind that is moving the cold naked trees outside. Leaning against the east wall inside the door, I gaze lazily out the west window. Spindly shadows lie across the mossy covered soil and the neatly stacked piles of seasoned oak, hickory, and maple firewood.

Ama looks up from her desk for a moment, "What's on your mind, Billy?"

I snap out of my dream state, "Tryin' to figure out how all this is going to unfold."

"Come on, I just know it will . . ."

"But . . ."

"It will! Remember when our neighbors said you would not last the winter when you first camped out on this very spot seven years ago?"

"Stayin' here and building the house was the easy part. I know construction. I know nothing about bike riding! We have to leave August first if I heard you correctly?"

"Where is your faith, Bill?"

"Let's leave religion out of this, okay?"

"Okay, but are you with me? On the same page?"

"Babe, I am on board and we'll do our "darndest" to leave in August. I'm just tryin' to piece together how to finish our house, complete all the jobs on Jackson Street in Berea, the tasks at the KOA in Renfro Valley, make plans for our building in Mount Vernon, visit Israel to be with friends from my previous life, see my kids in Bristol, not to mention, get a bike, learn to ride the crazy contraption, get in shape, build a website . . ."

Ama rises from her desk, walks over, and puts her arms around me.

"Hey, it will all work out! Who's your buddy?"

"You are."

"I'll take care of the bike stuff; you just get the customers' work done. Wherever we get our bicycle, it probably won't be ready till spring anyway. I can build a home page and set a detailed route in place."

"Have you thought about the route?" I ask.

"Take a peek at this," she says with a grin.

At her desk, she pulls out a Cracker Barrel map. Open on the desk, I see a yellow highlighted path that curves over the southern portion of the country before it turns west, then north in California, and ends in the northwest where the map ends.

"I thought we were going to Alaska, why are we going south to go north?" *I knew better then to ask her such a question, but I could not resist the fun of it. When it comes to navigation and maps, she is relentless in her precision.*

"I chose the route so we can miss most of the summer heat. If we head north, winter will intersect us in the Colorado Rockies and the higher elevations will be brutal to climb. If we were to leave in May in order to beat cold weather, I don't think we can get all the logistics in place. If we follow this southern route, we can be one step ahead of fall and then winter until we make it to California. We can hang out at Todd's place in San Diego until we're able to follow spring as it moves up the Pacific coastline."

Looking down on the map as her plan ricochets in my head, I am speechless. She and I stand in silence, letting the map's image soak in. To say you're going on a 7,000 mile voyage does not compare with seeing it on paper! Especially when you realize Alaska is not even included on the map.

"Is it too late to back out, Ama?"

"Yep," she says in a mocking sort of way. We both know that what we have set into motion is irreversible.

CHEYENNE CAME INTO THE WORLD in Amarins' third floor apartment in Culemborg, the Netherlands. It was a cold and sunny Dutch winter day in January of 2003. As Amarins pushed, flat dwellers moved around in the fading sun foraging for the evening's meal in stores under her complex.

Cheyenne arrived as bright and vibrant as were Amarins' doorways, all six painted by her own hands of different primary colors and combinations thereof. We bundled her up in the same green and white bunny blanket that once held her mother. With hands trained from three other miracles of birth, I laid Cheyenne in her bassinet. Thinking of this new life and her amazing mom, I knew our incredible journey together was only beginning.

In January of 2005, Jasmine greeted the world on a cold and sunny Kentucky winter day. Experienced now, within minutes of this delightful girl's arrival, Amarins was sitting up and wanted pizza. I ordered pizza and had it delivered to the hospital where we celebrated this momentous occasion, American style. We were eager to head home to show Cheyenne her new sister. The hospital staff agreed to let us leave the next morning. The following night as the sun faded, Ama and I wrapped Jasmine in the bunny blanket and laid her on a homemade soft pallet in our bedroom. The locked, insulated glass door near her provided a wonderful splash of natural lighting and openness for her to bathe in.

Jasmine, Robin (two weeks old) and Cheyenne. November of 2006

Robin came into the world on a warm and sunny fall day in south Florida where I had a teaching position in 2006. As her feet were imprinted on my t-shirt with black ink, as is my tradition, I sensed a rebel spirit in her expressions. With her eyes open from the beginning I could see a spark in them and a smirk draped across her lips. The next evening in our cramped rental quarters, Robin, our "red tail fox squirrel" reminiscent of some squirrels that live in a tree outside our bedroom window in Kentucky, lay between us. The wind blew sounds of the Atlantic Ocean's crashing waves through our open windows and lulled all five of us to sleep.

OUR KENTUCKY HOME IS A beehive of exploration and natural noise. Moving from the sanctum of Ama's office, we head to the play room. The girls have been unaware of our internal struggles and now it's time to share the outcome with the girls.

"Hey girls, get down here!" I holler.

From upstairs in the house, Cheyenne responds, "Why Dad?" Curiosity leading the way, she doesn't wait for an answer.

I hear the footsteps stampede downstairs.

"We'll tell you when you get down here!"

We gather in front of the world map on the wall before Amarins begins. "We are going to take a bicycle journey!" she announces proudly.

Cheyenne asks, "Where to?"

"Alaska. We will ride from our house."

"Can I ride mine and what will Jasmine ride? Her bike is too small for her legs. Can Robin ride too? How long will we be gone?"

"Hold on Cheyenne. I think we are going to get a bicycle with five seats on it so we can all ride together."

"Do they make one that long?"

"Your mom has been looking online for a bike that will fit all of us," I add.

Speaking up, Jasmine asks, "Where is Alaska?"

Amarins is standing next to the map and points out where it is.

Cheyenne says, "Yes, I remember where that's at, I saw it in a National Geographic on the shelf over there. They have polar bears!"

Jasmine looks at me with a bit of fright on her face, "Will they get us?"

Robin tries to figure out what is going on. She hears bears and doesn't like it, so I reply, "No, Jasmine, we are not going that far into Alaska. We will not be seeing any polar bears in the wild."

"Your dad and I think we will be gone for about two years. We will camp and stay with friends we have in Florida and California. We will probably stay with other people we meet along the way as well."

Cheyenne's eyes narrow, as she often does when her ever-expanding brain is churning, "Are we going to see Hal and Tonya?"

Amarins traces a route with her finger, "As you can see, we are going through South Carolina and we will try to stop by."

"We could sleep in his boy's room again!"

"Listen, we cannot make any promises. Mostly, we will be on our own and enjoy seeing America. Can we do this?"

In unison they let out a primal shriek, "Yeaaaaah," as little girls do. Once my hearing returns, we hug and bask in this moment of joyous expectation.

By mid-January, we are on our way to Kansas City, Kansas. It's a marathon of miles and rolling landscapes in our gray Toyota Previa to check out a quint Amarins found on the internet. I was not willing to borrow and then hand over fifteen thousand dollars until I touched one. Like doubting Thomas was to Jesus' scars, I wanted to touch the tandem's steel frame to abate my mind's ramblings that "the picture of the bike on the internet is a fake!"

As we pull up to a house in a typical suburban neighborhood, we see it leaning next to a full-size mid-eighties Ford van. It appears longer than the van. So long that it scares me a little bit and I'm ready to head home. Amarins, though, is grinning from ear to ear. A smile that would drive any man wild, but I am the lucky one.

Ama, the kids, and I anxiously get out of the van and stand around the massive contraption. Mark, the owner who is also the bike company's representative, comes out, and we exchange the usual greetings. Close up to the bike, my mind starts spinning. A can-do attitude about this 14.5 feet of bicycle sitting atop two wheels replaces my initial nervousness. How is it possible to turn it, hold it up, or even mount the beast? These are all questions that need solutions. Overcoming challenges is my forte and I begin to warm up to this kind of vehicle. Asking him questions about the bike's durability and if there is some kind of trailer we can pull our belongings with, he offers very little in the way of answers. Shrugging off the vague answers, we push the bike around the cul-de-sac with the girls sitting on it (holding on for dear life). Mark tells us about the cross Kansas trips he has taken on it. It seems that they use sag wagons to haul the tandem riders' overnight gear. A vehicle following us is not a luxury we've planned for. He is not sure what we can use to haul our clothes, sleeping gear, and food. I start to wonder if we are doing something that has not been tried before with such a large bike. Puzzled, I ask him, "Will a bike like this endure the kind of ride we are considering?"

"Yes, it will," he answers matter of factly.

The dream is dreamed. While the girls play with various toys in his yard, Amarins and I walk to the side.

"What do you think?" she asks.

"I like the bike. It looks and feels strong. It seems to hold up on cross state traveling. Flat terrain, that is!" I catch my breath before I add, "Ama, this is a lot of money; there ain't no turning back once we hand him our dough!"

"Let's do it!"

"Alright, write the check for the down payment then."

I can see Amarins' hand trembling slightly as she writes out "five thousand dollars" for the down payment. What I see in Amarins' trembling I feel in my tightening of the gut, once the signature is on the check.

Less than an hour after we arrived, we're heading home. Not much is said at first. Amarins squeezes my hand while I move the van through traffic. I glance at her and see a very familiar smirk on her face, one that clearly states that she's very happy with herself. Adventure is in the making.

Mark will call us for measurements so a new quint can be custom built to fit us. We are looking at June as a possible delivery date.

THE PHONE RINGS ON MAY first. It is a beautiful warm day. The redbuds fill the woods with dark lavender hues. The dogwoods are beginning to bloom with white flowers and occasional pink ones.

"Hello?"

"This is SAIA trucking company. We have a shipment for the Harrisons. Are you Mr. Harrison?"

"Yes, I am," I confirm.

"Our driver just called and said he is headed up highway 1249, can you meet him at your mailbox?" the lady on the other side of the line continues.

"Yes, I will head out there now."

"Our driver says the road is pretty windy. Do big trucks travel your road?"

"They do. In fact, Cromer Trucking is our neighbor and his trucks come up here all the time. He'll be fine. Thanks for calling."

I head outside to find Amarins on our white oak porch. "Hey Babe, our bike is on its way."

Knowing he has to come up Smith Hill, we hang out in the yard that is positioned on the point of a ridge until we hear a truck engine strain in the distance. That must be the one we're waiting for. We pile in our pickup truck and head down our 1,200 foot gravel drive that once was a wagon road. It ends at our mailbox on the main road. At the time we get there, so does the truck.

Amarins and the girls sit in a grassy field behind our mailbox just beyond an electric fence that keeps the neighbor's horses in. They have a bird's eye view of the unloading. The truck driver verifies that I am Mr. Harrison before he throws the rear trailer door open. The inside is empty but for three large thin rectangular boxes.

The girls are wild with excitement. I reverse the pickup so the tailgate is up against the opening of the tractor trailer. In minutes we have the bed of the pickup filled with the boxes. That was easy. Once again we pile in to head back to the house.

It isn't long after we put the boxes on the porch before they're open. Saddles, saddle posts, handle bars, wheels, and three strong looking, bright yellow pieces of frame. The girls are most excited by the plastic water bottles that came rolling out.

My hands are itching to put this puzzle together. The yellow pieces of frame are simple to attach to each other. There is a front, center and back piece. Each connects to the other with three stainless

The arrival of the quint.
May of 2009

steel couplers. The way it is set up we can actually make the bicycle into a tandem, a triplet, a quad or a quint. Adding the wheels, saddles and handle bars is a piece of cake. Connecting the brake and shifter cables doesn't cause troubles either. Before our eyes the quint is materializing.

In the evening I make the first solo run on our newly assembled bicycle. Like a wobbly colt trying to rise for the first time, I weave and bounce down the gravel driveway. With Amarins and the girls in my wake I turn left onto the asphalt. The smooth surface enables me to travel with less zigzagging. This first half mile is fantastic. Despite the wobbliness caused by the quint's length, it handles amazingly well.

Before the road drops down the ridge, I make a big U-turn. I need the entire two lane road to do so, but I manage. It's an exhilarating experience. The girls and Ama are cheering me on. Filled with pride at this big step we've taken, I pull up to the end of our drive, coast down our grassy yard and park the quint against the white oak porch of the house.

Cheyenne is begging to ride, "Dad, can you take me?"

"Not today," I reply.

"Why not?" she wonders.

"Well, we don't have helmets yet. Second, I want to ride it more so I am comfortable with our yellow beast before adding you kids. Besides, you are going to be the first one to ride with me. Can you wait that long?"

"I guess, but it's hard, I want to ride!"

"Just remember, we are going to be on this thing for over a year, you will get plenty of riding time!"

Ama moseys over and grabs the rear end of the quint. Together we lift it onto the porch so it is out of any wet weather that might come while I am gone for the next ten days. I give the girls a stern warning not to mess with it unless we are with them. I say, "This thing weighs about one hundred pounds, and it will crush you if it falls on one of you." Their curiosity is somewhat diminished by this fact. Taking advantage of the setting sun, we herd the girls inside, leaving Yeller to herself.

As THE WEEKS ROLL BY, we become more and more comfortable with our quint. By late June, the rest of the Pedouin clan is riding behind me.

After riding the same ten mile loop for several weeks, we decide to spice it up. Ama and I are tired of hearing that the girls are bored with the same road. Instead of taking our normal training loop, I follow our highway to the right off the ridge instead of turning onto the gently rolling Cleftrock Road. Immediately the girls go nuts with a buzz of questions.

"Why are we going this way?"

"Dad, you missed the road!"

"Where are we going?"

We live on top of a ridge, so the only way we can go is down, in any direction. For two miles we go down. We accelerate without pedaling. Gravity is on our side. Our clothes wave in the wind. Except for the sound of the wind in our ears, we hear nothing. Our digital speedometer registers 41.5 miles per hour. It is incredible. It took us less then five minutes to go two miles. Our record speed ends at the bottom of the hill as we roll past Buffalo Baptist Church sitting on a creek bank to our right.

Now, we have to get back up the mountain. That is a different story. Pedal, pedal, pedal . . . We are going 3.4 miles per hour and it's a long way up. Our new pace feels like standing still after flying down the mountain. The girls ask if we're still moving.

It's time for a break when we get to the first flat spot.

The girls are not out of breath at all. They get off the bicycle and run around in a beautiful field full of round bales of hay. It takes a good five minutes for Amarins and me to get our breath back.

On the bicycle again, we are in the lowest possible gear, gear number twenty-seven. Around and around we spin. It is slow going but we're keeping it moving. The end of the hill is in sight, but I am dying. We're at the steepest portion of this intense hill. We come to a stop to rest up for the last part. We did this many times on our ten mile training loop, but this incline is five times steeper than anything we have climbed before. Jasmine screams a scared cry. The bicycle is leaning too much for her liking. She does not like stopping, especially on a hill as steep as this one. While we rest, Amarins walks over to hug and comfort her.

Sweat drips down my nose. My shirt is totally soaked. Amarins thinks we need to push it up the last part of the hill that includes a sharp left onto a side road that will take us home again. There is a rise at this transition that might be a challenge for our long bike. I am curious if our middle pedals will drag on the asphalt when we turn left. I convince Ama to hop back on.

To start with momentum we put the left pedal up. On the count of three, we push down at the same time. I lift up my right foot and take a stab at the right pedal in motion. Bracing for a fall, I hold my breath. But, it works. We actually start from a dead standstill and move 750 pounds of bike, humans, and trailer, full of water jugs, up a wicked hill. As we return to the house, something clicks inside my head and I realize, "We can do this!"

All aboard on our training route: Captain Bill with stokers
Jasmine, Robin, Amarins (taking picture) and Cheyenne.
June of 2009

With the down and uphill victory fresh in our minds, we decide to give ourselves our first real test: the Fourth of July celebration in Renfro Valley. Early in the morning I fine tune the gears because over the last several weeks, shifting has become troublesome. Instead of making it shift better, it actually gets worse. In the first few miles of the ride to Mount Vernon, I keep readjusting the derailleur until the shifting improves. The chain still comes off three times during this process of adjustment.

Days earlier, I told Marty, the owner of the KOA, that we would be at his booth at the fairgrounds around two o'clock. I feel the strain of this decision on our ride today. Pedaling on, it starts to rain and we didn't pack any rain gear. We ride on pretending that it isn't happening and I feel fortunate, because it tapers off.

Ten miles into the ride we take a long break at the side of the road. Since it is narrow and winding, the girls stay on the bike where we have a great view of our local wet weather spring in which the spring's water appears to be bubbling out of the rocks. Holding Yeller, I catch my breath. I never realized how many hills there are between our home and Mount Vernon.

Carrying about 750 pounds, we give it our best to traverse the scores of hills in one haul without stopping. At the point that my heart is about to jump out of my chest, I stop and we take a couple of minutes to catch a breath. The steering, shifting and braking is all in my hands. The pedaling we all do together. It is in my hands to choose when to take a break. I know that Amarins will speak up when she needs me to stop.

Then we start again. All the climbing during our training has improved our ability to tackle hills with efficiency. We've come up with a system of commands so that everyone knows what is going to happen next. "Three, two, one... Go!" is the command we use to get the bicycle rolling again.

In exactly 15.4 miles and a bit over two hours, we make our grand entrance at the Blast in the Valley event. I make a beautiful turn around the KOA booth, but I do not see a hidden groundhog hole. Our front wheel drops in the hole and all five of us tumble over! A crowd of onlookers stares in disbelief. We look like a turtle on its back.

Ama and I hop up and untangle Cheyenne and Jasmine from their foot cages, push the quint back up, and get Robin out of her seat. We are all fine but a little startled from the experience.

We receive a lot of strange looks. Yeller is a total aberration to folks at this event. Even so, her uniqueness stirs up conversations. All manner of questions arise and we take the opportunity to share about our journey. In our minds, the more people who know about it, the more they will keep an eye out for us on the road. We hope this will result in a safer ride. It is also our goal to encourage others. We want to challenge folks to work toward their own dreams, to think outside the box. Maybe we will even inspire people to throw out the box and do something new.

Throw away a box we did. In all the preparation leading up to our August one start date, we were bombarded with one basic question, "How will you pay for this endeavor?" This is becoming a theme question as people respond to our story. Our only answer was, "We do not know."

We leave in less than a month with little cash on hand but a heart filled with faith. We are just blue collar mountain folks heading out with a dream in our souls and the Universe as our support.

We decided against the non-profit route. With so many people saving the world in a myriad of ways, it seems crowded around that trough. We don't want the government entanglements that come with this path either. In keeping with past American dreamers, we don't think it is necessary to justify our chance to live one of our dreams by cloaking it in a *not for profit cause.* American history demonstrates that humanitarianism has generously grown out of her people's financial successes.

If people want to support us, they will, not because we beg for it, but because they believe our dream is worthy of their support. We will provide visual stimulation and mental inspiration as we jump off the cliff called risk. Whether the outcome of this fantastic voyage is success or failure, at least the choice is ours to make.

Still, embracing this adventure from the support angle is not easy for us.

I grew up in a home that preached and lived its sermons of self reliance. From the time we could work, my eight siblings and I were groomed for labor and its rewards. My problem is the ingrained idea that earning a living involves the sweat of my brow and most often is void of pleasure. I have sweated many years.

Amarins grew up observing her parents. They are inventive folks who understood that if you want something different you have to fight for it;

whether it is to build a boat from ferro cement or to build a business based on one's expertise. They knew that if you don't have the knowledge to fulfill your goals there is no reason not to find out what you need to know.

Our journey involves faith, art, and pleasure with traditional blue collar values. It will surely throw unexpected surprises on our path. But with our combined upbringing of self reliance and inventiveness, it will enable us to pass a unique experience on to our girls.

Our first encounter with a quint.
January of 2009

Adam has designed part of our logo.
February of 2009

Robin observes our shadow.
July of 2009

Cheyenne, JonJon, Nathan, Robin, Erika
and Jasmine on a spring hike.
April of 2009

Barbara and Glenda are on the
journey with us.
July of 2009

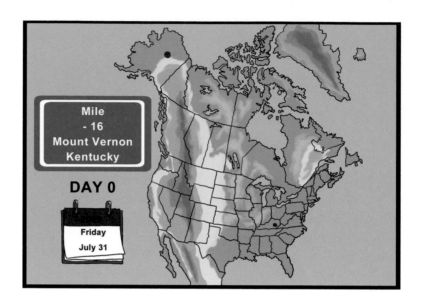

Mile
- 16
Mount Vernon
Kentucky

DAY 0

Friday
July 31

CHAPTER 3

IT IS THE DAY BEFORE D-day. We leave our home to head for the KOA campground in Renfro Valley, Kentucky. We will camp there tonight. The training is over. The fruit trees that will greet our return are planted. Tanner, who will house sit for us, begins to move in today. We lock the front door to our yellow house, and we breathe a long sigh of relief. The wait is over. The journey begins. Ama and I hug before we step off the porch. It's reality now.

The girls surround the quint in the gravel driveway and carry on like jumping beans. For seven months we've told them that we'll be leaving on our journey before they know it. The moment is upon us.

On this muggy, cloudy, final day of July we are ready to roll. The twelve one-gallon jugs of water that we've lugged around in the trailer for training purposes are replaced with actual survival gear.

The Burley Nomad, our two-wheel enclosed trailer made with two compartments and an aluminum rack on top, looks like a dirty clothes basket piled high and about to spill over. It is filled to bursting.

We have five cinch bags the size of footballs once they are closed and compressed, each with a different person's clothes in the rear compartment of the trailer. Each bag has several pairs of underwear, socks, one extra pair of pants, shorts, and two shirts. It is our plan to change out the undergarments and hand wash or find a laundromat when possible. Also, in the back are two stuffed animals—Cheyenne's Dogge, which she's had since she was one, and Jasmine's year old purple kitty cat. Robin's Binkies, small square rags with an animal head in the center of each one, are pinned to her seat so she can have them whenever she needs to. We've learned to pin them to her seat, otherwise they'll keep falling off. In the front compartment are wipes and diapers, toiletries, a first aid kit, metal eating utensils, and neon color bowls and cups from IKEA.

On top of the trailer we have more gear. On it we have bungeed three weatherproof bags; one with the REI Kingdom 6 Tent, one with our sleeping mats and the last one with down sleeping bags and our Indian blanket. I picked up the Indian blanket on my 2001 trip from Alaska and pack it here as a talisman ensuring our safe passage back to the Last Frontier.

We chose the six person tent because it is going to be our home for the next year. Like the Bedouin canvas and woolen tent design, we too have a room divider. The desire for separate compartments is not based on seventh century Islamic Law but rather on the need to have some parental privacy. If we're stuck in one place for days under a spell of bad weather, we're going to need not only the extra space, but also the option to separate the adults from the children. The next step down would be a four person tent, and that would be too small. We learned from our camping experiences, that when the package says a tent is built for four, what they really mean is four kids or four half starved adults. The added weight will be a small price for the added space.

On top of these three bags are two of the most important items, one cultural—an old 10-inch porcelain, gray wash pan; and one vital—a new white plastic kid's potty for the girls. The wash pan is a piece I picked up on a junket of mine along the New River flowing between the North Carolina and Virginia state lines back in the late eighties. I still remember seeing Amarins wash Cheyenne in it while the pan sat on an old piece of rough sawn white cedar plank that had hundred year old musket balls imbedded in its grain, while we lived in our shed on Pongo Ridge. It has a ton of character and deep sentimental value.

I have always enjoyed antiques. Some of my best memories as a boy are of picking through old barns or digging under old outhouses and coal piles for treasures such as old soft drink bottles, cork top medicine bottles, and earthen crocks. I bring the wash pan along in celebration of my boyhood and for my Grandpa Byers' sake. He raised me and his input still bears fruit. Somehow, the gray wash pan reminds me of him or some part of his nature in a way that comforts me as I head into uncharted territory with my family. Just as the porcelain wash pan has endured years of use and survived, so has he. He was always there for me. In this porcelain pan I wash my hands and in Grandpa Byers I washed my soul. I can't wait to arrive in Malibu wearing my Red Wing work boots with the wash pan sitting atop the trailer.

A selection of tools necessary for any breakdown sits atop the bike rack positioned over the rear wheel. It is a five by twelve inch black aluminum shelf of sorts.

Tucked into two panniers there is an assortment of food to fuel our start; granola bars, Rice-a-Roni packages, bread, a block of cheese, and a bag of Jolly Ranchers. We give Jolly Ranchers to the girls at the start of a tall climb.

Jasmine and Cheyenne make sure the water bottles are filled.
July of 2009

Ama and I need their silence so we can focus on pedaling our way up a hill. As any parent will attest, snacks are key to a peaceful motor journey... doubly so when the journey is self-propelled.

Our quint Yeller leans against a telescoping walking stick I bought at Wal-Mart. She has no kick stand so I had to improvise before the journey even started. At about nine-thirty, I lift the tongue of the trailer and hitch it to the bike. It is so heavy it almost gives me a hernia.

My brother Eddie and a friend drove from Illinois to see us off. They are on their lightweight racing bikes and will ride with us this day. In the yard I see Eddie sitting on his bike next to ours. I stroll over and we talk.

"Eddie, we are going to be very slow, so don't count on getting to town too fast."

He nods and says, "I am well aware of the fact."

I have my doubts. The Harrisons are known to be lightning fast at getting jobs done. Whether rebuilding carburetors, pouring concrete, or delivering newspapers, "Get-r-done and fast" was our unspoken motto. As he circles us like a vulture zeroing in on road kill, I know he is raring to go.

Even so, he offers moral support for our ride to town. I let the matter of an overweight trailer pass for now. We've started this trip, in part, to see how little we need to live, not how much. For now, these are the items we think we need. Our travels will be the judge. Perhaps our load will lighten as we go.

THE MOMENT ARRIVES. We gather around the bicycle and start the launch procedures. This is the real deal. I feel like I'm going to puke. I'm no stranger to adventure and stress, but this moment is tough. As I mount the captain position on the quint, the weight of the venture crushes me. We're about to embark on an experience that's never been tried before with 7,000 miles of road ahead.

One by one, Ama hoists each of our daughters on. Cheyenne and Jasmine each have their own purse on the handle bar tube in front of them. The purses hold little trinkets and space for treasures they'll find as we float along the highways and byways of this vast continent. Their current treasures are change, pencils, and some candy.

Robin doesn't have a purse. She's too small to need one and her seat is totally different from her older sisters'. Robin's seat is like a car seat, but then for on a bicycle. She has a five-point buckle to keep her in her seat as well as leg rests to support her legs. In front of her is a head rest. Since Robin doesn't have any handlebars, she doesn't have the space to hang a purse.

As the secretary and historian of this expedition, Amarins has a purse too. She has the real power—the money, the map and a phone. We found a map in the Cracker Barrel of London, Kentucky. All their restaurants along our route are marked. We love to visit this restaurant for its family friendly atmosphere, mountain like décor, and for plenty of home cooked grub. The phone is a gift from my sister Beth. It is an important connection between us. When Ama and I traveled through the Western United States in my red, 1987 plain jane Toyota pickup truck during the summer of 2001, I called my sister often to give her updates on our adventures and whereabouts. This journey we'll do the same.

The girls laugh when they see that I also have a purse. Mine is exactly like the others and we just can't come up with a better name for it. My purse provides easy access to small tools for simple repairs. A Payday candy bar lies on top as a source of quick energy.

So THERE WE ARE: the girls are on their mounts, the trailer is hitched, and we are good to go. The bicycle jostles from side to side as the girls teeter back and forth in expectation of blast off. The excitement hits me too. Amarins walks over to me. There is no need to speak. We put our foreheads together and give a last kiss in our front yard to signal a goodbye to what we leave and a welcome to what awaits us. Then she too climbs aboard.

"Three, two, one… Go!" We press the left pedal and off we ride.

WE CAREFULLY MANEUVER OUR GRAVEL driveway to the pavement. The neighbors watch from their porches and yards as we pass through our domain. I can only imagine what runs through their minds. For months, we've been the gossip of Pongo Ridge and Mount Vernon. Rumors that there are bets we won't make it to the town of Jellico, sixty miles to the south on the Tennessee and Kentucky border, and that we will return in a few short days.

We coast down the first hill. The air is not only thick from July heat and humidity, but from the weight of our expectations as well. Before long, we coast down Smith Hill. I feel some sorrow when we round the right hand curve at William McClure's home. He recently passed away and is quite famous in our part of the world. William was a true mountain man who raised twelve kids in and around his holler. He taught me to rive shingles. William traveled the world as an ambassador of Kentucky Mountain Crafts and Lore. His work is displayed in the Smithsonian in Washington DC, a claim most folks can't make but one of which William would never brag. I wonder when I'll see this home again. My emotions move like the bike, up and down with the rise and fall of these hills.

Behind me the jostling has stopped and only the voices of my girls remain. I can hear their excitement about camping at the KOA. They are looking forward to swimming and enjoying the new playground.

After a round of curves we hit our first real climb. I start to shift, but Yeller's rear derailleur is acting crazy, not letting the chain shift properly. Last night I decided to tweak the shifting mechanism, but today it doesn't pan out as I thought it would. I've worked on it several times over the past months. I even had a bicycle mechanic look at it. I just can't wrap my head around what's going wrong. We would have never imagined that we'd make our first repair stop within three miles of home.

Following us since we hit asphalt are Bob and Jane Larkey in their Yukon. In their early 70s, our neighbors offered to ride behind us on our way into town. This stretch of road is narrow and windy, and they felt better knowing they could act as a buffer between us and traffic. We are delighted to have them as our "guardian angels" today. More than this, they have been friends of mine since 1995, when they were directors of a rural retreat not far from where we are pedaling. At the end of the previous century I made some tough decisions, a divorce being one of them, as well as a change in vocation. Many of my previous friends and associates had a hard time accepting the former. Being raised Catholic, divorce was a no-no. My choice to leave my first marriage earned me the "going to hell" label. But Bob and Jane Larkey remained friends. To get my feet back on the ground, they rented me an acre of land with an option to buy. Amarins and I eventually bought it and built our home on it.

WE CREST THE HILL AT the turnoff for High Dry Cemetery when I see what looks like a huge raccoon carcass in our lane. It's too late to swerve around it.

The quint clears the carcass, but the trailer latches on and we drag it for several yards before we come to a halt.

"Hey! No passengers allowed." I shout. I tell the girls what we've hit. They all break out in loud laughter and then start to gag when it finally settles into their heads.

Cheyenne sits on the last seat of the quint and can see the carcass beyond the trailer, "Dad, it's not a raccoon, it's an opossum!"

I see that Eddie stopped up ahead, and turned around to roll back toward us. "What's up brother?" he asks.

"You ain't gonna believe it, but we hit that dead opossum that was back there!"

"You dummy, why'd you do that?"

I hold the bike steady and it's up to Amarins to evaluate the situation. She tells us, "We hit it dead on and the guts are stuck to the front of the trailer with a blood trail down the road. It's nasty!" Ama grabs our baby wipes and cleans opossum parts from everything as well as she can.

Six miles from home and the second crisis is solved, bike repairs and gutsy cargo. What next? I joke to Ama, "Maybe we can make you an opossum hat from it." Having had cleanup duty, she does not find it funny.

IT BECOMES APPARENT THAT WE'RE chugging as we pedal, even on level ground, like walking in a wet peat bog. Amarins and I tried to anticipate the weight of the gear we could efficiently pull. We're dying as we near the climb that leads to the top of the mountain before the drop into Mount Vernon. All food and water seem to evaporate from our bodies. Every fifty feet we stop to catch our breath and let our leg muscles calm down. While regrouping, my brother rides past us several times, and I interpret the motion as, "There is no way they are going to make it to Renfro Valley, let alone Alaska!"

We finally work our way to the top of the hill. A long break is in order. We feast on the cheese, bread and granola bars. By this time, Eddie decides the show is over. He needs to head to Louisville and is running out of time. We say our goodbyes and they go on.

Energized from the rest and snacks, we descend into town. If the uphills are arduous and exhausting, the downhills are a symphony from heaven. We go like an Olympic bobsled. I hold the brakes as tight as I can, and the girls squeal and laugh all the way down.

Some weeks earlier, the Mount Vernon Signal, our local newspaper, did a story on our upcoming adventure. Today, the locals watch it unfold. Mountain folks throw a wave in our direction. This is our town and our starting point, and we all feel proud.

By late afternoon we fly south on the long grade of North US-25 that will take us under interstate 75. The interstate replaced highway 25 much the way interstate 40 rendered highway 66 obsolete. Hundreds of times I have traveled this I-75 corridor, connecting the Upper Peninsula of Michigan all the way south to Naples, Florida. Either it was going north to work in Berea, Kentucky, or heading south to see my children from my previous marriage: Sara, Adam, and Jesse in Bristol, Tennessee.

Just a few days earlier, the whole Pedouin clan was in Tennessee for the birth of my second grandchild, Lindsay. Adam, who was about to head off to college and my younger son, Jesse, were around for this special occasion.

In between the joyful chatter of the recent birth and our impending journey Adam says, "Nothing you do surprises me, Dad."

"What? Why do you think that?"

"You are always doing crazy stuff. You're turning into a hippie!"

"You know better than that—it's a bike ride, not a rolling commune, Adam. Besides, you know I ain't just wandering off without a purpose!"

"So, what's all this about?"

"As I have said before, we want to share this great country with the girls and put ourselves in

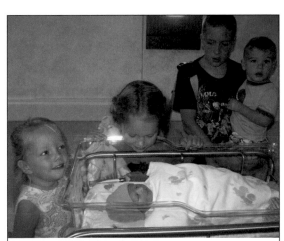

Jasmine, Cheyenne, Jesse and Christopher surround
the new arrival, Lindsay.
July of 2009

a different flow of opportunities before we are legislated to death."

"That's something I can agree with. Still, it is not something I would do."

Shrugging my shoulders, we agree to disagree.

After my divorce, I did not think I would marry again. When I met Amarins in the bottom of the Grand Canyon, an awesome thing happened. I got a second chance. In the process I fell into the lap of intimacy for the first time in my adult life. Today is but one expression of that intimacy.

Still, there are my kids that pre-date Amarins. For a second time, I am leaving them. The first time was a horrendous departure that remains seared in my mind. Over the years, each of them has forgiven me in their own special way and those cauterizations have healed some.

Riding today, especially under this I-75 overpass, Sara, Adam, and Jesse are with me just as sure as if they sat behind me.

RENFRO VALLEY IS ON THE east side of the interstate. It has its own post office, but if you're not aware of it you'd think you're still in Mount Vernon. Renfro is

The final ascent of the day.
July of 2009

famous for being the cradle of early country music before Nashville became what it is today. The barn dances and music were famous in the Valley. There still is the Big Barn and music, but they are only a whisper of their former glory. The old folks here, like in many places, miss the old days.

Another mile and a half and we're at the entrance to the KOA. Perhaps the biggest challenge of the day greets us—the steep ride up to the campgrounds. Emotionally and physically, we are worn out; our bodies not yet acclimated to the punishments of biking distances that a lot of folks do commuting to work. We decide to push Yeller up the hill even though our egos want us to pedal the whole thing. Ama helps the girls off and they cheerfully run up the one-way road. They know the campground well from visiting me often while I worked on the men's bathroom last winter.

MARTY COMES OUT OF HIS office to greet us as we arrive. He is a round, happy Jewish man from the Northeast. He and his broad smile found this place as a business venture and fell in love with the South and its people, an unlikely marriage. We became acquainted with each other over some small jobs I performed on the campground. He became enamored with our journey before most people knew what we were planning. Understanding tzedakah (Hebrew for grace in action, i.e. acts of kindness), he supplied the funds for our trailer. Because of his energy, Marty's friends from New Jersey to Florida are hearing about our journey.

He leads us into a prime spot for the evening. The whole campground is full of hickories, oaks, maples, and ornamental pear trees on a rolling hillside. We are near the playground, pool, and the restrooms, all great features for children. It also saves the host a ton of work guiding visitors to our spot since most vehicles have to go by us to check in at the office.

We catch our breath while eating some Wendy's burgers brought by the Larkeys. This is where we say our goodbyes to them, as we will do so often with friends, old and new, in the months to come. We note that saying goodbyes is going to be a difficult leg of the journey. We wish each other safety, health, and blessings.

Refueled, it's time to set up camp. We put the tent up once before and it proved fairly simple and straightforward. Soon, the colorful REI Kingdom 6 is up, sleeping mats are inflated and sleeping bags are inside. With all the immediate items inside the tent we turn to the trailer. What can we leave and what do we truly need?

In a flurry of movement, novels, silverware, tools, deodorant, tires, a Jewish Bible, small play toys, and some clothing get stuffed into two black bags. In a short ten minutes, it's over. We probably lost twenty pounds.

We feel akin to the pioneers depicted in old western movies. As they headed over the Rockies to their promised land by wagons, mules, horses, and by foot, they often chucked books, pianos, rocking chairs, and the like if the load became too much. All of a sudden, necessary items are not so necessary anymore.

One of the things we keep is Stephen E. Ambrose's book *Undaunted Courage.* Cheyenne, Jasmine and Robin all cut their first teeth while listening to its stories. They're on the verge of experiencing similar events they have heard about, like camping under the stars, pulling together as a team to finish the journey, or meeting new people that will be different from them.

The girls enjoy the playground with their cousin Zac, and his dad, Bob Barnes, who is married to my oldest sibling, Gale. By this time the summer evening is filled with sun and conversations about our journey. Figuring that a lot of people will be milling around our bike, I lean it up against a small tree.

We spend the evening entertaining our guests which include many of Bob's brothers. They have come to help Zac set the rafters on his living quarters located a couple of miles from our house. Like neighborhood strays, the girls visit the surrounding campfires and listen to the campfire stories. With no wind, the fires' smoke rises toward the stars in lazy streams of grays and whites. The girls are the brightest lights of the evening. My brother-in-law's family is amazed at the size of the quint and by the fact that the girls are up to the task.

A fellow from South Carolina looks especially puzzled as he saunters to our spot just as the sun fades away. Steve is passing through and is spending some days at Marty's campground. He is an earthy, blue collar bloke, who erects the advertisement signage that beckons people off the road when they are tired or hungry from a long day of travel. I jokingly call him Steve the Sign Guy. He is no different from the ancient blacksmith or broom maker, doing things our society needs or desires so it can function more smoothly.

He asks, "How long have you been on the road?"

"Not long," I reply. "In fact we begin our journey tomorrow."

After I lay a thumbnail sketch of our plans, he says, "Wish I didn't have to work tomorrow, I'd love to see you off."

He is touched that we are blue collar people like him and not a silver spoon family on vacation. I give him our card and he says, "I'll leave you my number on your website. If you need anything when you arrive in South Carolina, just give me a call."

Parting, I note the ease with which a stranger became something more. I wonder at the friends we have yet to meet.

Around ten o'clock we finally turn in. The crackle of flames, the whisper of hushed chatter, and shrilling June bugs fill the heavy night air. Overhead, tree branch shadows dance over our tent. The girls fell asleep a little while ago. I lie next to Ama, my stomach churning with anticipation. I close my eyes and fade away. Tomorrow we'll start our journey of 7,000 miles with one stroke of the pedal.

Our journey is about to begin.
July of 2009

Our Burley
Nomad is
fully loaded.
July of 2009

Our trailer is
full of guts.
July of 2009

Marty at Renfro Valley KOA.
July of 2009

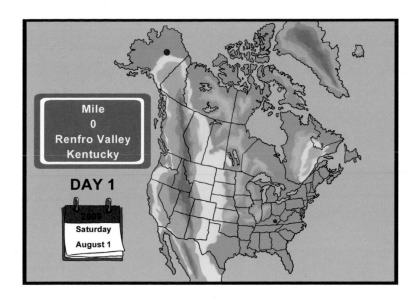

Mile
0
Renfro Valley
Kentucky

DAY 1

2009
Saturday
August 1

CHAPTER 4

I WAKE TO THE CHEERING chorus of robins and dawn washing over our tent. I lay for a few moments as the girls' breathing turns my mind towards them. How awfully lucky I am to have such gifts. Amarins and I were surprised by each birth, not knowing their gender until birth. In our civilized state of living, in which routine and order are paramount, we prefer some age-old unknowns. This, too, seems to be a sliver of the reason why we embark on this journey. What is beyond the river bend? Sure, our roads, states, and country lines have been mapped out, but to us they are unexplored. How will our bodies, brains, and bike hold up over the long haul? Questions only time will answer.

I look for Ama. She's not next to me. Where is she? I already feel the pinch to get on the road. I crawl out of the tent as Amarins returns from the bathroom. She used the internet there to make the first entry on our website, Pedouins.org, to let everyone know we are heading out. It is about seven-thirty and a fine, peaceful morning greets us. We begin to work on getting things ready on the bike and trailer. The girls start to roll out of their sleeping bags. They sit at the brown picnic table and have some mild cheddar cheese, club crackers, bananas, and orange juice.

Folks on their way to and from the restroom stop to wish us well. A husband and wife from Berea give us a stun gun they used years earlier on a cross country trip. We graciously accept it. I feel better knowing that if in the grips of a black bear or a rabid raccoon attack, I can zap them into stillness with our close combat, gazillion volt, palm sized weapon. I tuck it in a front, right hand corner pocket where it will travel out of sight, but within reach.

A gathering of folks prior to departure.
August of 2009

I am intoxicated from the chaos. Family, friends, and strangers surround us creating an affirming atmosphere of our unfolding dream. At the same time, I feel like I might have swallowed a cup of pulverized glass. All the events unfold in a surreal silence. It's as though I'm having an out of body experience. I wonder if this is how I got through my crazy childhood; being teased for wetting the bed until twelve, being told what a dummy I was, that I would never amount to anything, and that I was grandpa's little pet. These harsh words from my parents and siblings still reverberate deep in the dark spots of my mind. As I must have way back then, I block out all distractions, and we pull our bike from under the tree, off the grass, and onto the waiting asphalt.

The quint is pointing downhill now. I strap the brake lever to the handle bars. The brake engages and the walking stick under Robin's seat will keep Yeller from leaving without us. Between breaking up camp and getting everything loaded, we proceed to hug some of the familiar folks milling around in the circus-like atmosphere.

Amarins seems to go about her business with ease, but I can see from the watery look in her eyes that it is hard on her. My eyes start to sting with the awareness that we may never see these people again. Many of these friends are up in age and I fear that if death comes, we will not be there to be a part of any closure ceremonies.

It is nearing ten o'clock when I straddle the quint. The girls give their friends another hug before climbing on. Cheyenne seems to understand the gravity of saying goodbye to her friend Nathan even though she knows she's going to see him again this evening. We'll still be in the area then. Jasmine and Robin seem to think this is just another training exercise. Under the awe-struck eyes of our friends and fellow campers, each of the girls gets situated. Amarins makes sure all our safety rules are engaged.

I ask Bill Stolte to offer some words of blessing for our trip. Bill is one of the Jackson Street folks I had the privilege of rubbing elbows with. Jackson Street runs perpendicular to the Daniel Boone Square on Berea College's campus. It is home to many professors, many also happen to be clients of mine. Years earlier during my studies he was the Dean of Berea College. He is a tall, starchy man with heavy Scottish and New England traits that to me epitomize a university dean. He prefers things mapped out well in advance. We worked on his patio together this past spring and we had a hoot. Together we were like a twenty-first century version of "The Odd Couple." I did get him to laugh and let his hair down some by the project's end.

Just a hair after ten on this muggy morning, I release the brake and we coast back down the hill we walked up, officially launching our trip. A round of cheers and "Go get 'ems" rise from the crowd. Just like that, we are down the hill and entering highway 25. Trucks from the Mount Vernon Fire Department greet us and escort us past the industrial part of town. We turn southwest on highway 461, leaving Mount Vernon behind us, and are finally on our own. The silence is immediate. A peace descends, and we push down on the cranks while moving into the day's rhythm.

A journey of 7,000 miles starts with the first mile.
August of 2009

THE PREVIOUS MONTHS WERE FILLED with activities to prepare for this undertaking. Now we can look ahead to our new goal. The entire journey is broken down into baby steps. We're taking it day by day, town by town, and state by state. Like the climbers who start the ascent of Mount Kilimanjaro in the dark of night, barely seeing what lies ahead, we, too, simply embrace the day. Right now, our eyes stay on Kentucky. Alaska will have to wait.

The sun is bright and the air is damp. The grass lining the road and standing in the rolling fields seems to be an extra deep green today. It feels exhilarating to float down the roadway in total freedom. Robin has already settled into nap mode, face pressed to the pad in front of her. Cheyenne and Jasmine have broad smiles on their faces as we pedal away. The road lies like long ocean waves before us. In a motorized vehicle, the road is mechanical. On our quint, the road is alive. I look down and notice red and black ants, fat bugs, long skinny worms, and other creatures I have no names for.

Some four miles from town, we spot a news van beside the highway. They're setting up on the road's edge waiting for us—the Pedouins! Channel 27 from Lexington has come to catch us in action. We pull over to share our story. It goes smoothly with the who, what, where, when, and whys. They follow us for some miles to capture enough footage to match the sound bites. On what we think will be the last camera action, we all throw a wave and plod on down the road. It feels strange to be a news piece. The fact is that we are private people on a very public journey. We don't have cable or an antenna for our television at home. It is our opinion that books and the natural environment provide the best classroom. If not for the internet, we would have been completely disconnected from the world.

TODAY, WE AIM TO ARRIVE at Burnside State Park, but it's too far. We are at the end of our rope. The past months' preparation and excitement have taken its toll. We settle for a grassy field near the BP filling station off highway 80. Before setting up camp, we sit down for a while and let the day sink in. We did not get as far as we had hoped, but it's a start.

After some deep breaths, my old survival instincts kick in. *We'll settle here for the night, but is it all right to stay here, I ask myself.* I decide to check with the cashier.

I explain who we are and then ask, "Can we camp for the night across the way in the tall grass?"

After some dialogue with her co-workers, they give the go ahead. They don't know who the land belongs to, but seem to think it'll be fine.

I thank them and say, "We will be gone by eight in the morning, and you won't even know we were here."

We set the tent up in a light breeze with the blazing sun beating down on us. Robin and I crawl inside for a nap. Amarins takes Cheyenne and Jasmine into the cool, air-conditioned food area for a game of Skip-Bo. Robin and I do our best to nap in the tent, but to no avail. The inside gets so fiery hot that all we do is thrash around like someone in the midst of a bad dream.

THE GIRLS JUMP UP AND down when the Munguias arrive in our old van with their four energetic children: Nathan, Erika, JonJon and Victoria. Regina is a local country girl from a family living in a mobile home down the road from us. Her husband, Julio, is a green card holder from Mexico. He makes dashboards at an automobile parts plant near Somerset on the banks of Cumberland Lake, where pontoon house boats were said to have been started. They work hard to eke out a living, which isn't always easy.

Amarins got to know Regina when her son, Nathan, was in the same pre-school room as Cheyenne at Mount Vernon Elementary School.

Regina said to Ama on the first day of school, "Ain't you always pushin' your kids around in that wheelbarrow?"

Ama simply replied, "Yes, I am."

After some laughter, a friendship was born. Since we live in the woods, a normal baby stroller is useless. One day, out of necessity, Ama stuck the car seat in our wheelbarrow and headed to the mailbox. In time, she just kept going farther.

The Munguias seemed to follow a streak of bad luck with the cars they drive, often leaving Julio stranded on the way to or from work. We decided early on that a vital part of the journey would be about giving as well as receiving. We had a choice of letting our van sit for some years or passing it on to folks who might need it. Ama and I talked it over with our girls, and we decided the van would be better served with the Munguias. We had our 1991 Toyota Previa cleaned and serviced before giving it away. An important family value is that when you give a gift, you give your best.

JonJon is having a birthday today, and they brought us food and cake to celebrate his third complete revolution around the sun. Lying on a tarp next to our tent are dishes with meat, deviled eggs, fresh tomatoes, cucumbers, beans, and a cold, ripe watermelon. This could be a Fourth of July picnic with seven children running around like banshees. The adults enjoy each other's company and eat heartily.

Supper with the Munguias.
August of 2009

THE SUN BEGINS TO SET and our friends say their goodbyes. Our girls cry for their playmates; they are starting to realize that this goodbye is going to be a long one. I myself am exhausted and ready for bed. In our solitude, we clean the area around the tent of all trash to leave the place better than we found it. The girls jump with gusto, cleaning well beyond our tent's perimeter. Once teeth are brushed and a last potty stop is made, it's time to turn in. The sunlight is disappearing. We nestle into our spots on the tent floor and unpack what just happened.

"I already miss Nathan; he is my best friend in the whole world!" Cheyenne says.

Jasmine chimes in, "I miss our house."

Holding Cheyenne and Jasmine, Amarins tries to comfort them, "Nathan won't forget you, Cheyenne, and besides, you can call him from time to time."

"I'd like that."

"Mommy, can we visit the house?" Jasmine asks.

"No Jasmine, not till we have finished our bicycle journey."

"Will we keep our house?"

"Why, yes, Tanner and Jenna are only staying in it until we return."

"I sure am glad," Jasmine says.

Cheyenne adds, "At least I have Dogge, right Mom?"

"Yes, and he will be with you the whole way, too. Think about it, we will make lots of new friends and do all kinds of stuff that not many children get the chance to do!"

Once the tears are dried I let them know, "Girls, you can visit all your friends and places in your dreams. Let's close our eyes and drift off to dreamland. Maybe we will see each other as well."

Like a closing episode of "The Waltons," echoes of "good night" ring out and mingle with the sounds beyond the walls of our tent.

The girls are in a deep sleep.
August of 2009

A lesson about barnacles in the middle of Kentucky.
August of 2009

Trash clean-up around our campsite.
August of 2009

Our first campsite.
August of 2009

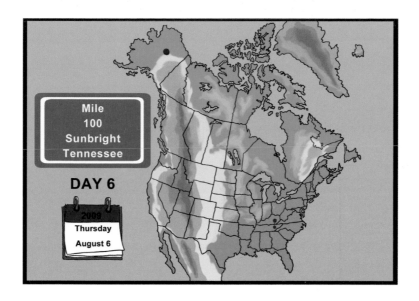

Mile
100
Sunbright
Tennessee

DAY 6

2009
Thursday
August 6

CHAPTER 5

OUR DAYS ROLL COMFORTABLY ALONG into the unknown. Under the mid-August sun we define our Pedouin days by the rhythms of the ride and the landscapes we pass through. They are rhythms that center on waking and sleeping along roadways that began as prehistoric animal and native foot paths. They are rhythms that involve new dietary habits that cater to bicycle travel and the availability of jot-em-down grocery stores. Food in our mountain abode consisted of home canned meats, vegetables, and fruits. Now we are relegated to pre-packaged Vienna sausages, shriveled as well as overpriced fruits, and muffins in shrink wrap. Even our girls question our diet.

THE DAY IS CLEAR, HOT, and muggy as we cross the high peaks of the Big South Fork National Recreation Area in the foothills of the Appalachian Mountains.

With an elevation of 1,300 feet, this path was once an ancient route used by Native Americans. It moves between modern day Nashville and Knoxville, Tennessee. Beneath this asphalt road lay the more primitive paths that hoofed animals and moccasin clad feet once trod. Our muscles ache from the gradual but steady ascent of the past few days since leaving Whitley City, Kentucky.

I readily imagine the ancient voices that still echo through these woods. I share these with the family, "Hey, see that creek bed; it was probably a place where Natives hung out." In my mirror I can see the girls turning their heads to catch a glimpse.

Cheyenne responds with, "This is kinda like where we found our arrowheads on Buffalo Creek Road. Remember when we found a black and a white arrowhead?"

Amarins says, "Absolutely. Cheyenne, these are the places they hung out and did their daily routines."

The summer heat and rolling landscapes keep us suspended between peak muscle fatigue and jubilation. Traveling through areas filled with tall red oak trees with leaves of deep green, pointed lobes, and tight grained bark, we find comfort in their familiarity. Cheyenne, Jasmine, and Robin spy trees that they see back home. Cheyenne informs me, "Dad, these trees are like ours in Kentucky!"

Ama chimes in, "We are in the Big South Fork where we share similar geological features."

I think *ain't that kinda deep for the girls?*

Actually, Ama's shared knowledge is schooling at its finest. On this voyage, the girls are living what textbooks can only attempt to convey with printed text. Instead of studying geological features in the abstract, the girls are experiencing the similarities and differences in the geography of the states we ride through. They notice when landscapes change and when they are familiar. Like the red oak trees from back home, Cheyenne makes inferences as to what that means about this new place. When there is something new, as there is at every stop along the way, as well as in the spaces in between, it opens opportunities for conversation and ultimately potential research at the libraries we frequent along our route.

When I am tired, I get a little cynical. Chugging up these monstrous hills in the heat, I need to focus on pedaling and my brain coasts away as my body struggles to run on autopilot. The chit-chat can wreck my concentration. Then BAM, *bike schooling on the roll* enters my head! I give in and enter the fray of words. We play games involving "name that tree," which builds on lessons learned in our mountains and hollers. Stirring my thoughts, I remember sitting between Grandpa's knees as he squatted next to a spindle with drum brakes of some old car. There is no substitute for hands-on learning. Riding onward, I appreciate this truth on an ever deeper level.

Pedaling and playing, we crest a hilltop of amazing character. The road lies ahead of us like an arrow. There is a dip in it midway, like the sagging back of an old nag. To the south, the land rolls off the road bed and slopes gradually down into the distance. The trees, three to four-foot diameter oaks of various kinds, spread out in a meadow. The grass under the trees seems to have been recently cut; there are faint tractor marks in the leftover legume stubble. West of our bike route the land moves slightly upward and has

Enjoying the view over Tennessee.
August of 2009

large patches of open grassy spaces. In the distance, thick woods resume.

Before the swag in the road, we see a sign, "Sunbright." We had noticed this town on the map, but there's no evidence of a town to support the signage. The girls are raising questions about it too. It is Amarins' habit to let the girls participate in ascertaining directions from her maps. The topography lends itself to a town, but time has erased all but an old log cabin that hugs the road's edge up ahead on the right. Pulling up to the mailbox, I smell fresh cut grass clinging to the sultry summer air. We have been traveling for several hours without a serious break. Past noon and nearly out of water, we decide to stop in Sunbright. There is something mystical about the place, calling us to rest. Thirty feet past the cabin we spy a fine shady spot on a knoll. Between it and the house is a hose bib sticking out of the ground. We stop our ride and talk about what to do.

The girls cheer at the pause. We do not want to trespass even though it seems inviting. I ask them, "Do you see anyone around?"

Amarins points out, "I notice an old man milling around behind the old cabin at the tree line."

I holler several times, "May we stop and have some water?" He appears not to hear us. After a minute or two we ride a few feet farther and dismount near a grassy knoll on the same side. It looks so inviting that I take a chance he won't mind if we enjoy some rest, while I get his attention. We climb over a rusty cable blocking the driveway and make our way to the shady hill. As Amarins spreads our Indian blanket and gets the girls situated, I head off toward the man and what looks to be a tool shed off in the distance.

When I approach him, the old fella startles. If I had to put a number on his age, I'd guess him to be in his late eighties. After an awkward greeting on my part, he smiles. I ask him if we can sit a spell and have some water.

He is very agreeable and says, "My name is J.P. Morgan. You have to speak loud 'cause I'm hard of hearing."

I invite him to join us and then rush back to the girls and Ama to tell them that we can stay. I grab the empty water bottles from the bike and fill them at the shed where I met J.P. We all nestle down on the blanket and grass. Then he begins to tell us about this place called Sunbright.

He starts: "This old place belongs to me now. In the beginning the Cherokee roamed this hilltop. To the southeast of this cabin here in Sunbright is where the first old log cabin sat, built before the Civil War. When I was a small boy, I remember the stories the owner of this property used to tell me. His name was Mr. Barnes, and on entering the war he walked all the way to Kentucky to join the Union Army. After the war he came back and bought that old place. Somewhere in the late 1890s he built this cabin we are next to and used the old cabin for firewood over many years. After his death, my family came into possession of the place." It is a narrative that fits into a box, as if he has told it several times before.

I ask him, "Do you know of any Indians that still live in the area?"

Listening to the stories of J.P. Morgan.
August of 2009

"They are all gone now, but I remember hearing stories from my mother about her seeing natives around in these parts when she was a little girl."

Sitting in this spot, we are fed secondhand stories of Sunbright's history from an old man's lips that too, will vanish.

Cheyenne asks, "Can we see the log house?"

"If it is alright with your dad, we can," he responds.

"Follow J.P. I'll be behind you girls."

While Amarins cleans up our picnic area, the girls and I get a tour of the old cabin. Amarins does not share my love of old things, and some quiet, alone time has infinitely more value to her at this moment.

The cabin was a one-room house once, with an attic sleeping area. J.P. takes us in through the kitchen on the back side, which is a later addition to the main ten by fifteen foot living area. It is cool inside, despite the heat and humidity outside. The furniture, of an era not ours, is still in place. The mattresses lie on bare springs. Only a few white, homemade cabinets line the kitchen walls, and a plastic-like material covers empty sofa chairs. No one has lived in the place for about forty years. The old place is like a museum whose only regular visitor is Mr. Morgan. Entering one of the downstairs bedrooms,

Cheyenne, Jasmine and Robin
on the hunt for adventure.
August of 2009

we find a door to the attic. I'm not surprised that the girls want to go upstairs.

We cautiously climb the rough lumber steps as our host follows us up through a wall of heat. Hanging around the hand-hewn stone chimney where it meets the roof line is an old picture frame and a couple of old fiddles whose handlers are part of the whispers on this hilltop.

"Hey girls, do you see those fiddles up there?" I ask.

"Yeah," they reply in unison.

Cheyenne says, "They look like violins, but why are they cracked?"

"Because they are very old and the attic's heat has caused them to split," I answer.

Jasmine inquires, "Can we play them?"

"I don't think so. We better leave them alone. Hey, look up there!"

Upon seeing loaded wasps nests clinging to the rough cut oak rafters and our gasps for air in the heat of the non-insulated attic area, we make a quick exit.

We walk out the front door, and the girls sit on an old swing that hangs under the porch roof. As they play, my attention is drawn to an area of the porch where a single step leading to the walkway meets one of the main posts. There is the most unique collapsible gate bridging the opening between two posts. I ask Mr. Morgan, "What is that funky metal gate?"

He throws it back into my lap, "What do you think it is?"

I touch it and play with it for a while, then venture a guess, "Is it a gate from an old turn of the century dumb waiter?"

He laughs and says, "No."

He tells us the story before we jet off, "My dad said it was from an old mid-teens Buick. This being the old road from Knoxville to Nashville, there was early car traffic. One spring a family was on a trip when their car got hung up over there." He is pointing to the hill we had just climbed about an hour earlier. "They had to get home. So, they left their car and walked to the next town where they caught a wagon to the big city. They never came back for their car. Over the years folks pillaged it for useful items. The luggage area on the rear of the Buick had this as the gate to keep the bags from falling into the road."

Cheyenne brims over with questions. I see by the way she narrows her eyes and cocks her head that she is processing what she overheard, a talent she has developed well, "Why did they leave their car?"

I venture a guess since she spoke too softly for J.P. to hear, "Since all the roads back then were mostly dirt, it was probably muddy and it got buried in it. They did not have wreckers then the way we have today. It would have taken a team of horses to haul the thing out."

"Oh," she responds.

Hanging on this 1890s log cabin porch post is a 1913 to 1918 Buick luggage rack that bears witness to stories, like ours, of folks who have traveled this ancient road system. The girls open and close the gate a bit before I put a stop to it, fearing they will get their little fingers caught in its workings.

We thank J.P. Morgan and bid him farewell. Leaving his hilltop, I wonder how long he'll still be among us. And like the ancient oral traditions, what was said to Mr. Morgan has now been told to us. The story of this place, however minute, is etched into ours. We too, will repeat it.

Arrival in Tennessee – state two.
August of 2009

Road schooling in Burnside
State Park, Kentucky.
August of 2009

Flat tire number two.
August of 2009

J.P. Morgan's cabin in Sunbright, Tennessee.
August of 2009

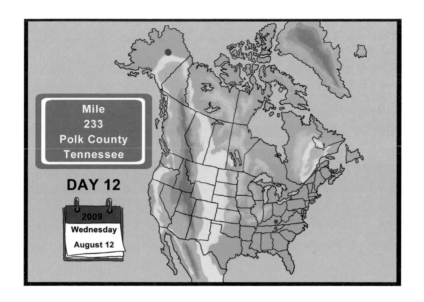

Mile
233
Polk County
Tennessee

DAY 12

2009
Wednesday
August 12

CHAPTER 6

STILL FOLLOWING ANCIENT VOICES THAT whisper to us along the tree lined country roads, we cross into Polk County, Tennessee. The temperatures were brain frying hot on the Tellico Plains Plateau. Now we find ourselves in higher elevations with cooler mountain air. Crossing yet another county line, this time we have stepped into a time warp. We see fewer new autos and the houses seem dated. Contemporary home designs and double pane windows are scarce. Skeletal remains of big round TV dishes as big as a full size pickup truck bed from the 1970s are visible.

Deep in the Appalachians, I feel a quiver of uneasiness. Passing a dilapidated log cabin, we are charged by a large brown pit bull as his owners look on like marble statues from antebellum days. I order, "Pedal with all your might!" I sense a panic in the girls. The dog stops at the property's edge, just one lane of asphalt from us. We fly downhill past him. Our hearts race as we pull to a stop some three hundred yards beyond the encounter.

Amarins says, "This county is different from the rest of Tennessee."

I agree. There is something different, but we can't discern what it is. Amarins passes out some Jolly Ranchers to bring back some normalcy after this bizarre event.

Just after noon we pass an old fort. Fort Marr was one of the Trail of Tears' holding areas. Because of the Indian Removal Act of May 1830, the Cherokee were taken from their lands. Many perished on their forced walk to Oklahoma.

SEVERAL MILES UP THE MOUNTAIN from Turtletown, we begin our descent. Working the brake and eyeing the road for obstacles, I notice a man next to a beat-up white Ford van trying to get our attention from high above in a parking lot. We stop for no one on a free downhill ride. We fly on by. At the intersection with highway 68, near our Turtletown destination for the evening, we stop for a break on the opposite side of the road in the parking area of an old abandoned, white painted store. The van had passed us as we were descending and is in the parking lot as well. Its owner comes over and starts asking questions about our journey. I try not to judge by appearances, but his does not speak in his favor. He's greasy, and dressed in a haphazard sort of way. I notice he has a camera tucked under his arm and appears to be filming us. Feeling uncomfortable, I finally bid him farewell.

In the outskirts of Turtletown, we roll over some overgrown train tracks and pedal on up a curvy incline. Coasting down the other side of the grade, we spot a local park to our left. There is a horseshoe-shaped entrance and exit to it. I call out to Ama, "What do you think of this spot for the night?"

"Looks good," she replies.

I carefully pull Yeller across the oncoming lane and gingerly coast down the gravel entrance to a covered picnic area. In front of two rows of long tables is a freshly bush-hogged field of grass about six inches high. Running parallel to the road, next to one end of the pavilion and along the grassy field, is a small creek. Dismounted, the girls run and play. They soon find the swiftly flowing water. Sounds of glee can be heard as they wade up to their ankles in its coolness.

"Hey Ama, let's put the tent over here by the creek." The hill behind our potential camp site gives it a secluded feeling.

A local stops by as we finish putting up our tent. Looking up, I go over to our visitor who's admiring the quint leaning against a post.

Our home for the night in Turtletown, Tennessee.
August of 2009

"Jim is the name," he says, extending his arm. We shake hands and automatically I start my spiel about our outing. Concluding, I inquire, "How 'bout you?"

He explains, "We wanted to get out of the city, so my wife and I moved here from Jersey."

"How is it going for someone raised north of the Mason Dixon Line?"

"Not too good, really."

"Why not?" I ask.

Jim goes on, "A couple of weeks ago our house burned to the ground sometime after midnight."

Shocked, I ask, "Where was the fire department?"

With an expression of defeat he says, "They came and ran out of water within minutes. They just watched it burn to the ground. I later saw the report stating they used a total of six gallons of water on my fire. They left without saying a word when it was over."

I could see the emptiness on his face.

Despite his pain and loss, Jersey Jim (a name we gave him based on his bio) isn't one to stop living and still enjoys an opportunity when it arrives. He goes into town alone because his wife is in Jersey for some medical reasons, and brings back a hot rotisserie chicken, Coke, cookies, and water for supper. He stays to eat with us, temporarily forgetting that painful night of the house fire. As our bellies begin to fill, the fireflies gather in the grassy field sending signals with their small glowing green lights. One by one, the girls run off to catch some.

Darkness comes early in the mountain holler. We thank Jim for his goodness and wish him all the best. Leaving, he says, "I'll bring some tea tomorrow. What time do you expect to head out?"

I reply, "About eight I guess."

Ama reminds the girls to thank our host. They all yell in unison, "Thank you Jersey Jim." Their voices echo in a high shrill tone, fading into the early evening air.

Exhausted from grueling hills, heat, and humidity, we turn in. Amarins and the girls nestle into their pieces of the tent floor. I find it hard to sleep. My mind is afoul with anxieties. What if the guy in the white van was some kind of nutcase? What if we are attacked tonight in our dark, secluded camping spot?

Looming too is a visit to Fort Benning, Georgia, to see my son Adam. He is to graduate from basic training a few days from now. He asked me before we departed if I would be present. I assured him I'd do my best. Our imminent arrival in Ducktown signals my brief planned departure from our travels. It was the spot Ama and I picked out as a place for them to hang out until I returned. That was then and this is now. We will have to see what tomorrow brings.

Another thing on my mind is the flashes of lightning I see off to the northwest. The tent fabric glows with the soft flashes given off from the distant storm. I unzip the tent opening and quietly slip into the night air. It is as thick as soup, swimming with sounds of June bugs, crickets, and frogs. There is no hint of a breeze, which leaves me to assume the storm will not pass our way. Just in case, I secure the Burley under the front fly of our tent so it will stay dry. Moving toward Yeller, I make sure she is well covered by the roof of the pavilion. The brake is on and the walking stick is securely in place.

A LITTLE PAST ONE IN the morning, the sound of wind wakes me. The girls and Ama are still asleep. I lie awake counting the distance between the lightning and the sound of the distant thunder. Flash. One thousand one, one thousand two, one thousand three, one thousand four, and so on until… Kaboom. As I count, the numbers decrease as the storm comes closer. Since there's nothing I can do, I roll over and crash into a fitful sleep agitated by light, sound, wind, rain, and prayers for safety.

R AIN AND FOG SURPRISE THE girls when we wake them. Jasmine says, "I thought it was clear when we went to sleep."

"It was, but we had a bad storm sometime early this morning. Did you all hear it?"

They all say, "No."

They wonder what we are going to do as the light rain softly splatters on the tent fabric. When we established ground rules for our journey, we determined that we would not ride in the rain. The girls know this rule. The fear that some busy body, well intentioned or otherwise, might call on law enforcement or social services was in our minds a real threat.

I poke my head outside and see that the sky is getting lighter and, more importantly, the rain has stopped. We peel out of the tent. The girls head for the pavilion. Amarins and I pack up the tent and its contents. Within minutes of getting all our stuff on the tables, the rain returns. Blowing in with the rain is Jersey Jim. Just as he promised, he has tea and donuts.

Hunkered down on the concrete tables, we eat and watch the rain. We wonder when it will end.

Waiting for the rain to go away.
August of 2009

Jim informs us, "The weather report says we are on the tail end of this stuff."

Ama and I feel optimistic despite the water that washes over the concrete pad of the pavilion. The sky lightens at mid morning. I shoot a look in Ama's direction. She too, is ready to roll. We all hug Jersey Jim and load our belongings on Yeller.

"Three, two, one... Go!" We're off and yell "Thank you!" to our Northern host.

It is only ten miles to Ducktown where we plan on grabbing a motel. From there I'll hitchhike to Georgia to see Adam. Hitchhiking is something my family has seen me indulge in on other occasions. While I'm gone, Amarins and the girls have a date with electricity and indoor plumbing, not to mention a bed and television.

As soon as Yeller's tires hit the asphalt, the drizzle begins. We choose to ride since it is in the seventies and town is only ten miles away. The rain quickens as we enter a desolate Turtletown. We pull off the road. Ama secures the girls' rain jackets and pants a little more snugly while I hold Yeller steady. A woman in an SUV stops. She rolls down her window. A small dog is sitting in her lap. With a faint smile on her face she says, "Can I help you?"

"We are fine, but do you know if there is a motel around?" I say.

"Not here, but you will find one in Ducktown."

She inquires several more times if we need help, as though she is probing for more information, perhaps wondering why we are in this rain with our three little children. Losing her smile, she speeds off.

Pedaling in the hide and seek rain showers, we are stopped about one mile from Ducktown, Tennessee. In my rear view mirror I see blue lights. I instinctively turn my head and tell the girls to be quiet, "Let me do the talking." Jasmine is not happy we have to sit here in the drizzle so close to our destination and voices her disproval. My mind freezes with the watery image of a man stepping from the unmarked blue Ford Crown Victoria.

As we wait, paralyzing jolts of numbness run down my legs in their attempt to steady Yeller.

MY MIND RACES THIRTY YEARS back to a similar event along the Floyd's Fork Creek in Kentucky. While enjoying the sunshine and working on my Ford

Fairlane, an officer pulls up and startles me with, "Are you William Paul Harrison?"

"Yes sir," I answer.

"Son, we've been looking for you for some time. You are one hard person to track down!"

"What is this about?" I ask the officer.

"You are wanted for a felony count of receiving and selling stolen merchandise."

I searched my mind to figure out what he could be referring to. The peaceful atmosphere at Iron Gate Country Club in southeast Jefferson County was fractured by the police officer. I had lived there off and on since 1976. It was where early Kentucky travelers forded on their way to Louisville. Graves on the property date as far back as the early 1700s. Except for the fifteen acres or so hugging the banks of the creek, the other four hundred acres are hilly and covered by a large stand of second growth timber. It was a teenager's perfect hideaway; from bathing in the creek to keeping baloney and milk in the spring. Living in an old dilapidated homestead was a carefree life on the land, like a mountain version of Tom Sawyer.

I was mystified as to why this officer was after me. After he read me my rights he sat me in the backseat of his car for the twenty mile drive to Louisville. Trees and fields gave way to urban sprawl and then cityscapes. On the way, I was informed that my offense was with regard to a small dirt bike I had sold some years earlier. This motor bike, which was given as payment for some mechanical work on an old Ford truck, turned out to be stolen. Not wanting to give the name of my brother's friend in an effort to protect him and his children, I ended up paying the price. A night in jail, restitution, counseling, probation, and a decision not to rat, still sits heavy with me.

THE PLAIN CLOTHES OFFICER STEPS to the front of our bike. As water falls from the bill of my helmet, I ask, "What's the problem officer?"

Without identifying himself or what law enforcement department he is with, he answers, "In Tennessee it is against the law for children to be in the rain. Did you know that?"

"*Hell no!*" is what I want to tell him but I just say, "No sir."

He proceeds, "You have to be actively getting them out of the rain, or we can take your children."

My breath catches. Then the officer asks us, "Where are you all headed to?"

I think better than to tell him our whole story, so I say, "We are heading to Ducktown, sir. We were told there are motels there."

He agrees there are and then says, "Why don't you put your three small girls in the back of my cruiser and I will take them to the motel. You can pick them up when you get there."

Wondering what loon would turn his three girls over to an anonymous man in an unmarked car whose only connection with law enforcement is blue lights on his dash board, I say, "Officer, my girls ain't getting off this bike until we get to the motel."

After a painful pause, he says, "Then I will follow you to the Ducktown Motel to make sure you check in."

"Whatever you need to do," I reply.

By this time, the kids are scared to death. I am seething. The gall of this supposed law man. I thank the girls for their patience and urge them to hang on until we get there. We take off with Johnny Law on our tail. Ten minutes along, we pull into the motel parking area. The clouds are already beginning to break and the sun peeks through. Amarins makes a beeline for the office door before the officer gets out of his car. He steps over to where we are parked and pulls out a small spiral notepad and asks for my name and date of birth. Next thing I know he hops in his car and is gone. The whole mile long event unfolds so fast, I forget to ask him for his identification. I kick myself for not being more alert.

In our room, we fall on the beds. The girls switch the television on. Gathering our thoughts, I decide to call a friend in Kentucky. When Bob answers the phone, he can sense something is not right. He asks, "What's wrong?" I share what happened and ask him to say some prayers for us. He assures me he and Jane will.

Amarins and I retreat to the bathroom to talk so the girls won't be privy to our conversation. Knowing I have to start thumbing to Atlanta this afternoon, Ama asks me, "Go to the grocery store and pick up what we will need for the next several days while you are gone."

We want to err on the cautious side. Ama wants enough supplies on hand to last until my return. If she decides to truly camp out at the motel, not venturing outside until I get back, they can survive. It's hard to believe we're feeling this afraid in our own country.

Walking back from the Piggly Wiggly grocery store behind the motel complex, I receive a call back from Bob. "Hey Bill, you need to get out of Polk County now. Jane and I just realized that we lived near there. I worked with the forestry service for several years. Those people do not like outsiders. While there we heard rumors of people passing through who got arrested on trumped-up charges. That place is not friendly at all."

My gut is constricting. This day is not improving. How am I going to break the news that Marty in Kentucky called and said that a sneakily filmed video was put on YouTube that was not flattering to us from this same area? I should have kept riding when I saw the white Ford van.

Stepping into the room I drop the two plastic bags of groceries on the night table and motion Amarins back to the bathroom. Having filled her in on what Bob said, we are more convinced that Amarins and the girls should not venture outside. I know neither one of us has easy days ahead. I'd almost give up on my departure, if not for my promise to Adam.

We've only been gone for twelve days and anxiety has enveloped our journey. Amarins keeps the phone for safety reasons and she tells me to call her when I get to Atlanta for the evening. I promise her that I will call her every time I get a chance. I head out the door to catch a ride about two in the afternoon. Amarins shuts the door part way leaving a viewing crack; the girls are trying to squeeze through the crack like puppies trying to get out of their cage. With a backpack slung over my shoulder, I throw a blind wave and disappear.

DAYS LATER, FIVE RIDES PAST Atlanta on my way back to Ducktown, I am dropped off in the town of Elijay, Georgia, on the side of highway 515. After I walk through the main intersection, past the city limits sign, I stick my thumb up. Eying some police cars down the road, I figure that since I'm now outside the city limits, I am free to catch a ride. I'm wrong. The blue lights ignite and move toward me.

From behind, an older officer exits his car and asks for some identification. There is another police car in front of me. They have wedged me between

61

them. I wonder if that is a testament to the degree of my "crime." I am well dressed, clean shaven, and have short, well kept hair. I wonder what marks me as suspicious. In three days I have been stopped twice while minding my own business.

I was in some scary situations in the Middle East, but I'm caught off guard feeling this level of tension in my own backyard. As I hand over my driver's license, he asks, "What's your business here?" I tell him that I have been to see my son and am heading back to Ducktown to meet up with my family. To add to the story, I fill him in on our bike journey with hopes that it might soften his attitude. Looking at me in mild disbelief, he heads to his cruiser to run the numbers.

Figuring I am going to be here in the sweltering heat for a while, I set myself down on the asphalt at the edge of the grass. Picking some grass and chewing on it, I reflect on the situation. Our ride to Polk County was wonderful. Since we crossed the county line, we have been plagued with everything from rain to police. My head spins with questions. *Are we nuts for taking this trip? Is something trying to tell us to go home? Is American freedom only a distant fable?* I halt the downward spiral. *Bill, you have done nothing wrong other than living out a small portion of the American way of life that so many others have given up on.*

After what seems like hours, the officer gets out of his car. I stand up, a little weak in the knees. He says, "We have called someone to carry you to the next town." I dare not ask him what the problem is. On the bright side, I am getting a ride. A long-haired middle aged man pulls up in a rusted Chevy pickup truck. I hop in and we take off.

Riding along, I share my story. John relates that hauling people from the jail, usually at midnight, is his ministry "from the Lord." He goes on, "If any of the other police officers had picked you up, you'd be sitting in jail until I picked you up in the wee hours of the morning." I feel lucky, though still wondering what's wrong with this part of the country. I reach no conclusion as we ride to Blue Ridge, Georgia; the last town before Ducktown, Tennessee.

John drops me off on the highway just inside Blue Ridge. Within moments I get a ride from a young couple. The boy drives with his wife scrunched up next to him and me at the passenger door. They say they moved here from Pennsylvania about ten years ago, wanting to get away from the high taxes.

Here, they have been in and out of the trucking business. I ask what they think about this part of America.

He responds, "We steer clear of the law, even here on the Georgia side. The people around this whole area are not too keen on outsiders. Even though we have had some problems, being outsiders ourselves, we like living here. You know, the lack of restrictions and the like."

Pulling into the Duck-town Motel, I direct him to the room. The young

A pile of girls in Ducktown, Tennessee.
August of 2009

couple waits in the truck while I fetch Amarins. After I knock on the door, I see Ama peaking around the curtain. I hear a chorus of cheers from the girls as she closes it. Once she is outside, we grab an awkward hug and turn to thank them for getting me home safely. We wave as they leave. In the room I am mobbed by three girls with three days of pent up energy and love to be shared.

Once the kids are asleep, Ama and I discuss the next day's travel plans. To get out of Polk County, we either head two miles south to Georgia or eight miles east to North Carolina. I am concerned about going into Georgia because of what happened in Elijay. Our original route was to take us there, but we think this whole area of Tennessee and Georgia is too problematic for us to travel by bicycle. We decide to shoot for the North Carolina border at daybreak and take our chances with the more mountainous terrain.

IN A CLOUD OF APPREHENSION, expectation and literal fog cover, we prepare Yeller for departure like Dillinger preparing for another jailbreak. The fog will protect us from distant eyes. We get the girls fed and ready. My stomach feels like I'm blindfolded and on a roller coaster for the very first time. Amarins is focused and methodical as she attaches all our gear to Yeller and the Burley.

We mount Yeller in the cool air. I inform the girls to be silent and pedal with all their energy until we reach the North Carolina line. I say, "There will not be any stops for potty or snacks. All we want you to do is pedal."

Quietly, I count off, "Three, two, one… Go!" We sail down the motel's parking lot and make a dash for the border.

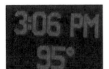

A hot day in
Tennessee.
August of 2009

Friends from Kentucky have come to visit in
Kingston, Tennessee.
August of 2009

Robin enjoys a comfortable nap.
August of 2009

Jasmine awaits the sunrise.
August of 2009

Finding refreshment at a roadside spring.
August of 2009

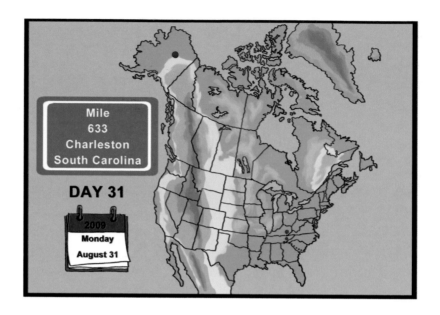

Mile
633
Charleston
South Carolina

DAY 31

2009
Monday
August 31

CHAPTER 7

THE LADSON NEIGHBORHOOD IS AROUSED by a loud scream of "Thank you!" It echos through the damp streets, still wet from last night's vicious thunder storms. We are off again, delirious with expectations to put our feet in the Atlantic Ocean today on the battlement in downtown Charleston. It is our first huge milestone of the journey. The girls will put their feet in the ocean for the first time since we left and the second time in their lives. We can almost taste the salt in the air. Our load feels light and the cranks turn easily. Leaving the bedroom community of Charlestown behind, we are on highway 78 headed southeast. It is a straight shot to the battlements where the first shots of the Civil War were fired.

The traffic grows heavier as we approach Charleston. I pull over at a split in the road.

"What are you stopping for?" Amarins asks.

I say, "Do you want to stay on the main road or take the alternative road?"

"You decide," Ama replies. "It looks like the right arm is the old business route though. There could be less traffic on it."

I agree and choose the old route. It leads through the industrial area. There are aban-

To Charleston, South Carolina, we go.
August of 2009

doned factory buildings and smaller structures containing mom and pop muffler shops and the like. People who drive by look at us as if they are seeing something from a circus. They seem to be dressed in work shirts advertising the local businesses. Laughs, thumbs up, and general bewilderment greet us.

After crossing several sets of railroad tracks, I notice a set that is not perpendicular to the road. They move at an angle across the road, sort of like the left arm of a lower case "y." To keep our tires from slipping off the wet rails into the trough, I swing out near the center line before swinging back in, so as to cross them closer to a perpendicular angle. Moving at about four miles per hour, the front tire crosses just fine. I sigh a breath of relief when I'm across the tracks. I adjust slightly to go back in the direction of the road again, but the rear tire is not across the tracks yet. It slips off the wet rail into the trough causing the entire bike to come to an unexpected stop. Yeller crashes to the hard wet asphalt, taking us with her. The fall is so sudden that there is no way to stop it.

Our movements seem to unfold like a movie scene, one frame at a time. I pick myself up out of the cockleburs—small thorny balls the size of raisins that grow on a low ground cover bush I'd landed in—and assess the situation. Getting the kids out of the road is the first priority. Cheyenne kicks her feet out of the foot cages and works herself from under the frame. Then she hurries to the shoulder of the road. Amarins grimaces as she slowly gets up. Blood drips from her elbow onto the asphalt. Jasmine screams. She's stuck and needs help to get off. I hold Jasmine under her arms and shout to Amarins, "Untie her foot cages." I am frantic to get them up. When Jasmine is safe, we move to a crying Robin. I fumble around until her harness unsnaps. I pull her out and give her to Amarins. Like a lioness protecting her cubs, Amarins shields the girls with a strong embrace, as though she's trying to squeeze all the hurt away.

My focus turns to Yeller and the trailer, which is still in an upright position. The hunk of yellow steel composite is sprawled out over the entire lane of the two lane road. On the intersecting side street just past our crash site is a motorist who is stopped and is looking at us. He offers help, but I wave him on. We've got it covered. A few other cars pass slowly in the opposite lane. The entire contraption needs to get out of the road before we assemble an ingathering of helpers. Although we have had no trouble in North or South Carolina so far, I'm not taking any chances. The sooner we can get the bike up and in order, the better. The cockleburs pierce my skin as I walk to the bike. I grab Yeller in front of Robin's seat area by the supporting gray, 14-gauge metal channel and heave. It's amazing how strong you are in times of great necessity. Up pops the bike and I yell for Cheyenne to grab the walking stick fastened under the bungee strap on the trailer. She rushes it to me and I secure the bike in an upright position on the shoulder of the road.

We sit, huddled together, on the side of the road and survey the damage while Yeller stands guard between us and traffic. It appears our helmets saved us from serious injury. All of the girls' helmets have scrapes on the right side from tapping the pavement. Cheyenne and Jasmine have scrapes on their right knees also. Robin escapes physical damage by virtue of her protective seat. Ama's elbow has swollen and continues to bleed. She gets up and grabs the first aid kit from the front of the trailer and patches scrapes and bruises. I begin to remove cockleburs from my skin and clothing. Ama and I exchange a look that says, "We just dodged a bullet." It takes about ten minutes before we get up in order to start the remount.

Focusing on the bike, I see four of the five crank arms on the right side are bent, a fact I did not notice from the sitting position. Handlebars are twisted in their sockets. Shaking my head, I grit my teeth and start yanking on the handle grips to straighten them up. What can be done about the bent Gossamer crank arms? I don't have tools for this kind of problem. We have to get to a bike shop.

"Let's see if we can make it to the Civil War Memorial down by the water's edge," I say. We push the quint well over the troubling tracks and get back on. We ride onward, more cautious and a bit nervous, wanting to leave our first real spill of the journey far behind. My right foot wobbles in and out as the warped crank system propels us forward. I remember an old Buster Keaton movie where he humps across the screen on some busted contraption.

THE EARLY MORNING RAIN AND the fall put a damper on this momentous day. It is hard to force ourselves out of this negative spiral. We can't do anything about the weather, but hopefully we can learn from the fall. We have to put our focus on what lies ahead.

Nearing downtown Charlestown, our spirits lift upon seeing the pre-Civil War homes in pastels of every color. The girls call out when they spy a favorite color—Cheyenne claims green; Jasmine claims pink; Robin proclaims her love for blue. Charlestown's residents seem as diverse as the houses. Using our surroundings as the backdrop to illustrate history lessons, we share with Cheyenne, Jasmine, and Robin some of the town's importance. They look around with intent as we tell them that people watched from these very windows when the first shots were fired at the Battery where heavy artillery and men were stationed on a small sand bar in the Charleston harbor. The Rebels watched in the way we watch TV today. Absorbing our surroundings, we find ourselves at the water's edge where the Confederate Defenders' statue stands as a reminder of that war. Good guys and bad guys can change, depending on which side one claims to be on. By now the air is warm and the sky threatens rain the way grandma threatens discipline: full of rumble but with no delivery. The battlement sits at the edge of Charleston Harbor. Fort Sumter is visible in the distance. Beyond the fort lies the Atlantic Ocean. We're almost there.

Robin, Jasmine and Cheyenne enjoy the cannon at the battlements in Charleston, South Carolina. August of 2009

We spend time at the waterfront; snacking and playing. I reflect on the world that once prevailed here. The girls climb on the old cannons. Amarins picks gravel from her elbow and wonders if there is a park for the girls to play in. It's not what we had in mind when we envisioned this day. There is no place to put our feet in the water. We decide to head for Folly Island south of town adjacent to the ocean.

Moving in and out of narrow streets, we stumble upon a horse drawn carriage full of tourists. We tail them on Yeller eavesdropping on some of the city's history as we go along. Before long we stop at a garden area to use the public restrooms. While we are hanging out in the gardens under the shade trees, a middle-aged gentleman dressed in slacks and a polo shirt stops and asks about the bike. After a few more questions he says, "How do you support yourselves?"

"By the generosity of strangers who find joy in our story," I reply. "By the way, I am Bill and this is my family," pointing to the girls as they run up and down the paths between the flowers and plants. "What is your name?"

"George," he answers.

"Nice name. It is my grandpa's name as well."

George, who would not have had any freedoms before the Civil War as a black man in the south, reaches in his pocket and hands us a fifty dollar bill from his wallet. "In return for a picture of your bike," he adds with a grin.

After he gets his shot he says, "I wish you well on your journey."

I hand him one of our Pedouin cards before he leaves in his truck.

His curiosity and support, which just played out here in the Deep South, demonstrates to me how far we have come from Charleston's uglier beginnings. His actions punched all kinds of holes in the views of "people of color" that I was raised with and which later I came to know were inaccurate.

Feeling encouraged by this encounter, Amarins and I turn our attention towards the ocean. With maps from tourist magazines, Ama pieces together the road to Folly Beach. She is the compass of this adventure.

A view of the marshes on our way to Folly Beach.
August of 2009

SAILING FROM TOWN, WE SEE before us a road system that looks like a plate of spaghetti. The concrete roads pile up and twist in all directions. Motorists speed past us as we climb the tall mound of noodles. Trying not to be totally overcome with fear, I force myself to look forward and pedal. On top we have a commanding view of the city to our left and lush, green marshes to our right. The shoulder is at least eight feet wide along the bridge. Leaning against its wall, we admire distant waves and the sea of green below us.

Coasting down the overpass near the bottom, we see someone in front of us taking lots of pictures. As we pass the tall, thirty something, slim photographer, I holler at him in a half joking way, "Hey, we need a place to stay in Folly Beach, can you help?"

He yells back, "Let me make some calls!"

About a mile farther we see him again as he passes us. I pull Yeller to a screeching halt. The rotors, warped from heavy usage in the foothills of the Appalachian Mountains, make the bike shimmy as it ceases forward motion.

"Hi, I'm Mark. I work for the Charleston Bicycle Company here on James Island. Does your bike need anything?"

We give him the short version of our run-in with the tracks, and he responds, "I know our company would love to get your quint back in shape. I'll also call around and find you a place to stay."

We exchange phone numbers and get back to pedaling.

IT IS THE MIDDLE OF the afternoon and hunger sets in. An Applebee's comes into view. We whip in with hopes of a great meal plus a place to relax before we reach the beach. Our wish is granted. It is not crowded. The girls play about while we wait for the food. Brandy, the manager, comes over and asks about our story. As we share our adventures, other patrons eagerly listen in. Our story strikes a chord with someone. When we check out we discover that a customer has paid our tab in full.

Brandy meets us at the exit and says, "Would you like to stop by tomorrow for a meal on us?"

Amarins and I look at each other and say "yes" at the same time.

Brandy adds, "You guys are great and I admire the opportunities you give your girls."

Deep inside, her words resonate. Today is a lesson in overcoming obstacles and loving your neighbor as yourself. With the exception of Grandpa Byers' unconditional love, I found little redemption. A childhood full of criticism, void of physical and emotional safety, can have a detrimental impact on the trajectory of one's life. Family systems are as old as life itself. They can be very hard to break away from, even when necessary. Today, a day peppered with unexpected kindness from many different directions, I take another step away from my past.

Brandy and some waitresses watch from the entryway as we load up. A light rain begins to fall. Amarins puts the girls in raincoats under the restaurant's eave as I get the bike ready to roll. Robin, not having a rain jacket, gets mine. Her rain coat was one of those things that fell between the cracks as we prepared to leave Pongo Ridge. Wrapped in mine, she looks like a pig in a blanket. Now that everyone is shielded from the rain, I say, "Three, two, one... Go!" Then we let our customary "Thank you!" echo behind us.

With full stomachs and high morale, we ride toward the Atlantic and Holiday Inn. Somehow, Mark has arranged for a free night. Pulling into their parking area the girls are bouncing all over the place. I try to contain the bubbling expectations of ocean front play time and freedom. I hold the lively bike and wait for Amarins to return. With a smile she says, "We have a ground floor with a patio to the beach."

YELLER IS RESTING AGAINST THE outside wall under a warm cloudy sky. Our belongings are tucked inside our spacious room. We walk hand in hand to the great water. We inhale the salt air and listen to the restless waves lapping towards our feet. After 633 miles, thirty-one days, five states, and countless amounts of *tzedakah*, we triumphantly put our feet in the Atlantic Ocean.

Our feet are in the Atlantic Ocean.
August of 2009

If you can't ride it, you push it.
August of 2009

Cheyenne brushes her teeth
in the great outdoors.
August of 2009

Surrounded by mirrors at the
Aiken University.
August of 2009

New friends in South Carolina.
August of 2009

Fun in the Chattooga River, South Carolina.
August of 2009

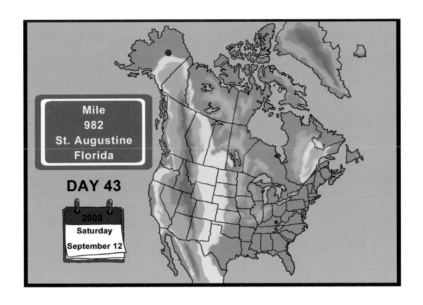

Mile
982
St. Augustine
Florida

DAY 43

2009
Saturday
September 12

CHAPTER 8

WE ARE PEDALING DOWN THE east coast of Florida when our spokes start breaking, front and back. We have less than 1,000 miles of tension on the wheels. I have a mind for how things work, but this bike is driving me bonkers. I just can't seem to figure out why this thing keeps breaking down.

This is not the first time we've had problems. Just three weeks ago in Hiawassee, Georgia, we did major bike repairs at the Spin-Lite Cycling shop. Lyle, a former airplane mechanic and now owner of the bike shop, had a sleepless night after we pulled in with our ramshackle bicycle. It wasn't the spokes then. They hadn't started popping yet. That time it was a badly stretched drive chain (due to dirt, heat and climbing mountains), used-up brake pads (the Appalachian Mountains have their name for a reason), a wobble in the rear rim (caused by spokes that had worked themselves loose), and shifting trouble (the result of a 9-gear sprocket not lining up with a 10-gear shifter).

When we came back to the shop the next morning, Yeller stood outside in the sunshine, ready to ride again. Lyle fixed what he could, installing a new drive chain and brake pads and tightening the spokes on both wheels. He'd also installed a rear rim brake so we'd be safer crossing the Rockies. The shifting trouble we'll always have. We have a road gear system that requires minute movements that the long tandem shifting cable cannot deliver. That was a faulty setup by the manufacturer. When I went to settle up, he said, "You owe me nothing. It was all taken care of. God bless you all." There was nothing we could say except "Thanks!"

I've always been too busy working to follow athletic pursuits. Most jobs kept me active, so I never felt like I was missing much. Acquiring a bicycle of any kind was initially a rather insane prospect to me. If we were going to ride to Alaska, Amarins and I figured, we'd be better off buying from a custom bicycle company rather than some chain store. We'd told Mark (the middleman) and Co-Motion what our plans were with the bicycle. We were informed that the bicycle is built for five grown-ups. Our weight at last count was only that of three grown-ups. We figured this would actually be helpful to the quint's performance and longevity. Reality has proven differently.

Yeller has performed just fine, not counting the fall in Charleston, since Lyle worked on her. We've been riding with more stability and less sway. But now things have changed. Broken spokes are making the wheels feeble.

WE RIDE AROUND THE DOWNTOWN area of St. Augustine, the oldest Spanish settlement in Florida. There are beautiful buildings, old narrow roads, and horse drawn carriages. The old fort still stands.

As we skirt the Spanish buildings from the sixteenth century, we are stopped and quizzed.

"Are you here for the Cycling Festival tomorrow?"

Questioning what that is about, I ascertain that there might be vendor tents set up at the amphitheater where they sell everything imaginable for the biking community. The booths are there today, and the bicycle event is tomorrow. As I shoot a look toward Ama, we both know where we're headed.

Castillo de San Marcos in St. Augustine, Florida.
September of 2009

At one of the many traffic lights, Amarins gets directions to the amphitheater. Shortly after, we pull up to the event at the local fairgrounds. We
ride Yeller up a curved ramp as people part like the Red Sea did when Moses
touched the water with his staff. The girls are quick to get off into the festive
atmosphere. They want to find out what is happening here. While Amarins
stays with Yeller and the girls, I head up toward the vendors' area to find help
for our ailing spokes. Immediately I see a familiar face—Jeff. We met him at
Champion Cycling in Jacksonville, Florida.

"Hey Jeff, man, am I glad to see you again. We're the Pedouins. We met
you in Jacksonville."

"Yes, I remember, how are you all doing?"

"Not too great. We got lots of rain and some broken spokes. Can you
help?"

"Absolutely, I can't stop the rain but let me get my tools and I will get
down there as soon as I can and see about the spokes."

"Great. Take your time."

Cheyenne, Jasmine, and Robin play with some kids in the grass. Amarins
tells me that we have our first flat tire on the trailer. When it rains it pours. As
I fix the flat, Jeff makes his way to our bike. With the trailer tire fixed, I spend
time with our mechanic at the front of the bike. He informs me, "These
spokes are too light for this bike's weight."

"Yes, I know. Lyle from a bike shop in the mountains of Georgia said that
as well. We're realizing more and more that this bike was not made with our

intentions in mind. If we had the money and time, we would change or fix the rims." Jeff changes out several broken spokes and we both seem confident that it will be fine because we are in for some nice, smooth, flat road riding ahead. He will not take any money. He just says, "Ride on!"

WHILE REPAIRS ARE BEING MADE, Amarins calls Ryan and Jenny whom we met via our website. They want to show us their town. Since we can leave Yeller at the bike show, we take them up on their offer.

Off we go for an afternoon of sixteenth century Spanish history lessons in St. Augustine. We appreciate standing next to the oldest wooden school house in America.

The girls ask if lessons are still held here. Ama tells them they are not. Instead of reading about this place in a text book, Cheyenne, Jasmine, and Robin are touching the bleached, hand-hewn weathered boards covering the school's exterior. They also try to peek in the thin, wavy window panes. I say, "Girls, you are also making history. You are the first girls to travel on a five-person bicycle across North America." With this realization, Cheyenne grins.

The oldest wooden school house in the U.S.A.
September of 2009

Coming to the end of our tour, we talk about grabbing a motel for the night. The campground next to the show costs as much as a cheap dive and we really don't want to put up our tent in a mud hole since it keeps raining off and on.

Our hosts drop all but me off at a motel about one mile from the fairgrounds. I get a ride back to Yeller. By now it is getting dark. I thank Ryan and Jenny and wish them well on their journey as they seek new directions for their lives. They have been contemplating changing careers and have started a business in photography. Our hosts are very encouraged by our "leap of faith" and ability to make ends meet while being self-employed back home. It has impacted them to the point that they need to be more proactive concerning their future.

There are still people around our bicycle. Looking on as though I'm just another stranger, I fill with pride. Our efforts are bringing joy and wonder to so many others. At the vendors' area, I see Jeff again. As I thank him, I am introduced to his friend Joe, a retired officer from the Northeast. I soon dub him "Boston Joe." Joe is stunned by our gumption to take such a trip.

"Hey Bill, have you seen "Endless Summer"?" he asks.

"No, what is it about?"

"It's a classic surfing movie about two guys who follow the summer around the world, surfing the coasts of Africa, Hawaii, and Tahiti and such. It's showing in the outdoor theater tonight. You need to see it man. They're your kind of breed. If you want, I will come and get you."

"Yes, why not, maybe I'll bring Cheyenne."

I ride off in the evening, heading back toward the motel. The drizzle feels warm on my skin. I once again realize how blessed we are to be living out this dream. At eight-thirty tonight Boston Joe will come to the motel to take Cheyenne and me to the theater.

Cheyenne is excited about our "date" as she labels it. Even though Jasmine and Robin are worn out from the walk through the historic district, they are sad they can't go. Ama and I decided it would be better for them to rest and watch some Discovery Channel.

Cheyenne and I sit in the covered, outdoor theater and enjoy the movie. Since the show is short on dialogue, Cheyenne and I talk about the cars and music in it. I tell her about my first truck, a fiftieth year anniversary special, 53 F-100. She loves the part about the round glass-knobbed radio and the six chrome teeth that lined the front grill. She is surprised that I would push it out our driveway at night and go for rides before I had my license. Still holding my hand, we both enjoy my trip down memory lane as I share other things I did as a boy contemporary to the movie.

Taking us back to the hotel, Boston Joe hands me a generous gift and tells me how wonderful it is to meet us. I assure him it has been our pleasure.

EARLY IN AND EARLY OUT. The clouds greet us as we prepare Yeller for the day's adventures. There is a ride to attend at the bicycle expo. By seven-fifteen we glide through hundreds of bikes and their masters. Jerseys of all hues, from sunny neon to classic black, drape the contestants' backs. There are tandems, road bikes, and mountain bikes filling the gravel parking lots. We enjoy the others as much as they enjoy us. We work our way to the front and lean against the metal gate on the left that leads out to the highway. Jasmine feels like a princess as all eyes are on us. We have a prime front row seat for the start.

At seven-thirty the throngs of riders shoot out of the gate's opening and onto the roadway where local police have held back traffic. The whoosh of wheels overpowers cheers and conversation. Metal clicking sounds of gears changing and chains rattling, reminiscent of the sounds of squirrels chattering in nut-laden hickory trees, rush past our ears. The girls are mesmerized by all the bike wrap and jersey colors. Once the largest mass of riders has flown by, we slip into the crowd and enjoy the company of fellow cyclists for a couple of miles. The girls enjoy the many comments of "Great job!" and "You guys are awesome!" as folks ride past us to their day's unfolding.

Soon we are alone once again.

A fuel pump overhang at a weathered filling station is our first stop of the day. We mill around and eat donuts under the eave when we notice other bicyclists stop to take refuge like us. We're curious that they have taken a wrong turn, because once we broke off from the group, we haven't seen any cyclists. Amarins walks over to some riders standing close to us and inquires about the situation. There are several routes for the ride. We happen to be on the shorter, thirty-mile loop.

Though the clouds seem angry, the warm rain slacks off to a drizzle. We mount Yeller and bolt. A couple of miles farther, we are flagged down by a race official. Surprised, yet curious, we follow his lead. We have arrived at the turning point for the riders. Fresh fruit, cookies, and ice cold lemonade greet the participants. The covered pathway leading from the road to a marine biology center makes a dry place to relax and socialize. Amarins explains we are not part of the tour, to which one of the volunteers replies, "Now you are."

We mingle with fellow riders while snacking. Our girls take the oppor-tunity to enjoy the company of other young riders in the group. This event is a charity ride plus race. The leg we are on has novices and families with kids around Cheyenne's age and up. We have a chance to hand out cards and talk to folks about our journey. The girls look like bees going from flower to flower, person to person, handing out cards.

As the crowd breaks up, we push our bike into the rain and head back south. We've decided to just ride through the rain. The tepid drops fall straight down. The concrete roadway has the distinct smell that comes from being baked by the sun and then quenched by rain. The smell reminds me of our driveway at 9900 Fern Creek Road, where I was raised. Grandpa Byers lived with us in our orange brick tri-level house on a sloping lot cut from the Aldridge farm that once provided hay and farm goods for Louisville residents. He had formed up and poured a concrete masterpiece of a driveway in the 1960s. It was adorned with concrete curbs, drains, staircases, and walkways. Folks would drive by just to view his concrete art work. Many warm summer days were spent lying in the gutters as a deluge of water from a thunderstorm washed down the rough surfaces. The bodies of many of my eight siblings and I formed temporary dams until the gushing water spilled over and around us.

Immersed in a childhood scent, the kids wrapped in rain gear, and with a nice wide shoulder as a buffer, we ride off, leaving the sights and sounds of distant riders in our wake. They are returning to their starting point as we venture on the seemingly unending surface of South A1A.

FOR MILES THE RAIN PELTS us. The girls keep their heads down and complain little. To our left is a sea of saw grass and splotches of sea oats. Just beyond it is the Atlantic Ocean, of which we get an occasional glimpse. On our right is nothing but palmettos and more grass as far as the eye can see.

A gunshot sound pierces the late morning. Through the pouring rain, the sound scares the living daylights out of us.

"Billy! Stop! The rear tire is flat!" Amarins yells over nature. There is so much runoff on the road's edge that I couldn't feel the flat tire on the rear of the bike.

I pull the bike to a stop and straddle it, holding it upright. Amarins is already off before I go through these routines. She instinctively gets the girls off Yeller and sends them across the drainage ditch to the edge of the foliage. She comes back with the kickstand.

When I finally get off, I grab the blue tarp and together we throw the tarp over the girls. Jasmine calls out, "Dad, what are you going to do?"

"I've got to fix the flat tire girls, just stay under the tarp!" I have to yell over the thunder of rain pummeling our shelter.

At the bike, I realize we are hosed. More than just a sand spur puncture, the inner tube has blown out through the tire. I won't be fixing this one because the tube has a hole the size of a dime in it. At 800 pounds of total weight, a makeshift patch inside the busted tire will not hold. To make matters worse, we have no spare tires. We hoped to make it another two hundred miles to Fort Pierce and buy some Nimbus Armadillo tires there. These tires by Specialized are bulletproof according to Lyle.

My gamble to carry no spare tires of any brand has backfired. I decide to hunker under the tarp too. It is a Sunday afternoon and there is little traffic on the road. Now what?

An hour passes slowly while we hunker under our makeshift canopy. We all sit close to create some atmosphere of comfort. I try to keep calm, attempting not to let bad habits boil over. The girls point out cars in the distance when they become visible through the fog of rain. Their actions demonstrate hope that help will materialize on this lonely stretch of road. When one stops, it is Officer Ryan. Off duty, but spotting trouble from far away, he pulls over to inquire about our situation. Finding out that we are not just one stranded cyclist, but five with only one bike, he asks, "Where are you from?"

"We hail from Kentucky. A thousand miles from home and now we are out of tires. I gambled and came up short. Do you know of any bike stores around where I can find some?"

"Yes," Officer Ryan says, "but I don't think they're open on Sundays. There is a Wal-Mart in Palm Coast, twenty miles south of here. It's the closest I can think of. I can check for you and see if they carry tires, if you want me to."

"That'd be great Officer. Take down my number and let me know what you find out." I hope he can find some, but doubt it since we have an oddball tire size.

His gift of time is soothing. On his way north he didn't hesitate to help strangers in need, even if it took him south again. About thirty minutes later, he calls and confirms my doubts. There are no tires of our size available.

It is time to call Boston Joe. He gave us his number in case of trouble. Well, we're in trouble now. He answers his phone on the first ring.

"Boston Joe," I say, "Bill with The Pedouins here. I hate to call you out on a Sunday, but we need some help."

"What's going on Bill?"

As I explain the situation, I sense that help is on the way. It isn't ten minutes before our phone rings. It is Jeff. He's back in Jacksonville, some hundred miles north of us. He's heard of our trouble and is already on the hunt for tires which he thinks he has at the shop where he works. He lets us know he'll be with us in a couple of hours.

THE TIDE HAS TURNED. As though in celebration, the rain stops and the sun peeks through breaks in the clouds. I crawl out from under the tarp to go exploring. Surrounded by heavy, humid air, my eyes search for a path to the ocean. Salt catches in our noses, and the hush of crashing waves tickles our ears. The girls want to go, but we feel safer with them at the edge of the vegetation rather than walking along the road's edge, especially in this long curve. Riding, they are under the control of the bike. Walking, they might take off like rabbits.

Across the road I find an abandoned building lot and a trail that seems to lead to the water. Doubting the intent of the "No trespassing" sign, I motion for my family. There appears to be a well worn path towards the ocean, an egress to the water's edge that we have seldom seen in Florida. The building

Jasmine traverses the rocks with elegance.
September of 2009

that once stood here is nothing but a rubble pad and poses no danger to us. Together we walk to the ocean.

The beach is covered with volcanic type rocks and boulders. Up and down the sandy shore are layers of gray and black pumice-like surfaces with pores that absorb the sea spray which intermittently splash over them. Scattered among them are holes of varying sizes and shapes. Some holes hold water and others contain small sand boxes.

We play for hours. Sitting on a smooth rock that is shaded and striped like an old gray tabby cat, I watch with satisfaction as the girls explore the beach-front. They climb over rocks bigger than themselves. Our little girls fear nothing and are ready to explore the world. Each girl's compass is in line with her heart, unaffected by the magnetic pull of conformity. They don't know anything different than to live with an abundance of love and friendship, of giving and receiving. Amarins and I embrace on this beach devoid of humanity, except for us. We marvel. Our hearts swell as we watch our girls live, and love, life.

Mid afternoon I head back to the bike to wait. An hour later, our help arrives. I scurry back and get the family. Then we join Jeff and Boston Joe next to our crippled quint. They have brought hamburgers and cold drinks. The girls sit and eat in the shade of the tarp.

While we eat, Jeff puts the new tire on the wheel and installs it on the bike. He gives us another tire to take with us. He's also brought some extra tubes, but I assure him we have plenty of those. I tell him, "I would love to have them but the weight is a problem. We can carry only so much stuff. Every ounce counts, even here on Florida's flats." We bid thanks, farewell, and ride away with the retreating sun.

Seeking cover from the Florida sun.
September of 2009

TWO DAYS LATER WE HIT A sixty-eight mile stretch in one long twelve hour day to Titusville. Logging two more flat tires and broken spokes on the rear rim, it is time for us to have a serious talk. On the eve of the sixty-eight miler, we were in the home of a loving older couple. The girls enjoyed their pool until they looked like raisins. The Manns and their friends made sure we got our new Armadillo tires for the bike along with two spares. Those kinds of respites evaporate so soon when challenges pile up.

Our plan is to go all the way to Key West, the farthest island of the Florida Keys. But we're not so sure anymore. Most of the A1A highway property is off limits to camping. The campgrounds we've found are for RVs only. There is no tenting allowed. Even a local municipality in the middle of nowhere would not let us camp. It was not our intention during the planning stage to micro manage everything on the route. We wanted to leave room for mystery, uncertainty, and the freedom to linger or speed up if the situation dictated it. This decision does have its downside. Here in Titusville we are again forced to stay in a motel. It is breaking the bank. When Amarins says, "Bill, I don't know if I want to go to the Keys anymore," it's like she is reading my mind.

"Why not Babe?"

"Well, we have met some nice people in Florida, but the road is danger-ous. We have seen more than our share of aggressive drivers. We have had more people honk and shoot us the bird than in all the other states put together. It is almost impossible to camp. I just don't have a good feeling about going through Ft. Lauderdale and Miami. Just imagine the traffic and camping issues there. The accumulation of all this drains me, it is taking away some of the joy. Where is the simple act of flowing along the highway in all this?"

"Ama, you're probably right. I've been thinking about it, too. I feel a bit sad because you really wanted to go to the Keys so bad. Are you willing to give it up without regrets? What is the alternative?"

"Yes, I have already given up on it. I figure we can head west somewhere after Fort Pierce. I know we want to see the Brolmanns and you want to give John Hart a big hug."

"You got that right. If it weren't for these guys and a few others, we'd go west now."

"Let's get to Wally's and then we can turn west and skirt the top of Lake Okeechobee to the west coast of Florida."

"Sounds like a good plan to me."

The kids are fast asleep. It's good they aren't privy to this wrangling about details. Despite the mechanical troubles and a few selfish drivers, we want them to have good memories of Robin's birth state.

Sleep comes a little harder here in Titusville. My head still spins from our conversation. I hate to quit. I hate to give in, but Ama is right. We'll turn west in a few days to by-pass South Florida.

Once the sun is up, we find out that the local bike shop does not open until ten in the morning. Using most of what is left of our money, we pay early for another night's stay. By mid-afternoon the spokes are replaced, and Yeller is ready for tomorrow's departure. As evening approaches, we go to a park dedicated to America's astronauts. The girls run around placing their hands in the concrete casts of Neil Armstrong's hands. We reinforce with Cheyenne, Jasmine, and Robin that they, too, are on a fantastic journey doing something that has never been accomplished: one family, two wheels and 7,000 miles.

STRENGTHENED WITH OUR DECISION TO head west after Fort Pierce, we leave Titusville under an intense early morning sun. As we look to the east, the sun lies low on the horizon, and a bright orange streak reflects across the water, streaking towards us as if to say, "Keep going." The dark surrounding clouds are blanketed in an orange glow as well. It is a classic summer sunrise in south Florida, just brilliant enough to put our challenges in perspective.

The next evening, we arrive on the outskirts of Fort Pierce to see some familiar faces up ahead. Wally and a friend ride along with us on the south side of Vero Beach. A right hand turn takes us into a local park just north of Fort Pierce's jetties.

The Brolmanns are waiting with a sign that reads "Welcome Pedouins to Fort Pierce." They are the parents of my oldest friend, Wally, who emigrated here in the 1950's. In their eighties now, these Dutch immigrants joyfully show their support. Before I can get a word out of my mouth, the girls are already climbing off the bike like baby spiders leaving their mother's back. Wedging the walking stick under the seat, I leave Yeller standing alone and give our friends some big hugs.

Mr. Brollman shakes his head. He can't believe the size of Yeller and that we actually made it here. We mill around in the shade of palm trees, dodging ant hills, drinking juice, eating fruit, cheese, crackers, and delicious Dutch "stroopwafels" (sugar waffles with syrup in between), all the while sharing stories of the previous 1,190 miles.

This town, Fort Pierce, Florida, is where the smallest Pedouin was

Mr and Mrs Brollman welcome us to Fort Pierce.
September of 2009

born, and it is from this place we will head west after a long weekend with Wally and Betty-Ann Brollman in their waterfront home.

A warm welcome in
Woodbine, Georgia.
September of 2009

Camp Pedouin in Hollywood, South Carolina.
September of 2009

A shady lane in South Carolina.
September of 2009

Robin enjoys the beach in
Florida.
September of 2009

We're coming up on the Sidney Lanier Bridge in Georgia.
September of 2009

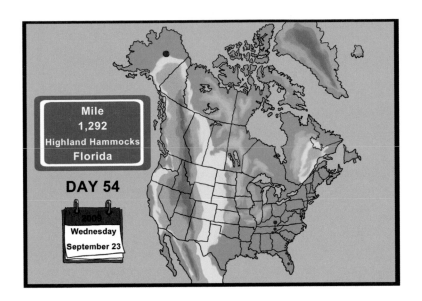

Mile
1,292
Highland Hammocks
Florida

DAY 54

2009
Wednesday
September 23

CHAPTER 9

WE CONCENTRATE ON PEDALING IN the intense Florida sun. The girls, quiet from the heat, begin to murmur when they notice the many dead armadillos. We think we are seeing a mirage as waves of heat dance off the endless black inferno of asphalt. Brown, football sized creatures with tapered tails, crushed heads, and plated outer shells, critters from prehistoric times, lay thick as flies in some spots. I swerve to avoid their rotting carcasses.

Cheyenne says, "What are those animals, Mom?"

"They are armadillos," Amarins responds.

Jasmine wonders, "Do we have them at home?"

"No honey, they live where it is very warm. I think they came here from the Texas area."

Cheyenne wonders, "Why are we only seeing dead ones, Dad?"

"They are night animals like raccoons, owls and opossums. They don't see well. As they cross the road they get hit by the fast moving trucks and cars."

"They're funny," says Robin.

"Yes, they are. I hope we see one that is alive," Amarins adds.

Cheyenne laughs as she retorts, "We can call them "darmadillos"."

"What?" I laugh. "Where did you come up with that?"

"They are dead, aren't they? I just put a "d" for dead in front of armadillo. That makes darmadillo. Hey Mom, what do you think?"

"I think it's a terrific word Cheyenne."

We all laugh so hard that the bike sways about on this scorching day.

PERHAPS THERE IS "WALT DISNEY" magic here in Florida. Back in January, with the help of a good friend in Florida, the "Pedouin" name was born. I called Wally, an incredibly smart Dutch man who started a business with a friend in the mid 1980's that he still runs today, to tell him about our plans.

"Classic Car Coating."

"Hey Wally, it's me. Do you have time to talk?"

"Sure, what's up Paco?"

"You ain't gonna believe what Ama and I have decided we're going to do."

"Let me guess, you're going to have three more children?"

"Nice guess knot head. No. We are going to take a ride from Kentucky to Alaska."

"A ride in what."

"Not in, but on. She has found a five person tandem bicycle from some company in Oregon."

"You are going to have one sore butt, Paco."

"Tell me about it. We plan to camp like the Bedouins. Remember when I used to work with the Bedouins in the West Bank? They are people of Arabic origin who move around in the desert, living in a tent. We'll haul our tent with us and camp along the way."

"Yeah, you are a nomad, that's for sure. I'll start calling you a Pedouin."

"What did you say?"

"I said Pedouin. You know pedal plus Bedouin."

"Wally, you are a doggone genius. You just coined a new word. If you don't mind, I think we might use it!"

"Go ahead. I'm not going to ride that thing."

BACK IN THE HEAT OF this Florida fall, the creative atmosphere continues. Cheyenne is just getting started, "Hey, we can call a dead raccoon a "craccoon" since it cracked its head."

The girls laugh hard enough to wake the darmadillos. Remembering a dead deer we saw draped over a fence like a piece of carpet, Jasmine ups the ante with, "Cheyenne, remember the dead deer that was hanging over the fence?"

"Yes, I do. It didn't jump high enough and got stuck in the barbed wire."

"We can call a dead deer a "zeerd"," Jasmine continues.

"Girls stop, you're killing me," I laugh.

Amarins gets into the fray, "You know what you call a squirrel that quarrels with a car and looses?"

Silence returns as our brains try to unravel her riddle. Straggling "No"-'s sound off, and then she says, "You call it a "squarrel"."

"Good one, Mom," Cheyenne says. "We can write a book about dead animals."

Still snickering from our word game, we make our way toward our destination. Pulling into the Highlands Hammock State Park, we see our first live armadillo.

RANGERS MIKE AND BRENDA ARRANGE a camp spot for us for two nights. It is a beautiful spot on the mossy grass under Spanish moss laden trees. The bathroom is right behind our site. We enjoy this because it allows the older girls to go there independently. The playground is within view, which also has its benefits. It is close enough to keep an eye on the girls and far enough not to perk up at every sound.

It is the first time we have a chance to use our tent in Florida. It has become our home, where we all have our own spots. Cheyenne sleeps all the way in the back. Jasmine is by her side. Amarins and I share a double sleeping bag in the front of the tent; no way did we want to sleep separate for the duration of this journey. Robin sleeps all over the tent. She starts out in the middle, between Jasmine and us. Sometimes she ends up in our sleeping bag. Sometimes we find her at the foot end of Cheyenne and Jasmine. The rain fly of the tent extends toward the back. This is our garage where we park the trailer. We can also add an extension to the front which comes in handy during rainy days.

Our stay at the park is thoroughly enjoyable. We have supper with Jack and Joy Spencer who are in their late 80s. They built their own trike-recumbent bicycles and ride them around a ten mile loop through the park several times a week.

There are several hiking trails to explore. Some lead across boardwalks, others through a "new" forest. The new growth is coming up quickly after a controlled burn in the area. One of the trails leads to the ranger station where we find Ranger Judy at her post. She tells the girls they can become Junior Rangers by working on Florida's Junior Rangers program. The girls don't need to hear this twice. When we get back to our site the girls go right to work.

Hiking the trail through a new forest.
September of 2009

Robin makes sure she colors on every page, while Amarins reads her different parts of the program. Jasmine works on the hidden words puzzle. She has a sharp mind and gets the hang of it quickly. Cheyenne fully submerges in the material. She reads every assignment and with little help figures out the answers to questions. After more than an hour she's still working on it. Luring her to take a playground break doesn't stop her. We let her follow her path of discovery.

Lessons about nature's litter (leaves that break down into tiny pieces and become soil) and people litter (bottles, cans, paper and other trash that can hurt wildlife) are easily understood and absorbed. The lesson about native plants and exotic plants takes a little longer to understand. The exotic plants invade the habitat of the native plants as they are competing for the same food, water and space to grow. The native plants and animals must find a different place to live if they want to survive.

In the afternoon we are in for a surprise. Rangers Brenda and Judy have made it possible for us to go on a tram ride through the park. We get to see where the exotic plants are invading the space of native plants. There is a leaning hollow tree which provides space for several plants to grow. This creates a small habi-

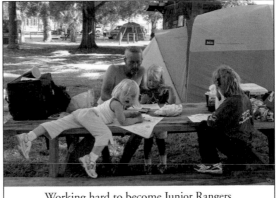

Working hard to become Junior Rangers.
September of 2009

tat by itself. We also learn about cypress trees. They grow in water. For the roots to absorb oxygen, they grow knees on them that stick out above the water. "Once a knee, never a tree," Ranger Judy teaches us.

We ride through a rolling landscape. The low parts are swampy. Here we keep our eyes open for al-ligators. We are rewarded with several sightings of baby alligators, a couple of turtles and eventually, mother alligator herself. She is huge. On the way back to the camping area we have to wait for a gopher tortoise to cross the path. He doesn't go fast. After all, this is his domain and we are only visiting.

Filled with new infor-mation the girls continue working on their ranger badge. Then we are off to

Junior Rangers Cheyenne, Robin and Jasmine,
with Rangers Judy and Brenda.
September of 2009

the ranger station once more. It is time for inspection. A little nervous and with high expectations, they wait for Ranger Brenda to check their work. Then, chests forward, they are rewarded with their first Ranger Badge and a certificate for completion. What a wonderful park, so full of lessons about life, death and survival.

THE NEXT DAY WE HEAD away from one of the finest state parks we've ever stayed at. Coming up to a bend in the road, I spy something in the field beyond a fence.

"Ama, what is that in the field up ahead?" At that moment, the smell is the clue.

I hear a chorus of, "What is that awful smell?"

"It is the smell of death." That is the truest answer I can offer.

"Where does it come from?" Cheyenne asks.

In the middle of a field of scrub grass to our right lays a large, bloated reddish-brown cow. Standing on the carcass are a half dozen black vultures, a couple with wings outstretched, as if claiming their piece of real estate.

Jasmine says, "Daddy, we've smelled this before."

"You are right Jasmine. We have passed a lot of darmadillos, craccoons, zeerds, and other dead critters, decomposing out of sight."

Cheyenne is curious, "Why is the cow so bloated?"

"Because when an animal dies and lies in this heat, gas builds up in its rotting insides. It blows up like a balloon. One of those birds has punctured the skin and we get to smell the rotten meat, like muscles, heart, and intestines."

"Do all animals smell like this when they die?" replies Cheyenne with a queasy look.

"Yep, it is a part of life's cycle, honey. Like that cow, we are all going to end one day."

"Then what happens?"

"That is one deep question, girls. We don't know when we will die. We have hopes of what happens after death based on our faith."

"I think it depends a lot on what you choose to believe," Amarins says.

Since I am the oldest, Cheyenne and Jasmine start crying, "We don't want you to die, Daddy."

"Thanks girls. If all goes well, I'll live to be an old man. By that time you might be tired of me anyway."

"Nooooo," they yell in unison.

Ama soothes the tender emotions bruised by one of life's hard lessons: mortality. She is great at letting them cry and encouraging them to explore their emotions, especially at moments like these.

When it comes to encouraging Cheyenne, Jasmine, or Robin to express their feelings, their mother is like a warm spring wind daring dogwood blossoms to take flight.

Captain Cheyenne sails on the Atlantic Ocean.
September of 2009

The girls at the jetty in Fort Pierce, Florida.
September of 2009

Enjoying the company of Wally
and Betty-Ann.
September of 2009

Clouds reflect in Lake Okeechobee.
September of 2009

Jasmine enjoys a "fishy" craft.
September of 2009

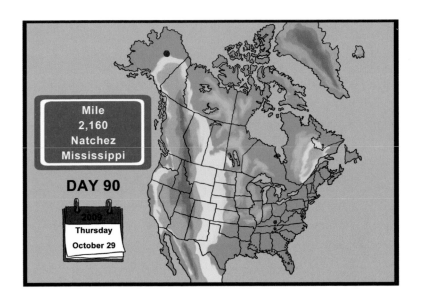

Mile
2,160
Natchez
Mississippi

DAY 90

2009
Thursday
October 29

CHAPTER 10

MY MIND IS AMOK WITH conflicting thoughts and feelings as we roll into Natchez, Mississippi. This city of layers sits on the banks of the fabled Mississippi River, where the stories run as deep as the river is wide.

One such story involves two persons from different generations that filled my desire for intimacy. Shortly after the death of my Grandpa Byers in the spring of 1984, I heard some wild tales about his birth and later about how he interacted with me when I was a baby. One of those tales involved his crossing the Mississippi River and how I retold this story to a beautiful woman I met out west.

IN JULY OF 2001, AMARINS and I hiked out from the floor of the Grand Canyon, each on a quest for different reasons and traveling alone. Walking up the South Rim we passed each other several times. At one point I offered to drive her to Flagstaff, Arizona, a town about eighty miles south of the rim where she could catch the Greyhound bus to her next destination. These miles turned into 16,000 miles. We embarked on a chance road trip that marked the beginning of our love story that played out over one third of the states. In western Oklahoma, we found ourselves cruising eastward on interstate 40, sucking on ice cubes from a cooler in my red, 1987 plain jane Toyota pickup truck. The temperature for days flirted around the one hundred degree mark, even warmer in our air-condition less cab. The mysterious blond European woman who sat behind the steering wheel, marked the only time since my childhood that I had ridden so much in the passenger's seat of a vehicle.

Decades earlier, Grandpa's love was demonstrated on long drives spent delivering the Courier Journal and Louisville Times newspapers. Most afternoons, we stopped by Huff's Bait Store at Thixton Lane and Bardstown Road. This man, who endured the Great Depression, would buy me lemon heads and Nehi orange soft drinks. In the company of our customers, he would lavish praise on me during his short conversations, while we were stopped at their round, aluminum paper boxes. Often, he let me hold the steering wheel as he worked the gas and brake pedals. Many hours unfolded looking through the windshield of Grandpa's 1964, blue, four-door Ford Falcon. Each change of scenery and each word spoken accumulated like a soft snow during my childhood years, creating the reservoir I would draw from in the years since. Just as Grandpa's love fit back then, looking out a different windshield almost thirty years later, Amarins' love fit just right too, and it still does today.

Signs counted down the approach to Weatherford. The closer we got, the more emotional I became. By the time we reached the sign that said twenty more miles to Weatherford, I was unhinged. I wiped at the tears.

"Damn, I don't know where all this is coming from."

"It's okay Billy, let it come out," was Amarins' common sense reply.

"But I feel so silly. It is just a town after all. The story of Grandpa might just be a myth."

"Yes, but your brother did say he found your grandfather's birth certificate which proves he was born in Weatherford, Oklahoma. And that is a fact."

Pulling off the interstate, we arrived on a broad street leading down the middle of town. It sure didn't look like a town from the 1900s. Just like many memories from our childhood that later turn out to be different, I had a vision of Weatherford being trod by horses with saloons on every street corner while cowboys leaned against white-washed buildings. We pulled up to a War Memorial and snapped some pictures. By then I had dried my eyes.

I suggested, "If you don't mind, let's drive out from town some, and I will tell you the story." Some inner compass guided our route. "I have no idea where we're going, but let's follow my instincts."

"Okay."

Several turns later we were riding into the setting sun. Amarins brought the truck to a stop next to a stand of scraggly trees lining the banks of a winding dry spring bed.

"I'll grab the Indian blanket. Let's hop the fence."

"Sure. I'll bring some water too."

Half a football field away from the truck, I found a wide shady spot and spread out the red and white woven cover. It appeared that there was some kind of homestead up the dry branch a hundred feet or so. The remnants of a wooden structure led me to believe that it was a home for share croppers. All around us were dried leaves clinging to thirsty trees baking in the relentless sun.

"Ama, I want to share a story about my Grandpa, George Washington Byers. I hope that by telling you his story in this place I can finally bury him.

"I had heard stories from Mom, Grandpa, and some of his kin folks that he was born in Oklahoma. They say his dad, Grandville Byers, used to follow the wheat harvest in the late 1800s from Kentucky, west through this area, and then back again. In this period of Grandville's life, he visited a lady of questionable character at a local cat house somewhere around Kentucky's Mammoth Cave area. Repeated proposals of marriage were offered, but she refused. In time he married the lady's sister, Lee. It is said that Grandville had married her to spite the sister for not marrying him.

"Imploring Lee to come to Oklahoma, she finally went. While pregnant in the summer of 1900, they set off on the harvest migration which took them across the Mississippi River into western territories. In October of the harvest, she gave birth to her only son out of her four children.

"Stories are told that my Grandpa was the first white baby that Indians of this area had ever seen. I assume they were the Arapahos. Whatever tribe, they offered to trade one of their babies for him. Great Grandma, filled with fear of kidnapping, would put him in a burlap sack and hang him in a tree at night in case their camp was raided. Up in the tree felt safer than on the ground. In time she got homesick and wanted to return to Kentucky.

"Once again across the Mississippi River and back in the Commonwealth state, life was not easy for Lee and the children. Grandville moved his family at arbitrary times and to random places. Once he forced them to live in a sheep pen without bringing along the food they had stored up for the winter. In spite of the abuse, all the siblings survived and created comfortable lifestyles for themselves.

"Grandpa made it to Louisville during the early days of the Depression. He had worked at many different jobs while hanging out with his cousins in Old Peth, near where he grew up. From being a core sampler in Bee Springs, to a foreman digging a shaft in an attempt to rescue Floyd Collins from his eventual grave in Mammoth Cave Kentucky, he kept active until the work dried up. Sleeping in wooden boxes downwind of steam vents on Market Street, he landed a job at the Kentucky Paint Company. He worked there till his retirement. He was not a man to sit still and do nothing. That's why he took on one of the biggest paper routes in the county.

"With firm love and a smile that consumed his Irish face, he saved me from childhood nightmares and probable teenage implosion.

"What's so hard for me, Amarins, is that a lot of the stories I never knew until he died. The darker family history, the way he attached himself to me when I was a baby, and his desire to keep the family intact no matter what, are things I wish we could have talked about. I have this space in my soul which I have not been able to fill. He was bigger than life. I found refuge in his presence. Looking back, anything I did as a boy, I did to please him. Even though he has been dead for over fifteen years, I still do some things to please him. I wish he were still alive so I could thank him for giving me the tools that have kept me from certain disaster.

"Ama, do you mind if I do something strange?"

"No, not at all."

Still facing west with the sun on the horizon behind her head, I turned up my hands to the sky and began, "Grandpa, I am so grateful for your love and lessons. There is no way I can repay you for what you have done for me.

I guess you couldn't know and didn't expect it either. I like to think I am near the place where you were born. I have come full circle on your life's physical journey and desire to let you go. Here on this spot of your birth, I release you. In doing so, I can get on with my life."

Ama and I embrace, taking in the Oklahoma sunset.

DRESSED IN SHORTS AND T-SHIRTS we let the warm Mississippi air flow over our bodies as we pedal closer towards Natchez, closer to the Great River. The warmth of the air coincides with our feelings for this beautiful state. The people have been warm and heartfelt from the time we reached Lucedale in the east and pedaled through Prentiss and Bude in the south central part of the state. We've met a string of wonderful people.

On the outskirts of Natchez, we see an officer with his lights on. He motions for us to pull over. He asks us, "Are you the Pedouins?"

"Yes sir, we are."

"We have been asked to give you an escort into town, would you mind?"

The girls are ecstatic with joy. Cheyenne says, "Can we, Dad?"

"Why not. Officer, we'd be privileged to follow you in."

Nearing the heart of the city, the homes are older and grander. Folks along the route wave and wish us a Mississippi welcome. Working the bike along the cobblestone streets and then onto pavement embedded with old street car rails, we turn off and head up an incline to the Hampton Inn. We feel like heroes arriving for our coronation. Janelle, the hotel manager, welcomes us with brightly decorated gift bags for the girls.

Unharnessed, Cheyenne, Jasmine, and Robin scatter like pool balls on the opening break. In all the excitement, I extend my hand and thank the officer for the lead in and, quicker then he came, he disappears out of sight.

We pull the trailer and tote all our purses, water bottles, helmets, and the bag from the bike rack up to a third floor room. We open the door to a grand sleeping experience topped off with a fruit basket on the desk. Two queen size beds with pillows so big, that if our kids were to hide in them, they would disappear from our sight. A flat screen TV as big as the tailgate on our old Toyota truck sits on top of a dark dresser. There is ample room for the girls to run around the beds as well as two pieces of furniture that the girls can work at. The Burley can even have its own spot out of the way of foot traffic. With

The girls eagerly reach for their gifts.
October of 2009

a panoramic view of Tom Sawyer and Huck Finn's river and the sun hanging on the Louisiana landscape beyond it, we have gone from rags to riches, from primitive tent dwellers to modern amenities that spice up our attitudes and our spirits even more. The girls plug into Dora the Explorer while Amarins soaks in an oversize tub.

I ride the elevator downstairs to figure out what to do with Yeller. The lobby is very cavernous, providing enough room for our ride.

"Janelle," I say, "What do you think about putting our bike in here?"

"Sounds like a great idea."

Pointing to the furniture separating the lobby and the sitting area, I ask, "Can I move some of this stuff to make a little more space?"

With her blessing, I carry the glass table and a couple of chairs over to the wall opposite the elevators. In their place, I roll our 14.5 feet of yellow steel into the lobby where it will park for three nights as part of our gift from Hampton Inn.

THERE IS A KNOCK AT the door. Screaming with anticipation of further surprises, all three girls rush to the door. I have to wade through them to answer it. A woman stands in the hallway. With a huge smile and a thick as honey accent, she reaches out to shake my hand.

"Hi. Welcome to Natchez Mississippi, the second oldest town in the Louisiana Purchase. How do you like your welcome?"

"We love it," all the Pedouins cheer in unison.

"I am Sally, the city's tourism director. We heard you were coming to town, so we wanted Natchez to be the best stop of your travels. We want to show you our town. I have all kinds of things lined up for you guys. Who wants to go on a horse and carriage ride?"

Our girls demonstrate their gratitude by swarming Sally with hugs. She fills us in on the coming days' events. We are overwhelmed by the city's gift to us and the desire to make our stay in Natchez the best one of our incredible journey.

Bringing the evening to a sweet conclusion, we have a meal with one of our Pedouin followers. The meal was arranged weeks earlier between two cousins. Barbara, from nearby Jackson, Mississippi, drives down to take us out to dinner at the Biscuits and Blues. Her cousin Barbara, one of my Jackson Street customers, has filled her in on us. She is anxious to meet us and find out if her cousin was telling the truth about her "handy man" and his "crazy family."

FRIDAY WE WAKE UP TO rain. Dodging drops of water we make our way across the street to the visitor's center. Here we enjoy its many interactive displays for all ages. We try out steam boat whistles, play with relief maps of the area, and trace the steps of the natives. Hours pass like minutes as we learn about the Natchez Trace, the early animal path that became an important Native route between

Sally shows Cheyenne and Robin the Natchez Trace.
October of 2009

Natchez, Mississippi, and Nashville, Tennessee. Amarins and I wonder if the Indians we heard about some months ago in Sunbright made it this far on trading expeditions.

The displays bring us through history, through the time of the vast cotton plantations. The cotton boom was possible due to the pioneering spirit in the Natchez District of hybridized breeds of cotton in the early nineteenth century. The strategic location of the city on the high bluffs on the eastern bank of the Mississippi River helped it develop into a busy port. Cotton was loaded onto steamboats at the landing known as Natchez-Under-the-Hill. The goods were shipped downriver to New Orleans or upriver to St. Louis, Missouri, or Cincinnati, Ohio. Here they were transformed into usable wares in the spinning mills.

The economic development of Natchez did not improve with the arrival of the railroads. The importance of being located on the banks of a major river no longer added value as it once did. In current times the tourism industry is an important part of the town's growth, remembering and preserving the past for the future generations.

HALLOWEEN ARRIVES IN BEAUTIFUL SUNSHINE. Sally treats us to a scrumptious breakfast at the historic Eola Hotel that served as headquarters for the annual antebellum home pilgrimages from 1932 until the 1970s. Many folks would tour downtown, soaking up the abundance of excellent examples of pre-Civil War southern homes. The Eola Hotel is on the National Register of Historical Places. Tours still go on for five weeks in the spring. For a small fee, some of the homes open their doors for tours inside these architectural wonders.

After 2,160 miles and three months of sharing eating utensils, we're not sure where to begin at this fine table setting. It is set with every utensil possible, spread precisely over a black on white table cloth. A Bordeaux red cloth napkin for each. A cup and saucer for coffee or tea. A glass for water, another for juice. Silverware to fit all needs. A teaspoon to stir your creamer, a small fork for fresh cut fruit. A fork and knife for your omelet, pancakes or other preference.

We start with coffee, tea and hot cocoa. I take some juice on the side. Amarins chooses a Spanish omelet. I take a triple stack of pancakes. French toast sprinkled with confectioners sugar is Jasmine's desired choice. A pancake with a whipped cream and strawberry face puts a smile on the faces of Cheyenne and Robin. What a feast.

With very happy bellies we walk the several blocks to the horse and carriage area near the old rail station. A white carriage with a black horse in front is waiting for us. We hop on board for a

It is Halloween at the Eola Hotel.
October of 2009

tour through the history of the town. The driver tells us about the many antebellum homes. Natchez, founded in 1716, is the oldest town on the Mississippi River, two years older than New Orleans. We stop at one of the homes featured in the tour. Sally hops off, runs up the steps, and goes inside. We're a bit baffled, but soon have an explanation. Sally's father lives here. From his porch, he throws us a wave. Sally returns and relays his greetings to us.

A visit to Longwood Estate finishes our tour in Natchez. Longwood is the only octagonal residential building in the world. It is four stories high and was never finished. Only the first floor was lived in for a little while. The construction began before the Civil War. The craftsmen laid down their tools in 1861 with the start of the War, and never came back. We can still see the hand tools and building materials, as well as the paper floor plans of the mansion.

I sit on top of a knoll surrounded by centuries old trees, admiring the old place. I feel at home. Home in the ancient voices that are calling from the door's unfinished and exposed headers, outbuildings still containing hand tools, and the grounds which were trod by characters long since buried in the same patch of earth. It is utterly amazing that this place even survived the War and the looting that followed. In 1864 Mr. Nutt, the owner, died of pneumonia. The collapse of the cotton barons' dominance faded and his wife was unable to finish the other floors. Windows and doors locked, Longwood slumbered until it was put into the hands of a historical preservation society. Now it gives silent testimony to a distant place and time.

Longwood Estate.
October of 2009

The eve of Halloween we split up. It has been a long day filled with new impressions. Robin and Amarins stay in the hotel. Cheyenne and Jasmine are going into town with me. Jasmine is dressed like a princess. Cheyenne transforms into a ninja. They are ready to Trick-or-Trunk.

Cars, vans and trucks are parked around the perimeter of a large parking lot in downtown. Kids dressed up in costumes go from trunk to trunk, van door to tailgate, getting candy. It happens just before dark. Afterwards, parents and children can then go off into the neighborhoods if they choose to. The girls pick up more candy in this one evening than they've had for the duration of our journey.

Robin is already asleep when we get back to our room. Tomorrow she will get her share of the treasure. But first dibs go to Amarins who doesn't shy away from the dark chocolate candy treats.

WHEN THE SUN SETS OVER Louisiana I walk to Natchez-Under-the-Hill. In its day, roughly 165 years ago, it was the most notorious river landing on the entire Mississippi River. Today it is a simple steamboat landing. I enter the last tame reminder of its history, a local watering hole. This old wooden building has been used for everything from a local store to living quarters and everything in between over the years. Hand blown cobalt blue bottles and many other antiques and collectibles from Natchez's past sit scattered throughout. A Bowie knife hangs on the wall behind the cash register.

Wetting my whistle on the porch, I can just imagine the spectacle that took place north of town on a sandbar in the river. In 1827 James Bowie became famous for his participation in the Sandbar Fight. What began as a duel between two other men, turned into a fight in which Bowie, wounded from a gunshot and stabbed several times, killed the sheriff of a Louisiana county with a large knife. His knife became very popular after his successful defense with it.

I take one last glance before I go back to the hotel. Tomorrow we are going to cross this giant river. Then we are really in the west and in the hands of yet to be known friends. Our lifelines from the east stop at the Mississippi River.

Breakfast: To each their own.
September of 2009

All for one and one for all.
October of 2009

Fairy tale tree in Florida.
October of 2009

Amarins at the Gulf of Mexico.
October of 2009

Friends: Harding, Hal and Bill.
October of 2009

We've come over 2,000 miles.
October of 2009

Remembering horseback riding
in Lucedale, Mississippi.
October of 2009

First bear
warning: in
Florida!
October of
2009

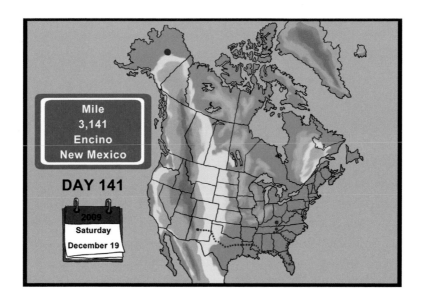

Mile
3,141
Encino
New Mexico

DAY 141

2009
Saturday
December 19

CHAPTER 11

IN THE MID-NINETIES I BEGAN a journey that involved mastering Arabic. Relationships were forged on meeting basic human needs. By repairing engines, helping build homes, and getting money to buy bread for hungry Arabs, I acquired a respectable level of spoken Arabic competency.

During a language lesson, my tutor Shadi asked, "Abu Adam, how do you eat an elephant?"

I said, "I don't know."

He responded, "One bite at a time."

I had been struggling with the enormity of Arabic's gazillion grammar rules, and he offered some humorous help.

Reflecting on our bicycle journey thus far, we are digesting this giant of a journey one bite at a time. Some days we bite off large chunks and take monster steps toward our goal, and some days we are full from the day before and simply stay put. Terrain and weather can wreak havoc on our appetite. In New Mexico it has been the latter.

Entering Texico, New Mexico, on highway 60 from Farwell, Texas, we feel the weight of cold weather. The winds become ferocious with winter's approach. At the visitor center and post offices along our route, the American flag hangs high and stands out straight—strong and full out from the forceful wind. Our hope of colder days broken up by warmer ones has not panned out since we rode out an ice storm with the Altmans in Slaton, Texas. It was time we used to rest, to put our new Burley Nomad together—a gift from the Burley company—and to get Robin her pedals. She'd grown so tall over the past couple of months that her legs had outgrown her leg rests and her shoulder straps didn't reach anymore. In the Altman's garage, Amarins sawed the leg rests off and put a plan together on how to still use the old seat and the hip buckle, but with the new pedals. I got to put it together. After mounting the child seat, I wanted additional safety features for her personal space. I decided to turn her handle bar backwards. It looked like a set of Texas steer horns pointed right at her before the modifications. On the end of these I screwed two twelve inch long, water pipe nipples and secured them in place with some JB Weld. JB Weld is to metal as duct tape is to every other problem in the world. When finished, a ring like a halo was circling Robin above her waist to help prevent her from falling off. With this seating arrangement also came her purse.

Winter is here to stay. It is amplified in the higher altitudes, with landscapes that allow the wind to move freely on open plains. As a result, the girls connect weather concepts such as jet streams they have seen pictured on weather maps to the actual winds of the Texas Panhandle and New Mexico— wild, forceful winds that want to push us back to the Mississippi River.

We are on a canvas where the sky transitions through a series of orange-reds that fade into dark blues and then black as far as our eyes can see. Crisp mornings waken our senses to distant gray mesas. We push our bodies and equipment to extremes we had not imagined. Each night's stop is welcome. The strain of these days causes Amarins' and my bodies to ache. With visions of hot springs and warmer weather beyond the Rockies, we purposefully move forward. Our girls are resilient. The concept of physical limitations is foreign to them.

Like riding on a giant tabletop into the distant horizon, the world feels flat. Trees appear only in towns. The highest objects on the horizon in any direction are water towers. These towers are our North Stars, guiding us to the next town. Moving on this barren landscape, it is easy to lose our sense of direction and distance. Cheyenne becomes adept

Amarins takes a break on the railroad.
December of 2009

at judging distances. With a knack about what a mile is, born from countless mile markers through ten southern states so far, she found a way to apply it to this seemingly featureless world.

"Hey Mom, I think it is about five miles to the water tower in Vaughn!"

"How do you know?" Amarins asks.

"I've been guessing how far the towers are after we first see them off in the distance. Then, I watch the mile markers," Cheyenne replies.

My pride is about to burst as I listen in on a stunning example of just how capable and ingenious our girls are. Cheyenne is becoming quite the navigator, just like her mother. Without a GPS or Google Earth, she is developing innate tools so she can find her way in most any environment. Knowing that Jasmine and Robin are watching this unfold, I can only imagine that they, too, will become self-orientating like the other women on Yeller, each in her own time.

In the panhandle of Texas, Amarins updated the website, letting all our followers know we were getting ready to enter our toughest state, New Mexico. Back east, many people live beyond a town's borders. Towns might be as little as ten miles apart. Starting at the Texas panhandle and getting more acute as we move farther west, the towns are stretching to thirty or more miles apart. In between the settlements, there is nothing but wide open rugged land. We were calling in the troops, asking for places to stay on our highway 60 route through that state. Little by little we got every little town covered.

Only two days before the Winter Solstice, we pull into Encino, New Mexico. Peggy, who put us up in the Desert Motel in Vaughn, prearranged for our stay at the Encino Fire Department. Here, we meet a local volunteer who lets us in. We stay in the office where the heater is. He warns us about the radio noise and the potential of the alarm going off. We tell him about staying in other fire stations and that if the alarm goes off, we'll be okay.

In our resting quarters, the girls enjoy some animated schooling time. There is a skeleton and a blackboard. Using white chalk, the only color available, Jasmine works on a beautiful self-portrait in which she wears a polka dotted dress. Cheyenne works on a detailed view of Adam and Jesse standing next to our Kentucky home. It would have been a fine time to use our bucket of colored chalk back at Pongo Ridge. Time and time again, our girls are great at using whatever medium they find in their environment for homemade art projects. Robin wonders how we can have so many bones in our body.

Road schooling in progress.
December of 2009

After several tries, I score some snacks at the only store in town. As we sit down for some rations, I wonder where we will find more groceries as we head farther into the countryside. For now, we eat and let tomorrow worry about itself.

With bellies full of bread and a hazelnut chocolate spread, the girls now squirm around in the beds they have arranged for themselves from tables, chairs, and sleeping gear. By seven, we try to get some sleep. About the time we drift off, there is a knock on the door. The girls jump, almost bumping their heads against the low ceilings of their self-made burrows.

Not expecting guests, I tell the girls to stay where they are as I go to answer the door. After opening the door, I see a short middle-aged man with gray hair and a beard.

"Hello, I am Mayor Gordo," he introduces himself. "How is everything?"

"We are great. My wife and our three girls are going to sleep back in the main office."

"We heard. I'm glad to hear you've made yourselves comfortable," he continues. "My wife, Martha, and I would like to invite you for breakfast."

"We'd love to come and eat. A hot meal sounds wonderful," I reply. Tomorrow is going to start out all right.

"Great, how does eight-thirty sound? It will take you less then five minutes to get to our home."

"Fine, we will see you then."

Jasmine, who apparently overheard the conversation, murmurs "Yummy" when I return. Then all is silent.

WE ARE READY TO RIDE by eight-twenty. The sun is bright and only a gentle frosty breeze brushes across our faces. This morning we pedal with a grand purpose, to eat hot food. Exiting the gravel lot, we turn right on the main thoroughfare. Nothing stirs in the town. Once a vibrant place when the railroad made stops here fifty years or so ago, it resembles a ghost town now. Countless adobe homes and businesses are collapsing in the dirt, returning to their origins. Turning left after half a block, we see a handful of homes looking as though people closed up and walked away. Dog houses appear to be waiting for their pets to come back.

After a few more turns, we pull up to the mayor's house and stop our ride next to a wooden fence that divides the grassless packed dirt parking area from the yard. Inside, the smell of homemade breakfast burritos and orange juice greets us. While we are enjoying food around their table, the mayor and his wife fill us in on their town's decline. Their story highlights a lack of jobs, limited resources, families leaving to find opportunities elsewhere, and a drought in tourist traffic. It sounds all too familiar. We've heard this same story and witnessed the same ravaging decline in hordes of towns along the way.

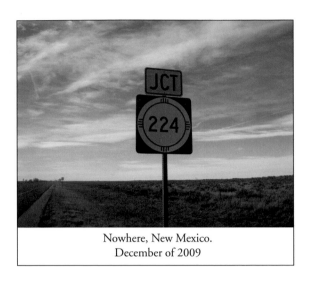

Nowhere, New Mexico.
December of 2009

Once we feel that the weather is ripe for moving out, we bundle up the girls with three layers of poly, cotton, and then down materials. Each one wears her Under Armor full face mask, down gloves, and a scarf. All wrapped up, they make for the quint. Martha hugs each girl as they climb on. When the clock strikes ten, we are ready to move out. We ride in the brilliant sunshine, with hopes of making Willard, which lies some thirty-eight miles west in this lonely space, just beyond the salt beds.

Moving by more crumbling mud brick homes, I feel a slight wind on my left cheek. I don't think it will slow us down too much. Still, we much prefer the tailwind of two days ago. Back on highway 60, we slowly make our way past the lone grocery store. We pull in to throw some trash away which we forgot to pitch this morning. I consult Amarins before we take off again.

"It looks like there is a turnoff up the hill a bit. Which way do we go?"

"I believe we take a left. If we go straight, we will end up in Santa Fe. Hey, do you feel the wind picking up some?"

"I do. It also looks like we have quite a climb to make to get out of Encino."

"I see it too; just take your time, especially at the junction."

"I will, Babe."

As Ama mounts the bike, I say to the girls, "Hey guys, the wind is picking up and we have a climb ahead before our turnoff. Let's keep quiet and pedal!"

"Three, two, one… Go!" and we cross over the eastbound lane to the westbound road's edge. Methodically, we move forward. The closer we are to the turnoff, the stronger the wind gets. One mile and ten minutes into the day's ride, we reach our junction.

While we wait for a lone car to clear the oncoming lane, I say to Ama, "This wind is brutal, what should we do?"

"Let's ride. Maybe it will trail off once we get past this cut in the road."

"Okay," I holler back over the wind.

Heading due west now, a twenty to thirty miles per hour headwind smacks us. It is an educated guess based on the wind's effects on our bodies. It is a number born out of 3,000 plus miles in her fury and sublimeness. How the wind bends the grass, blows certain sized flags, and pushes trash across our path, all paint a picture of her speed.

We are up against a wall. Our lowest gear is number twenty-seven. This is attained when the main drive chain is on the smallest of the three chain rings before the rear wheel and on the largest cog of the nine cog sprocket attached to the rear wheel. With this combination, we will move at three or four miles per hour. We have learned on other climbs that it takes over one thousand strokes for us to move our steel machine one mile.

The incline levels off to a slight rise. The temperature is in the upper thirties. We trudge along with incredible effort. With each revolution of the cranks, I feel exhausted. It is like we're trying to run a marathon through a swamp. The air coursing across my body closes out all sounds. All I hear is wind racing against my helmet. I no longer hear Amarins' labored breathing that normally accompanies a climb. The girls' voices have also been swallowed by the air movement as well.

I yell a loud, "Are you all cold?" But I get no response. I decide to stop. We have gone only half a mile since the intersection, but it feels like ten miles.

"Hey Ama, come up here, please." Dismounting, she pushes through the wind to get to me. I lean over and ask, "Do you think the girls are warm?"

"Yes, I think they are," she replies.

"Well, I am freezing. I guess my body is protecting them from most of the wind. I also think we are headed straight into this stuff. How are you holding up?"

"Fine I guess, but my legs are tired."

"Let's move on some more, and maybe this wind tapers off as we get farther away from the cut back there."

Without a further word, she leaves and gets back on. The girls are huddled up on their seats, trying to escape the wind's fury. If they added anything to our conversation, I would not know because I'm deaf, except for the howl of the air.

We battle onward, away from the small swale in the landscape that we believe is causing the wind to amplify its speed as it passes through it. Progress is painfully slow as we inch forward pushing the pedals with all our might at each stroke. Climbing the Appalachians was easier than this.

With forty minutes of ride time, we have only made three exhausting miles. *I am finished,* I think. I pull over once more and Amarins comes up front again, knowing it is time to talk once more.

"What's up?"

Time to reconsider.
December of 2009

"This is crazy," I answer. "I am worn out and I know you have to be, too. The kids have to be cold because this wind is cutting right through my clothes."

"What do you want to do?"

"I think we need to head back to the mayor's house."

Amarins overhears Cheyenne ask, "Are we going back?"

"Yes we are. Your dad and I think it is too cold to try for Willard in this wind."

Carefully, she holds the bike so that I can get off. In this wind I don't even want to try to make a U-turn on the two lane highway. We walk Yeller across the road. As we are perpendicular to the highway, it takes all our strength to keep her upright. With the wind to our backs facing Encino, we already feel warmer.

We notice a train approaching from behind, on our right side. The wind is on our team once we are rolling again. Keeping pace with the train, I am sure we are pushing forty miles per hour.

The girls scream out, "We are going almost as fast as the train." With the wind at our backs we can hear much better. It is good to hear the joy in their voices.

Within minutes, we are at the mayor's house again. I am beginning to understand why cyclists travel west to east. The prevailing winds move from west to east. That would certainly make riding much easier and warmer as well. We wanted Alaska to be the pinnacle of our journey and this meant going east to west. Today is an example concerning the price we are paying for this monstrous decision to go against unspoken bicycle protocols.

The mayor must have seen us coming, because as soon as we come to a rolling stop, he walks out his front door.

"What happened?" he asks.

"The wind killed us. Between the houses here, we didn't feel its strength. Once we were past the intersection it hit us in full force, right in our faces," I answer. "It went straight through our clothes. It took us over half an hour to make a mile. We just didn't think it was a good idea to continue onward to Willard in this wind. Can we come in and figure out what we can do?"

"Sure, come on in."

Martha meets us at the door. She is kind and supportive as she welcomes us back in.

"Mayor Gordo, is this normal, the wind?" I want to know.

"Yes, especially this time of the year."

I feel frustrated that we are stuck here. We are enjoying the hospitality, but we don't want to be a burden. Of course a challenge such as this arises when hotels, food, and communication are hardly within reach. "Do you have a way we can listen to the weather?"

"I do. We can catch it on TV."

It doesn't look good. The forecast projects a snow storm. This is not good news. Amarins and I walk outside to discuss the matter.

"Ama, what are you thinking?"

"I am not sure, but I know we can't ride in this or in snowy weather."

"I know. I was worn out by the time we turned around on the incline. I cannot imagine riding all day in this mess."

Amarins glances through the window, to where the girls huddle near the TV. "I am worried about the girls. This wind is brutal. We stay relatively warm because we pedal, but they do not generate a lot of heat when they pedal. Staying here in town does not do us any good though. I'd rather spend the time of the snow storm in Santa Fe with Fletcher and Rhonda. It would be a nice off-the-bike vacation there."

"I think we have to find another way to Willard. Maybe the mayor can haul us and Yeller there. What do you think?"

"I don't like it, but what other choice is there? You know we can't impose on them for days, and food becomes an issue even if we can stay longer in the fire department. Why don't you see if he can help us? Since Willard is a wide spot in the road, no bigger than a building and post office, we might as well go on to Mountainair sixty miles away."

Back inside, I pose the question of transportation, "Mayor, is it possible you can get us to Mountainair?"

"Let me make some calls and see if I can locate a truck with a hitch on it."

After about twenty minutes, he finds a Bronco he can borrow. With a trailer hooked to the Bronco, Mayor Gordo and I load the bike while Ama puts our possessions in the rear of the vehicle. When everything is secured, we load up and hit the road, warm and effortless.

It is discouraging to travel by truck rather than bicycle. To move forward without any effort on our part feels strange. Through the windows of the truck, the Rockies come into focus. Our stomachs churn. This is a sight we have been working so hard to see appear in front of our eyes while on Yeller. But, it is not to be. After climbing 6,200 feet from where the ocean's salty water laps against the sandy South Carolina shores, we are sad that we can't enjoy this beautiful view at our normal pace on Yeller. We had to give in to the elements. This is by far the hardest decision we have had to make up to this point.

While moving at sixty miles per hour, the ability to enjoy the view is far different from at our biking rate of three to thirteen miles per hour. The change in pace doesn't take away from the magnificence of the mountainous terrain, but it doesn't make it any easier either. We take a break at the salt beds where Amarins cries a silent cry for this lost experience.

Amarins takes a moment to herself.
December of 2009

On the edge of Mountainair we arrive just before lunch time at the Turner Inn. On Yeller, we wouldn't have arrived until supper time two days from now! We thank our hosts for their wonderful gift of food and rescue. They tell us we are always welcome.

Today we chose safety over our desire to ride.

We're crossing the mighty Mississippi River.
November of 2009

Jasmine shows what cotton looks like.
November of 2009

The Frogmore plantation in Louisiana.
November of 2009

Fishing lessons in Texas with Michael
and Amanda Cromer.
November of 2009

Portraits by Cheyenne.
November of 2009

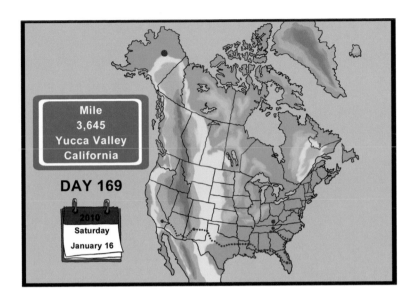

Mile
3,645
Yucca Valley
California

DAY 169

2010
Saturday
January 16

CHAPTER 12

D UMBFOUNDED WE SIT DOWN IN the sand at the far end of a wide spot
alongside state road 72 in Arizona. The demon truck is out of sight and
we are again stuck on the roadside. We have been broken down so many times
that Amarins, who keeps track of everything, has lost count. As I attempt to
figure out what caused this near disaster, the words of a friend from the past
spring to mind.

"Bill, you are a survivor. You can get out of any situation. There ain't
anything you can't fix!" Pat Brunner is a larger than life redhead from North
Carolina and was a great influence in my college years. Being an ole mountain
girl, she always saw the good in something, even me. I get mad when she
throws this at me, but this echoing assessment gives me courage to find a
remedy for our current trouble.

The three girls are wondering what happened, but I have no answers to give them. Amarins and I unhook the trailer and take everything off the back of the bicycle. Then we can begin to assess the situation.

She notices that the rear tire has the tread ripped from its casing. With a new tire sitting on the trailer we focus on the larger problem. The chain is stuck between the frame and the nine cog sprocket. It is coiled up like a rope on a ship's deck waiting to be thrown overboard. Seeing that the shifting device is okay, I rack my brain trying to solve what has caused the malfunction.

With tiredness born out of adversity and repetition of the journey, I sit next to the girls in the sand, wheel in hand, looking it over. Robin touches the tire at the broken tread and looks up at me as if to say, "Dad, can you fix this?"

Cheyenne and Jasmine enjoy the broken tire.
January of 2010

As I spin the nine speed cassette, it does not rotate freely. When we pedal, the chain causes the cassette hub assembly to lock some internal devices that make the wheel turn. When rotating in the opposite direction, it should spin unreservedly without causing the sprocket to turn. Yeller's hub isn't doing this. Somehow, the internal "stuff" isn't working properly.

I flash back to November of last year. Two miles from Groesbeck, Texas, the rear wheel locked up and we veered off the road like I had applied the brakes. I don't know how we stayed upright, but we did. Our chain had wrapped around the cassette sprocket. Once we got the chain unwound and back on, we figured out how to ride with no free wheeling motion. We had to pedal the whole time we were rolling and this proved to be a tiring exercise. When we stopped, I had to apply the brake while we were still moving the cranks until we came to a full stop. Adding insult to injury, the next day my right crank arm fell off. As we rode into the small lazy Texas town, we looked like a circus as I pedaled with my left foot and my right foot slung up on the top tube of the bike. We put the pedal back on in Groesbeck at Lynd Auto Parts. We limped to Waco until we found a bicycle store where we fixed the hub with some lubrication, and it has been fine since.

This can't be our problem now because when we broke down in Phoenix, Arizona, I lubricated the new hub and old guts before putting on a new rear rim. With the nine ring cassette assembly off of the spindle, I see no grit and plenty of lubrication. There has to be another problem which I am not seeing.

"Hey Ama, It looks like we can ride, but we will not be able to coast again, just like in Texas. I don't see any major problems inside this stupid thing."

"You are kidding me," Ama responds in frustration.

"I'm sorry for the bad news. I am so doggone mad I could throw this whole piece of crap over the fence. I just don't know what to do about this crazy hub!"

"Well, at least we can ride, right?"

"When we get on the bike, we will see," is all I can say.

Two hours later, we load the bike with our precious girls. Usually a time of chatter and stirring about, this time they are deadly silent. With apprehension, I wait for the road to be clear as far as we can see east and west before pushing Yeller across the road. As the cranks turn from Cheyenne and Jasmine's input, I pray that we will make it to Parker, Arizona—a bigger town where we hope to find a bicycle repair shop.

Miles down the road we ease into Bouse, a small retirement community of campers, trailers and double wide homes all lying on the south side of the highway. The sun is low on the horizon when we come out of a little café with bellies full of meat and vegetables. The question of "where to camp" remains unanswered. We learned that no tent camping is allowed in this wide spot in the road.

Leaving the café parking area we watch the sun disappear as we inquiringly look for a place to put our tent up. As we are slowly rolling past barren ground covered in low growing vegetation, the girls see an open area on a corner lot. Instantly, I turn the bike left on the gravel side road and we roll to a stop. Past a sandy ditch and surrounded by woody bushes is a rolling sandy area where we can pitch our portable home. It also provides some limited privacy from the highway. I figure once it is dark, we will be hidden from the lights of cars and the police, since we are rogue camping.

One of the road lessons is, it is better to say you are sorry than to ask for permission. Of course, we only apply this to camping. In these vast open areas it is hard to know where Bureau of Land Management land begins and ends. If it is BLM land we can camp up to seven days before we have to move. With the sun gone, we are left with few choices.

THE SUN REFLECTS OFF CONDENSATION that's dripping from the tent's ceiling. The sparkling lights wake us. Despite the very chilly temperature, we all slept very well. Looking up at the moisture and listening to the low-key chatter, I wonder what awaits us in Parker that might bring relief for our hub situation.

One of our journey's goals is to live in the now, be present today. Looking ahead for solutions to problems is the reason we're still rolling though. I really don't want to be spending my time foraging for bike parts, but it is what it is. Our lives are full of challenges, but we had no idea that Yeller would throw so many at us. With our funds running low, the solution might need to involve a miracle.

Yesterday I talked to the middleman we bought our bicycle from. He suggests the hub must be gummed up. Beyond that, he doesn't have an answer either. This is the last straw, another empty answer. It is not our intention to contact them again. They have not warranted anything thus far. Attempting to get information in the form of help has proven aggravating at best and not worth the mental energy.

As we turn north onto highway 95, the snow bird traffic is thick. Retirees from all over the States give us little room on our small shoulder as they roll past us in campers and trailers. On a rise just before Parker on the Colorado River Indian Reservation, we take a breather from the constant pedaling and ever increasing traffic.

Amarins tells us that we are at the halfway point of our journey; 3,500 miles of experiences are behind us. I want to be excited, but I can't. I have let the current mechanical struggles rob me of perspective and thus the ability to be in the now. All I want to do is to find a solution before we head off into the Californian desert beyond Parker.

PARKER IS ON THE WESTERN border of Arizona. The border between California is created by the Colorado River. This river finds its origin at the Continental Divide in the Rocky Mountain range of Colorado. From here it travels over 1,400 miles in a southwesterly direction, through the Grand Canyon before it reaches the Gulf of California in Mexico.

Being about a thousand miles downstream from the origin of the Colorado River, and having seen its majestic size in the Grand Canyon, we are surprised to find the river to be merely a muddy stream. To the girls this is just another river to cross. They are much more excited to play at the playground with some other children.

Amarins finds a good spot to sit in the warmth of the sun while I head to the bike shop. At the local shop the owner is very helpful. Together we pull the rear hub apart. It is clean and well lubed. I do notice something about the inner cogs though. They are two round pieces the size and shape of a quarter, about three quarters thick. The cog's edges, like the quarter, have grooves. These grooves are actually small splines that fit into the housing of the rear hub. The two pieces move in and out. The cog on the nine ring cassette side has some damage. The grooved lines have sheared and lost their straight shape. I figure this is causing it to lodge in the housing, locking up the hub. Determining that the inner cog travels in and out the least, I swap them.

We also see that the drive chain is stretched. The low and middle chain rings of the three ring set are worn. Their teeth are half gone and a few of the middle ring's teeth are nubs barely able to grab the chain. I am amazed that the chain has not been slipping. The repair shop owner has no chain rings to replace the worn ones, but he does have a new chain. We decide to wait till later to replace the chain rings.

Feeling hopeful because of the cog swap and the new chain, I ride away. I coast to a stop at the main traffic light. It works! I can free wheel. Buoyed by the great news, I continue on to the park and pick up the family. It is getting toward sunset. There is still a lot to do today. We need to pick up some supplies before we head for BLM land along the Colorado River for the evening.

Starting out slowly towards Wal-Mart, all seems to go really well. We are shifting and free wheeling. That is, until we reach the store's parking lot. The chain binds tight around the gears. New trouble is brewing. By now, I am ready to throw the whole contraption into the Colorado River. I am so mad that I can hardly see straight. I am thinking, "What in the world has gone wrong this time?"

I can hear the girls posing the usual questions, "What is wrong, Daddy? Is it the same problem? Why didn't you fix it at the shop? Can we go back to the playground while you fix it?"

Coasting into a parking spot closest to the traffic lane next to Wal-Mart, we dismount. Cheyenne grabs the walking stick for me and I shove it under Robin's seat bracket. I move back to the rear of the bike for a closer look. As I do, shoppers start gathering around the spectacle. I decide to communicate with the crowd about our journey to give me a moment to step away from the problems.

One fellow, in a white pickup truck says, "Do you need something to eat?"

"That would be great," I reply.

"We are headed to McDonald's, what would you like?"

As he takes off with our order, Amarins and I turn our attention to Yeller. "The chain is too tight and the rear derailleur is not in the right position," she says.

"Yep. It looks like the chain is too short. I don't have the extra piece he took out either. Let me get the bike shop's business card from my purse. I'll give him a call."

After explaining what happened, he promises to come by after work and put some links back in. While we wait, Amarins shops and I keep an eye on the children. Just before sundown, our help arrives as does our food. Double cheese burger, no onions, in hand, I watch the mechanic pop a link out and the derailleur springs back to its relaxed position. Baffled that the chain is too short, he adds two more links.

After the sun has set, we push Yeller to the southern edge of the parking lot. We decide not to test ride the bike. We will wait until tomorrow to give it a whirl. Across from the curb stones is an area the size of several football fields, leveled and ready for a new building project. Since it is well lit, we put our tent up. Our tent stakes barely penetrate the compacted soil. Ama and I are exhausted and the wind is light, so we drape the fly over the main tent and call it a night. With the inside of our tent glowing from the Wal-Mart lights, we play a game of cards. Jasmine beats us in a game of Skip-Bo.

Snug in our sleeping quarters, Cheyenne, Jasmine, and Robin slip into their routine sleeping styles. Oblivious to the noises of commerce next door, Cheyenne is snuggled in her bag, Dogge in her arms. Jasmine is lying on top of her bag, and a black and white stuffed puppy is her companion. Excited about her birthday in two days, she wears her pink dress from Natchez, Mississippi, as her gift to herself. Robin has snuggled to the bottom of her bag with her Binkies. Ama and I can hear her soft snoring. After a day filled with mechanical drama, this is our "now" moment together.

THE SUN BREAKS OVER THE mountains. All our belongings are loaded and we are ready to roll. The views of California in the west are breathtaking with their saw-tooth peaks and purple shading. These are energizing conditions. Over a hundred miles of desert lies ahead of us, desert that crosses the Iron, Granite and Cadiz mountains. Thousands of feet of climbing waits before we can roll down into Twentynine Palms, the first settlement on the other side of the desert. Calculating it will take us three or four full days to make it across, we decide to stay an extra day in Parker to rest. There will be no places to take showers or rest in a comfortable bed on the 110 mile stretch of desolation.

We plan to ride to the BlueWater Resort & Casino just north of town to spend the day and evening in comfort. Not pushing our luck where we had just camped last evening, we heed the information a stranger shared last evening. There are great rates at the casino's hotel. It will give us a little test run to make sure the bike is dependable once again.

Up the grade from the shopping center, the chain slips. With the push

127

of a feather we finally get the bike rolling. It isn't right, but it will have to do for now. To our relief, the hotel is downhill from here. In front of the massive entrance we come to a stop next to a Lexus that is just being driven away by a parking attendant.

After checking in, I help Amarins bring the girls and our gear to the room. We have to stay off the carpet, a rule that the girls abide by very well. The carpet is the area where the gambling machines are located. The route to the elevators takes us past the two story swimming pool with a water slide. The girls cheer in enjoyment. The room is accessorized with a balcony overlooking the Colorado River. We can almost touch California.

Once my women are settled into the room, I take off on the bike. Sure enough, as I pedal up the hotel's exit ramp, the chain is slipping on the medium ring of the front three ring cassette. My only guess is that the new chain will not fit over all the teeth that have been worn to a nub and whose spacing has been irregularly eroded. I make a U-turn pushing Yeller and then coast back to the building. I work her up against the wall to the left of the entrance and wedge it behind some shrubbery. If someone tries to steal it, at least they will have to work at it. Because we had none of these slipping issues before the new chain, I decide to get the old chain back. When I call the bike shop, I hear the old chain has already been thrown away and that the dumpster was emptied this morning.

I should not have messed with the old chain. I had it changed to prevent a future problem in the desert and now I have created a bigger one. To get new chain rings would involve several days of waiting and we do not have the money to wait that long here in Parker. On Ama's computer in the lounge area next to the gambling machines, I find various California bike shops online. Scoring two sources that have what I think I need, each one agrees to ship me a set to Yucca Valley, California, where we will stay with a childhood friend and his wife. One set is a gift and the other agrees to let us pay him when we roll through town in the months to come.

Back in the room, Amarins and I step onto the balcony. The girls are enjoying the Discovery Channel.

"What did you find out?" Ama says.

"Our old chain is history," I tell her a bit deflated. "I am sorry; I should have never replaced it."

"You did what you thought was best."

"Yes, I guess. Anyway, new rings will take several days to ship. We can't afford to stay here in Parker, so I had some shipped to the Hoeflichs in Yucca Valley, California. I figure since we will be riding on the small ring most of the way, let's try it. There are a lot of climbs to come

The day has come. California waits.
January of 2010

and we can coast down the other side. If we ease it along, I think we can do it," I say. "Does that sound like a plan?"

"It does. Now we can go swimming. Let's see if the girls would like to come," she adds with a grin.

Coming in from the balcony, Amarins asks the girls, "Anyone want to go swimming?"

"Yeah!" they cheer. The girls are already dressed in their bathing suits and run for the door. Now all they have to do is wait for us to change.

THE EARLY BIRD CAFÉ FILLS our stomachs with some delicious Mickey Mouse pancakes for Jasmine's 5th birthday. Hearing the stories of our trip, several customers give us some cash and pay for our meal. One anonymous benefactor puts a hundred dollars in my hand. He says, "This is from the Lord. It is wonderful what you are doing with your family."

We head out at eleven. Three ladies from the next door hair salon come out to see us off. A customer still has her cape and plastic dye cap on her head as she looks on. "Three, two, one... Thank you!" rings out to the folks left standing in front of the café. Meandering through the local traffic we come to the drop-off to the Colorado River. There, the bridge will take us into California. It is hard to comprehend that we've made it this far in less then six months. It's a good thing we travel slowly so we have the chance to savor this accomplishment while gliding across this river. It was a big achievement making it to the Atlantic Coast on August the 31ˢᵗ, 2009, but now the Pacific Coast is within our reach. It's just overwhelming.

Across the river, traffic is light. It makes for enjoyable riding. The road climbs out of the river bed and we're climbing with it, using our lowest gears. So far this works out well and it helps us get farther inland. Over a thousand feet in elevation we climb this way. Yeller feels good underneath us. Like always, it feels good to be on the road again.

A wide spot in the road presents itself to our right. The road has been very narrow and winding. This provides a good place to stop. Desiring to get us off the road, we send the girls up a path that looks like one that mountain goats might use. At the top the girls point out the town in the distance across the river.

Cheyenne carries a heavy rock for her rock tower.
January of 2010

The area is covered with rocks. It looks like pictures we have seen of Mars. The landscape on this side of the river has more rocks than in Arizona. Rocks of many different colors lay scattered. They are black, white, red, and green. The green ones are new to us. Like the markers in the desert used by Bedouins, the girls pile rock upon rock to mark our arrival in our thirteenth state. My hands are busy moving boulders for the girls, making the markers bigger and bigger. This scene is a great natural distraction.

The weather is great. We don't even have to bundle up. The girls are still wearing their ski pants and snow boots, gear they have been using since the panhandle of Texas. It provides good protection against the weather, and it makes for good play clothing.

As the afternoon progresses, the wind picks up. It is coming directly from the west, the direction we are heading into. With thirty-five miles into the day we feel very good about the chunk we've bit out of the desert crossing. It is time to keep our eyes open for a place to camp. The terrain is rolling, without tall rock outcroppings. When I see a large, man-made mound of dirt along-side a railroad track, I know that we can use it for a windbreak. It is about four stories high and seems to be an old loading ramp for the trains. On the eastern side of the mound the air flow is greatly reduced. The tent gets nestled well off the road and within a stone's throw of the train tracks.

The girls and I put some pennies on one of the rails in case a train rolls by tonight. I want to show them what heat and pressure will do to them.

I awake from my dream world in the middle of the night. The ground is starting to shake. I soon realize that a train is roaring towards us and it seems like it is coming through our tent. I push up on my elbows to see if anyone else is awake. Amarins stirs, but continues sleeping. The girls don't notice a thing. When they sleep, they sleep.

As the girls wake up I tell them about the passing train. They get dressed quickly, then scurry to the gravel bed foundation of the tracks to start looking for their treasures. Cheyenne finds the first one, "Dad, look what happened to it! It's so thin now, but I can still see Lincoln's head!" Together, we find three of the four coins. Each girl with her own souvenir runs down the gravel embankment to show their mother.

A light wind is coming from the north northeast. It is a tail wind. Time to load up and take advantage of it! No matter how fast we work, it still takes over an hour to get on the road. Our road parallels the railroad track. The girls call out the names which are written with rocks on the side of the elevated track. One of them is of Cheyenne's friend Nathan.

The road rises and drops over long, loping hills. It takes us in a relatively straight line closer to the Iron Mountains. It's hard to tell how far away they are. The sand in the air makes them hazy on the horizon. To the north we see more sand in the air. It appears to be a sand storm.

The next road sign warns us of drifting sand ahead. Cheyenne wonders what it means. As we get to the lowest point of the stretched valley we find out. The sand is blowing like a sand snake across the road. The wind has picked up in strength and is coming more from the north now. The twenty to thirty miles per hour constant wind is pushing us forcefully from our right-hand side.

It is past noon when we pull over for a break and some food. The sand is pelting us hard. I hold the bike up to keep it from falling. The girls head away from the road until they find a couple of shrubby bushes that give them a bit of protection from the sand. Behind the girls are distant mountain ranges which have been eroded away by time. Even though the sun shines brightly, the sky has a dusk look to it as the sand swirls around us and the mountains.

After a gritty lunch, Robin takes a nap in her seat. She doesn't sleep as much any more. Our little girl is growing up. All of them are. When we reflect upon the past six months we have seen them change and mature a lot. We understand that the same would have happened at home. But would we have noticed it as we do now?

WE CREST BETWEEN THE GRANITE and Iron Mountains after a steady ascent. Most of the climb, the girls were forced to turn their heads to the south in order to keep the sand out of their eyes. Off in the distance we see a valley where the mountains have been swallowed by sand. Only their tan peaks appear to be sticking out of the massive sand's landscape. It's an eerie yet beautiful sight. A road runs through this valley. We soon find it is the road we'll be taking towards Twentynine Palms. We actually are going to get an intimate look at the valley and the distant mountain peaks.

Between the mountains the sun will no doubt set quickly. We see two tiny hills in the distance, which look like a good goal for today. The first four miles are free miles, a nice descent into the valley. Down, down, down the mountain we fly. Not taking any chances with the rear hub, we keep on spinning the pedals.

We climb a couple more miles to be out of the flood zone of the valley floor. The two little hills are still off in the distance, so we'll save that for tomorrow. The whole family helps set up our camp in Cadiz Valley at the foot of the Coxcomb Mountains. Across the road is the outer boundary of Joshua Tree National Park.

Tonight we don't put the outer fly on the tent. The wind has died down and the sand has settled. This is the first time that we have perfect conditions for such night viewing. The air is dry; we have had no dew since Arizona. The days warm up nicely despite the cold desert nights, and this produces crystal clear skies for star gazing. There is zero light pollution where we are. We are at least forty miles away from any settlement in all directions.

The panoramic view of distant mountain ranges is breath taking. Securely off highway 62 we know that privacy is our gift tonight. Amarins and I both feel intoxicated with a feeling of isolation and the primitiveness that encompasses our family. In silence we drift off with the heavens at our finger tips. Each girl snuggled in her burrow, they fade into the penetrating darkness of sleep and night time.

Camping in the Californian desert.
January of 2010

WE ROUSE TO THE FIRST rays of light. The sun bathes the Granite Mountains with a soft yellow light that paints them a purple color. Each and every relief or fold is highlighted. Ama is outside with her camera, capturing the unfolding natural beauty.

The girls follow shortly to explore the dry washes around our camp site. Cheyenne and Jasmine find a can to play with. A hole is rusted in one side of it. When Cheyenne picks it up she realizes that a lizard is living in it. The cold blooded animal is not yet warm enough from the sun to take off running. It gives the girls a good opportunity to observe what it looks like. Robin wants to hold it for a bit. That goes well, until the lizard starts to move a leg. Then the fun is over for Robin. She shrieks and quickly works it back to Cheyenne.

After a while of playing with the lizard it is time to return him and his home back to the place they found it. Cheyenne would rather take him with us, but we quickly decline the request.

Every breakfast makes the panniers a little lighter. It does not help much when it comes to pulling our belongings out of the desert, back into the road. It is a chore shoving a hundred pound bike plus gear through the desert floor's sandy base.

We start the day with a climb. We're curious how far the two little hills—our aim yesterday—are still from us. Yesterday's late afternoon light distorted the far off places. Points on the horizon are much farther than they appear to the naked eye. One hour of climbing later we find out: still about four miles. Now that the sun is shining from behind us, they are barely recognizable in the morning light.

The wind is not blowing right now. What a difference that makes. We're going maybe three or four miles per hour. But we're making it despite the lack of a tail wind. Each time we stop to catch our breath and to look back we can see the incredible climb we've made. Stopping is part of our climbs. The grade and duration of today's uphill affair is intense. Lugging our 800 pounds makes it impossible to go more then ten minutes without resting. When we think we're going to crest, there is yet again another elevation to conquer.

On top of the mountain, the girls climb rock after rock in total freedom of exploration. Hand in hand they help each other. For 360 degrees, the magnificent mountains of Southern California wrap us in their beauty. The girls look like ants as they move farther up the mountain top to see what is on the other side.

Refreshed and refilled, today's ride is continued with a long downhill ride. For sixteen miles gravity helps us along. We are setting a speed record for sure. A sighting through a V-pass to the west makes us not want to believe our eyes. We see snow covered mountains. Where did they come from? As soon as we see them they disappear from sight, but not from our minds. Didn't we leave winter in New Mexico?

Roughly ten miles outside of Twentynine Palms we find a concrete slab off the road. I believe it used to hold a small shack or a shed. Tonight it will hold our tent. Our tent is long enough to stretch from one side of the slab to the other. This works out great to push the stakes down over the edges of the slab into the sand.

Inside the tent we talk about the desert passage and the climbing we've done over these past few days. Just this crossing alone is an incredible achievement. Tomorrow we will celebrate with a warm breakfast in town. From there we go on to Yucca Valley where new parts wait for Yeller. She has done great, but it is time to have it all fixed right again, at least for a little while until she breaks down again. And when she breaks down again, we will stop and enjoy the scenery, see what needs to be fixed, and fix it again. We will keep on going, because this is what we really want.

In the twenties at the Rio Grande River.
December of 2009

Decorating the Christmas tree with
Alicia in Santa Fe, New Mexico.
December of 2009

Jasmine enjoys a Coke in an
Arizona irrigation canal.
January of 2010

Warmer weather with Wâtte in
Tucson, Arizona.
December of 2009

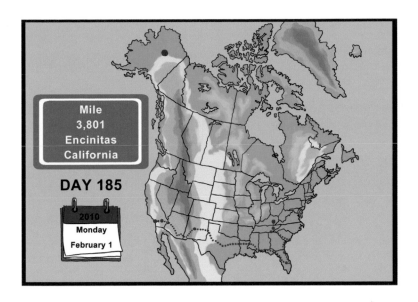

Mile
3,801
Encinitas
California

DAY 185

2010
Monday
February 1

CHAPTER 13

SOUTHERN CALIFORNIA IN FEBRUARY FEELS like Kentucky in May. The Kentucky Derby, on the first Saturday of May, ushers in the official start of planting. As the finest thoroughbreds in the world enter the starting gate ready to bolt on the first race of the Triple Crown, gardeners all over our region take this cue to set out warm weather plants such as tomatoes, peppers, and watermelons.

We're staying with the Register family in Escondido. Surrounded by yellow daffodils, light green budding trees, and emerald grass, we're savoring a vibrancy and warmth we haven't basked in since Louisiana. The weather here pops open our senses like the sun calling out red buds deep in our hollers back home. The Registers have treated us to the San Diego Zoo, fresh citrus, soft beds, and running water in the *Coyote Den* (a name they gave their guest house) behind their hacienda. Rosemary and her husband, Ray, created such an inviting space for us that we are tempted to extend our stay.

The Registers spent thirty years in service to the Arabs in Israel and the Territories. I met them there in the nineties. Dr. Register became my mentor of sorts for four wonderful years. Ray served his community through intellectual avenues while I served using the tools of various trades, such as mechanics and building. He liked air-conditioning, and I liked sweating. We both had a heart for service, bringing relief to the hungry, thirsty, and outcast. This common denominator kept me coming to his *fountain of knowledge* which was shaped by his lifetime of service in the Middle East. Their airy, concrete, whitewashed desert home was always open for me when I found myself near the Tel-Aviv area. Whether my visit was work related or a sanity check, a friendly welcome and thoughtful counsel graciously awaited me.

Well into their retirement years, they stand next to our bike as we get ready to shove off for our second ocean experience, the Pacific. With boundless young energy, our girls show their gratitude with hugs and expressions of thanks. Cheyenne and Jasmine leave the Registers with flower planters made from old cardboard boxes decorated with flowers that were colored with markers. The girls want to leave their mark here.

Ray leads the way in his white Subaru, from Country Club drive to Harmony Grove, onto Elfin Forest Road. The landscape around us is strewn with

Robin flies through Elfin Forest.
February of 2010

boulders and trees. It is hilly just like a fairy tale land. The road's name aptly describes this early morning adventure. We half expect to catch a glimpse of some fairy tale creature.

Javier joins us for the ride as we turn onto this magical road. In his twenties, this dental hygienist from Palm Springs found us online. On his mountain bike, he encourages us as we chug up the steep inclines. Ten miles into the day, we stop along the roadside for a break before San Elijo. As we goof off on the shoulder, Javier presents the girls with scarves that he and his mother made. Jasmine claims the purple one and Cheyenne the slight yellow one. Robin gets a speckled red and white one. With Cheyenne on the harmonica and Jasmine on the flute, Javier is serenaded with a musical performance. He is amazed, "These girls seem totally fine on the road. They are so creative!"

"We know. If they were not, we would not have been able to make this journey," says Amarins.

Eager to see the ocean, we mount up. Rolling along, we crane our necks at each crest to catch a glimpse of the big water. At each summit it eludes us. As we get closer to town, Javier offers to get our food so we have our lunch at McDonald's. While the girls tumble around in the colorful indoor play equipment, we meet Kevin McClave and his wife Melissa. They had contacted us through our website and offered us a place to hang out and, most importantly, they have two children close in age to our girls. Sitting in the play area, Ama and I seize a quiet moment to converse while we enjoy the still air and the warm sunshine. Sharing our story with Javier, the McClaves and other parents who happen to be here today, we're touched again by the riveted interest in our personal story. This same scene has played itself out many times as we have hop scotched from one fast food place to another on our coast-to-coast journey.

Amongst all the chatter, the McClaves affirm their previous online offer of a place to stay here in Encinitas for as long as we need. Kevin is going to ride with us the last miles to the ocean. He tells us that we should be able to see a glimpse of the water at the top of the next hill, after we leave the parking lot and before a long downhill stretch. As we all roll out and get situated on our respective rides, the local news truck stops by for an interview.

This last hill beyond the McDonald's proves to be a rite of passage. With fast food lying like a brick in our stomachs combined with a bit of premature jubilation, we stop multiple times, balanced on our bike like crows on a telephone wire, in order to get the courage and necessary rest to climb still higher. Despite the grueling climb, the ridge is worth the arduous ascension. The vertical line that makes up the crest of the ridge in front of us looks like the ground broke away and the crest or peak of the hill lifted straight up to its present height. The vertical walls are the color of red Georgia clay. Water over time has eroded sections of the lifted areas. Birds fly in and out of various holes along its face.

Without the encumbrances of weight and size, Javier and Kevin ride circles around us, yet continue to hover near Yeller. They can feel our elation.

Jasmine and Cheyenne are excited about reaching the Pacific Ocean.
February of 2010

The girls are giddy from the anticipation of reaching the ocean they have heard about since leaving Charleston, South Carolina. They also can't resist the chance to chat with our guests, disregarding our *no talk rule* that we usually apply to climbs.

"Say *Pacific Oceaaaaaaaan!*" Amarins cries out. I am so focused on the road below me as well as concentrating on pushing the cranks, I didn't notice the ocean spread out before us down below. Words cannot express how we feel inside as we crest this last hill. It hasn't sunk in yet, what has just taken place. The drive to push our bodies and minds for so long has numbed our response. Like sound to light, our emotions are slow to catch up to the moment.

Kevin says, "You have made it, can you believe it?"

Can we believe it? As soon as our feet touch the water we will.

It had been our plan to ride to the water's edge. As the road ends, we ride the sidewalk. The sand is heavy covering the concrete as we get closer to the beach dunes, and I move carefully until it ends. One hundred feet to our west, straight in front of our stretched bike, are no more roads. We can ride no farther west. A long way from Pongo Ridge, it is gratifying to be here at the Pacific. As we dismount, Ama tells the girls, "Wait, we will all go down and put our feet in the water together." Waiting has never been harder. Our guests stand around and let us have our space as they take pictures and roll some film when we finally tumble down the small sand dune which is ruffled with the depressions of others who have walked this way, leading to the beach.

With a crisp ocean breeze in our faces and sand between our toes, we walk hand in hand to the water's edge. The sun waves through the opaque clouds to congratulate us on this farfetched moment. The kids run and play in the cool surf's salty foam. Ama and I turn from the ocean and toward each other. We touch our heads together and grab on to the one sure thing: each other. We finally allow the emotions to run.

We soak up the realization of having made it to the Pacific Ocean. Three thousand eight hundred miles, six months, two oceans, thirteen states, nineteen flat tires, five falls, an abundance of broken spokes, six new rims, countless inner tubes and outer tires, two new chain sets (five chains each), several drive chains, handle bar wraps, nuts, bolts, bells, a new Burley trailer, too many warm, wonderful, generous, special, loving, incredible, kind people

Yeller stands fully loaded at the edge of the Pacific Ocean.
February of 2010

to count, and countless assumptions that proved totally wrong, from the landscape through people, the weather, Yeller, and everything in between. The constant remains: We are ordinary people on an extraordinary journey of giving and receiving. A hope we began with is a faith proven true.

AFTER AN HOUR OF SALTY sand and celebration, we peel ourselves away. The girls learned that the McClaves have a son and daughter about their ages. Now they, too, are ready to leave. Kevin and Javier lead the way. Once we cross the famous highway One, I am staring at a monstrous hill that shoots up for about the length of eight football fields. A six percent grade is common on interstates. We have traversed many six percenters on our cross continent journey. These kinds of climbs require us to be in our lowest gear and, at that, we stop frequently for breaks. I guess that we are looking at a fifteen percent one, at the least.

Kevin says, "Do you want to go another route?"

I grit my teeth, gearing up for the climb and say, "No, we can do this."

I ask the girls, "Can we do this?"

They respond with our favorite mantra, "Yes we can!"

It takes us almost thirty minutes to climb it. Amazingly, the brakes hold and, after more stops then we can count, we reach the top of the hill. Eight hundred pounds of machine, material, and flesh are king and queen of this mountain, and we have a killer view of the ocean behind us. Our girls never made a peep. I wonder if it was the pitch of this particular incline which held their tongues.

Since winter time, our journey has not produced many opportunities for Cheyenne, Jasmine, and Robin to play with peers. A kid friendly home is a treat

Melissa, Jasmine and Kevin.
February of 2010

sweeter than all the Jolly Rancher candies they have eaten. Toys inside and out, a concrete path around the house, and games galore await the girls' inquisitive minds. The McClaves' children, Kai (6) and Mae (3), take to our girls like an opossum to fleshy pink persimmons in the fall time after the first frost has turned them sweet. With friends for them to play with, Ama and I get to have some down time for one of the few times in our travels.

The openness of the McClave home is a continuation of hundreds of acts of kindness that have followed us from coast to coast. It is a microcosm of the larger story. Gratefulness is something we often speak about with the girls. As we lie down to sleep or when we rise in the morning, gratitude lingers in our conversations with each other and in our prayers. It is not difficult to pinpoint what we have to be thankful for. We are indebted to everyday folks of all walks of life that make up the collage that is America. Without them, we never could have made it this far.

AUGUST THE 25TH, 2009: Due east for six miles after leaving McCormick, South Carolina, and the girls help us find the correct mailbox number. We ran into a wonderful man in McCormick who invited us to stay at his house with his family when he found out what we were doing. We involve the girls as much as we can in the specifics of our daily travels. Even Robin looks out for numbers now. It is close to five when we park at the home of Reverend Bell and his wife, Carrie, under the close eye of the broiling sun. The girls jump right onto the playground set that has not seen our hosts' children on it for many moons. We set up camp next to a picnic table and under the edge of a large cedar tree. Tired of playing in the heat, the girls find the TV: Clifford, Dragon Tails, and Dora are always a good pick. As Amarins fine tunes the sleeping arrangements and cooks dinner, the Bell's son and his friend, Kurtez, stop by. They bring a surprise, two chickens and a rooster! No pen needed, they will roost in the trees

above us. The girls guess at how the hens will lay eggs. We can't help but enjoy their predictions. The girls immediately want to feed them. The TV is forgotten.

Life is good this evening with a meal of rice along with watermelon, oranges, and homemade cake provided by the Bells. It is close to nine when Cheyenne and Jasmine finally drift asleep on the couch in the house. When we carry them to the tent, Robin is already asleep. Amarins and I enjoy a good movie with the preacher who is as big as a tree and as gentle and kind as Jesus himself.

AUGUST THE 29TH, 2009: Our destination for today was Bamberg, South Carolina, forty-five miles from Aiken. When we arrive, it is still early. We look at the map. Our next host town is Ladson. If we can make it to Branchville today, we can make it to Ladson tomorrow. That would take us into Charleston on Monday, August the 31st, 2009. There is magic in that date, from Renfro Valley KOA, Kentucky, to Charleston, South Carolina, within one month. It is fourteen more miles to Branchville. It takes us an hour and a half. Oh, how we make miles on this flatter terrain. In the mountains the same distance would take us at least three hours. Branchville isn't a very big town. A couple of filling stations, an ice cream parlor and a Subway are in the center of it. We don't see shade at the ice cream parlor, so we choose to sit down in the Subway until our friend, Harding, arrives from Raleigh, North Carolina. He is going to spend the evening with us. As Amarins walks into the Subway with the girls,

a wiry black lady in her seventies jumps up and down with excitement to see us. She saw us earlier today in Bamberg when she passed us on the road, and hoped we were coming to Branchville. By chance, here we are.

Ms. Arlene lives around the corner, so she seems like the person to ask about a spot to throw up our tent. Immediately she offers her backyard! Once Harding arrives, we all head the few blocks to her home. Ms. Arlene is from the northeast and has traveled all over the states. We find a kindred spirit in someone who has also traveled much. Being in a rough part of town, we put our tent just beyond the chain of her big guard dog. The girls asleep, the four of us sit in the moonlight between the tent and the road and speak of things that people have spoken about for thousands of years in similar conditions. Where did we all journey from? What did ancient men and women talk about when they sat around at night looking up at this same moon? What are the hopes and aspirations for our children?

SEPTEMBER THE 4TH, 2009: We planned to go to Georgia today, but we decide to find a campground in Hardeeville, South Carolina. With the long days we start a little later, but the hot and humid coastal air is punishing. This is on top of a fifty-five mile day yesterday. We get different directions on how to get there. Some even say it has been out of business for many years. A Burger King with a

play structure provides a good stop to regroup and figure out what to do next. Here we meet a Hispanic lady, Miriam, with her two boys and a friend. They don't know about a campground, but if we want, we can camp at their place. What an experience! While we pitch the tent, Omar and Kerly Jr. share their toys with the girls. For supper we start with tomato base soup. It is their custom to eat around nine o'clock when her husband, Kerly, gets home from work. Miriam makes tacos filled with mashed potatoes and cheese, along with cream cheese and cabbage on top. The new tastes delight and fill us.

We decide to stay another day because it is Omar's eighth birthday tomorrow. By evening the next day, hamburgers are grilling. At the central table, a couple of ladies fix tostadas. Besides great food, we meet wonderful, hard working people. We share about our life before the bicycle journey. They share about their life in Mexico and their new life here. When the main food disappears, it is time to bring out the piñata.

It is already after ten in the evening, and Robin is in a deep sleep in the tent situated between our host's house and their neighbors'. A chain link fence and red ant mound border the other two sides of our portable home. Jasmine just fell asleep on a big stuffed animal in the living room while some other kids watch television. We can barely wake her up until we use the magic word: piñata! Bags full of candy collected from the ground signal bed time.

OCTOBER THE 19TH, 2009: At the sign for Alabama's Mobile ferry crossing, the bright red LED letters shout CLOSED. Not wanting to hang out for five days while they repair the problem, we take state road 59 to Foley where we pick up highway 98 to the west and head out on a different route than we had planned for. The road takes us over some hills and leads us through a landscape where we pass horse fences and see miles of Spanish moss draped over pinion oak trees. A Foley resident we speak with while taking a breather suggests that we go to Oak Hollow Farm in Fairhope. "They will have a place for you to pitch the tent." We arrive at Oak Hollow Farm and call the number we see on a sign. With one phone call, it is a done deal. We can put our tent anywhere we want to. On top of a hill, we find the perfect spot not far from a huge barn, a rope swing from yesteryear, and all the sunshine we can enjoy. Our campsite looks like something out of a camper's magazine.

In the morning we are treated to some citrus and a tour of the farm by Glenda, the owner's daughter. With offers of future hospitality we ride away, waving.

November the 4ᵗʰ, 2009: Unwrapping ourselves from the welcoming arms of Ms. Vicky and Ms. Vera in Natchitoches, Louisiana (founded 1714), we head for Texas. An hour or so out of town, our trailer falls apart. The main tow arm's vibration caused the frame tube to crack, dropping the front of the trailer onto the ground, making us come to an abrupt stop. It is time to get everyone off Yeller and to unload the trailer.

Amarins heads to the filling station to see if there are hose clamps we can use to hold the broken frame tube to the tow arm. The girls play next to the bicycle. As we fix the trailer, an engineer happens to drive by and stops to help us brainstorm solutions. Mr. Bergeron is a jolly Cajun and Vietnam Veteran now living on this stretch of the El Camino that the Spanish once used. It runs from Mexico to eastern Georgia. He lives seven miles down the road and on a portion of the original trail. He invites us to stop by as we head west and he gives us directions.

A temporary solution of hose clamps and a couple of tie straps makes us road worthy again. Our injured trailer makes every hump in the road a jarring occurrence. Our pedaling power is impeded because we are fearful of going over bumps too fast and causing our temporary solution to fail. When we see our Cajun friend again at his place, he invites us to spend the rest of the day and the night here.

I say, "Are you going to boil us tonight? I have watched too many shows about Cajuns."

Laughing, he says "No." He comes up with an even better plan than our tent. He puts us up in his bunkhouse used for hunters when they stop by, which has a laundry facility and cable television. Behind this are tables with all kinds of petrified wood he has collected from his property. It provides a great geology lesson for the girls and he is pleased to be the teacher. Amarins and the girls wash, clean, and relax. Mr. Bergeron and I go to the bicycle store for new tires in Shreveport, some hundred miles to the north. He will not let me talk him out of his very generous hospitality. We're running out of spares, and there are no bicycle stores on our route as far as we can tell until we get to Waco in the middle of Texas. I decide to leave the trailer the way it is for now until we can find a steel rod to put inside the broken aluminum tube. In the evening, we have gumbo for supper that he cooked up yesterday. It is the first time any of us has had it. Our daughters are not too impressed, but Amarins and I like it very much.

NOVEMBER THE 16TH, 2009: The outer tent fly slaps in the wind outside of Speegleville, Texas. Several hours before dawn, I decide to stake the guy lines on the outer fly of our new tent we picked up a few days ago in Dallas. This keeps the sides from flapping so much and helps the family stay asleep. The sun is up when our eyes open again. Jasmine has snuggled nicely in her new sleeping bag and sleeps well. With the weather getting colder, Robin's blanket was not enough to keep her warm. She was ending up in our double sleeping bag in the middle of the night. Robin slept until dawn before she decided to crawl in with Ama and me. This is her first night with Jasmine's old sleeping bag. At the filling station where we are camped, we have a biscuit breakfast with chocolate milk and coffee.

I talk with some of the older regulars who find our trip quite amusing. Amarins updates the website with the station's free wireless internet. The girls enjoy some cartoons. When Amarins goes to pay for the provisions, the owner, Ashraf, refuses to accept it. Our host is from the Middle East and is shocked when I inquire about his generosity in Arabic. We talk for sometime and then finish up posing for a picture.

He sends us off with drinks for the girls and biscuits for us later.

NOVEMBER THE 17TH, 2009: Iredell looks even farther away now that the rear hub is acting up. Pitching the tent alongside the road is tempting. We decide against it and keep limping along. We are beaten down by the wind and the continuation of mechanical problems. Yet, we keep on pedaling and arrive in Iredell in the late afternoon. The girls and Amarins wait in the filling station's convenience store while I ask around for a place to camp. There is a good spot to camp behind the Iredell Café next door. I ask the owners and they have no problem letting us stay there.

I talk with a motorcyclist for a bit before pulling Yeller around the back. With the help of Cheyenne, the tent is set up quickly and the beds are made. Back at the filling station to warm up our noodles from last night's meal for supper, the motorcyclist comes back with his wife. I take them to see the bicycle and share about our journey. They are inspired. This inspires me to ask the ultimate question that we have not asked before while staying in our tent, "Can you do a load of laundry for us?"

They say "Yes" without hesitation. Although we could use a shower ourselves, at least our clothes will smell fresh as we ride. Four days is the longest we have gone without bathing, but we usually find some way to clean up with diaper wipes and water along the way. We clean up in the restroom and head for the tent to pull our dirty clothes together. I hang out with the girls in the tent. Amarins goes back to the filling station to prepare some pictures and today's story for the website.

In the morning Amarins enjoys a moment to herself with a cup of coffee at the filling station. After a while she comes and gets Cheyenne and Jasmine. She tells me a couple of ranchers are having their morning get together in there. When Robin and I finally go in, a rancher speaks up and asks, "Who else are you going to bring in?" It leads us to talk about our journey and

last night's campout behind the Iredell Café.

The girls have their minds set on pancakes this morning. We saw the advertisement for them here yesterday. To our disappointment, they've run out. There is no consoling the girls this morning. Jasmine is especially disappointed. Soon the entire store knows. Rancher Mike speaks up again and offers to make the girls pancakes at his home. It's an offer we don't resist. We need to wait for higher temperatures to head out, and this is the perfect way to bide the time. Our girls get to see a real Texas ranch with horses and cattle and devour the pancakes fixed up by Mike himself. As we eat in the ranch house with décor of saddles and other cowboy stuff, we share our amazing journey with the rancher and his wife.

DECEMBER THE 15TH, 2009: We arrive in Yeso, New Mexico just after the noon hour. Jon, a contact from the internet, is already waiting for us with his Ford Power Stroke and trailer. These towns are small on the high plains, and the news of our travels had reached him through a television piece.

"Load up and let's head out," Jon says.

The girls have been waiting for this day ever since we told them. They know there are horses on the ranch and they're going to ride them. It's every girls dream, according to Amarins. The country we ride through changes by the mile until we enter the Salado Canyon. It is yet another different view, showing us more vegetation, side canyons, and boulders made from many shades of red. We look and stare. We could not have guessed from our travel route, highway 60, that it would look so different here. This is something that goes by unnoticed from the road. Jon and Suzanne are putting together a working ranch.

We get to stay in an old Ford travel camper, located on the top of the ridge, overlooking the Salado Canyon. Billy the Kid once outran the Law in this same place. We can sure see why. These canyons hide a person well once he is off the canyon rim's edge. It is surreal. We can almost see the outlaws riding through the canyon below while the dust lingers in the starry light.

The girls and I work on a fire. Firewood gathered with little hands roars toward the evening sky. The girls know how to handle a fire, though they do get carried away sometimes with the amount of wood to throw on it. Jon shopped and has stocked the refrigerator to capacity. Tonight we'll have meat, vegetables, and applesauce in the New Mexico countryside. Better eats than earlier travelers, I am sure.

Pictures cannot capture the tangible beauty surrounding us or the hospitality that rains down on us like the stars overhead.

Robin is ecstatic about California.
January of 2010

What a view: Cheyenne, Joshua trees
and snow-covered mountains.
January of 2010

One more mountain range stands between us and the Pacific Ocean.
January of 2010

Jasmine builds leaf castles in the sand.
January of 2010

Rosemary and Ray on Pacific Ocean Day.
February of 2010

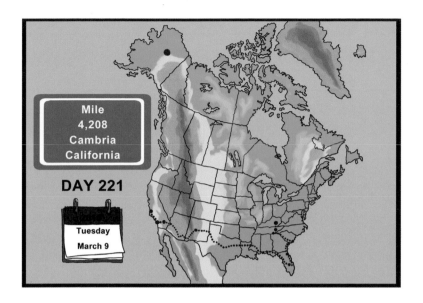

Mile
4,208
Cambria
California

DAY 221

Tuesday
March 9

CHAPTER 14

LIFE IS FULL OF RISKS. Here in the West, many of us build wonderful walls around our lives. We dream visions of nice houses, dependable automobiles, thick retirements, secure life insurance policies, and other trappings that scream to our neighbors how safe our existence is. Though we are affluent in this way, it is not the norm for the rest of the world. Any one of myriad events can change our fortunes faster than a bicycle tire blowout. Rolling along the highways of this vast continent, we have a deeper awareness of life's fragility.

For days we have skirted the chilly Californian coast. The songs and movies of my childhood about California life in the '60s must be an illusion. The world of the Brady Bunch and American Graffiti are missing from these coastal landscapes. Mountains, not hills, impede our forward movement. With combined strokes of two adults, two young girls, and a free spinning three year old, we make slow, steady progress. Beyond being pleasing to the eyes, the ocean does nothing for our sore bones and muscles. In our fantasies, we had hoped for accessible natural hot springs and a Pacific waterway we could play in as we courted the western coastline of America. Like passing ancient, painted landscapes in the Rijks Museum in Amsterdam, we see and admire, but are forbidden to touch, the fabrics on display, decorated from an endless palate of colors.

Finding places to stay in this illusionary world that teases our senses is problematic. Private property abounds along this rolling seaboard. It is a constant battle deciding where to pitch our home for the night since we do not want to make a habit of trespassing. I miss a more distant time when there were fewer fences.

The Californian countryside.
March of 2010

We roll through a long low pass before we come to a mammoth hill leading to Cambria. Hunger gnaws at our stomachs after many miles of stop and go. A crisp blue sky makes for a wonderful canopy as we slice through the chilly head wind. It has been with us ever since we left San Diego. When we finally reach the apex, we are famished.

Stopped at a junction, we try to figure out what to do. No businesses are visible north on California One. Cambria is down to the right. We debate about going down into the town, invisible beyond the straight drop down a holler. A truck pulls in front of us. I roll Yeller up next to it since there is plenty of shoulder.

Rolling down his window the driver says, "Cool bike."

"That it is," I admit.

"Are you out for the day?"

"You could say that, we rode from Kentucky!"

He and his girl friend's eyes appear to bug out of their heads.

"Do you know if there is a place to eat around here?" I add, "We are tired of eating granola bars."

"No man, we are not from here. We are just passing through to do some biking ourselves."

"Do you know if Cambria is down there to the right or does the road we are on meet with it down a bit?"

"Have no idea."

"Thanks anyway. Here, take one of our cards and follow us online."

I pull our lanky quint forward and turn around to catch Ama's attention, "What do you want to do?"

"Let's go down to the right. More than likely, the old California One used to go there before they made the new one we are on."

I look back at the girls, "All right girls, looks like you get to fly to the bottom!"

We sail for over a mile down the grade to the bottom, while the girls stretch their hands out sideways to catch the breeze. Beautiful hillside farmland streaks past our eyes. The California environment changes so much in every change of elevation. On top there was a scarcity of trees and down here they are abundant. The micro climates are intriguing. We find the town at the floor of a small valley, where the temperature feels much warmer. The wind has receded to a breeze.

We roll through downtown and park Yeller next to a bank on our side of the road. All eyes are on us. We can see there are several places to eat. While we decide, a local man, Mike, stands nearby talking to some other gentlemen. We strike up a conversation about a place to camp. He is not sure, but he will check with the local bike shop and get back with us.

For lunch we choose a family restaurant. After burgers, fries, soup and colas, we catch a glimpse of Mike at our bike again. We stroll over when he says, "You can camp out behind the Cambria Bicycle Outfitters shop that's just up the road."

Ama says with a smile, "Thank you sir."

THE BIKE SHOP SITS DOWN from the road on the left side. When we pull up to the door, Alan, the owner, comes out to greet us. He is quite taken with our mode of transportation. He tells us we can pitch our tent in the tall grass behind his shop, on the other side of the trees that make the border between the parking lot and the grassy field. We thank him for letting us pitch our tent there.

The girls are already off Yeller and observe the children's bikes through eyes filled with anticipation. One word from Alan sends them flying. Cheyenne hops on a black bike without training wheels. Robin finds a small black and orange one with side wheels to pedal off on. Jasmine has her eyes set on the pink one with the white basket and the streamers attached to the handlebars. The parking lot belongs to them. They spin the pedals and ride circle after circle, in control of their own direction and speed. The feeling of individual freedom surrounds them.

Amarins pulls her laptop from the trailer. It is time for her to update the website once more. There is internet reception in the store that she wants to take advantage of.

Jasmine and Cheyenne enjoy riding bikes.
March of 2010

I pull the trailer around to the rear of the shop and find a beautiful bowl area close to a creek to put our tent up. Ankle high, thick grass will provide a soft spot to rest on. Two big yellow sixty-liter dry sacks hold our home and our sleeping bags and another thirty-five liter blue one holds the mats we sleep on for additional comfort. I pull the tent from its waterproof package and position the opening toward a path that leads to a pedestrian bridge across the creek. The girls wave at me from the bridge. The slight curve of the bridge adds speed to their bikes on the way down. The camp spot is ideal. With privacy and delightful scenery all around, it is hard to imagine we are in a town.

The tapping of my hatchet on the stakes seems to coincide with the popping sound of a bb gun. The sounds come from nearby, but I can't detect the shooter when I glance around and over at our belongings. Nothing looks out of the ordinary; hence I keep on working. With the tent up, I place the sleeping gear inside. From the back of the trailer I pull our bags with clothing for each and place them in the tent. Amarins will make the beds once she has a moment to do so. The trailer can stay where it is for now. The evening dew has not yet set in; therefore I choose to wait before putting it under the fly of the tent. Looking around once more confirms my feeling that we have found some fine sleeping with the sound of the creek and the softness of the grass. We could not ask for a nicer spot. Again, we are blessed by the kindness of strangers.

Next my attention goes to Yeller who sits under a shed roof connected to the bike shop. I fiddle with the girls' purses, water bottles and Robin's Binkies. Gathering all the items under my arms to bring them to the tent, I stop at the sound of a loud boom, almost like a shot gun blast. Shrugging my shoulders I get back to collecting the items I need to take.

Not thirty seconds later, Cheyenne and Jasmine come running from the back of the building, hollering, "The trailer is on fire! The trailer is on fire!"

I drop everything I'm holding and peel off running. As I pass them, I say, "Go in the store and tell your mom, then stay put! Don't come back here until we say so."

Cheyenne says in a worried voice, "Get Dogge!"

Rounding the corner of the building, I see smoke and flames at the tent. Charging the trailer, I kick it away from the tent with my Red Wing work boots. The explosion sprayed hot stuff down the fly of the tent and put a thousand holes in it. I try to get the remaining items out of the burning trailer, but it is useless. The acrid smell of aluminum, plastics, and lighter knot fire starter creates a barrier to getting too close. The heat singes the hair on my fingers.

Amarins runs up with a fire extinguisher. She hands it to me.

I tell her, "Get back and take care of the kids. It looks like what was left in the trailer is gone."

Before she leaves, she says, "Is Dogge still in there?" I can see that she wants to reach in the flaming carcass and save Dogge.

I say, "Yes, I did not put Dogge or Rose in the tent yet."

I aim the extinguisher at the rubble and pull the trigger. White powder covers what remains of the trailer's belongings. In only a couple of minutes, the special beefed-up Burley trailer is ruined, along with its contents. An empty feeling enters my stomach as I hear the fire engine siren in the distance. *What will we do? How will I explain to the girls that their favorite stuffed animals are burned? My gosh, Cheyenne has had her Dogge for five years. If I had just investigated the noise when I was setting up the tent!*

A devastating moment.
March of 2010

The Cambria Fire Department stops by with two big trucks, but the damage is already done. It went so fast. A couple of firemen in their firefighter gear sift through the remains like CSI personnel sifting through the evidence at a crime scene. I feel helpless about facing the girls with the bad news. The fire chief does not know why the trailer ignited, leaving us right back at the beginning. What caused it?

My only summation is that our tracker set off a small fire, and it caused the camp stove canister to blow up. Jim, from New Mexico, gave us a homemade tracking device complete with a solar panel. We were excited about the use of solar power. This angle of the unit allowed us to occasionally speak about a practical green approach to meet some of our energy needs. It also enabled folks to follow us in real time which generated excitement among our followers. I figure that something did not click off the charge coming in from the panel and it overheated. The pops I heard must have been some of the solid state components bursting from the overcharged battery. Then, boom! It was on fire. Whatever the cause, we face a new and unforeseen obstacle.

In the store, Amarins cries with Cheyenne. The loss of her Dogge is a big one. Jasmine and Robin scoot as close as they can to seek comfort in each other. Out of the devastation we make new friends, Mike and Kathy. They'd offered to bring us supper tonight. Now they're taking us away for a bite to eat and some ice cream for the girls.

WHEN WE ARE BACK TO the tent, Mike and Kathy promise to come back in the morning. They want to help us figure out what to do next. The smell of charred plastic and fabric is still thick in the air. Lying in our sleeping places, the surroundings that made this place distinct are now distant. It is hard to find beauty in this moment. Sobs from the girls carry through the heavy night air and compete with the melodic gurgle of the creek. Without Dogge, Cheyenne snuggles up to Amarins. The sounds of their chatter concerning death lay heavy on my ears. I find my place between Robin and Jasmine who have their own sorrows about their lost puppies.

Exhausted from the day's physical and emotional events, we all fall asleep. My thoughts for the night are on sorrow and regret. *If only I had put their things in the tent. But if I had, then I probably would have put the trailer under the fly flap and all would have been lost. What if one of the girls had been reaching into the trailer when it exploded? It could have started burning while we were still riding, with tent and sleeping bags still on top. Then what would have happened?*

After a night of distorted dreams and true nightmares, we wake to the voice of Mike. He's here to pick us up for breakfast. We're going to eat at their house up on the mountainside, the same mountain that we descended to get here. Mike tells us it has a bird's eye view of the ocean.

The girls are enamored with Mike and Kathy's life-size female mannequin named Dahlia. She stands guard, looking out the window as if waiting for her lost lover to return from the sea. If we could cart the thing on our bike, I think it would make a nice replacement for the lost stuffed animals.

The first step is to try to figure out what to do next. A new trailer needs to be found; then we need to replace as many of the lost items as we can: pots to cook in, bowls, cups, silverware, fuel for the pocket rocket (a small steel stove top that survived the fire and attaches to a propane tank), tooth brushes, toothpaste, hair brush, dish detergent, shampoo and shower gel—items that seem to be an afterthought, but are necessities nonetheless.

I decide to ask Alan if he can help us find a new trailer. He is already ahead of us and has called around. There is a trailer in San Luis Obispo, a town an hour south by car. Alan says that the owner will let us have it at a discount since it is a demonstration model and because of our situation. Mike and I take off to pick it up.

Amarins and the girls stay with Kathy. The girls color at the table, basking in the sun that comes in through the floor to ceiling window. Amarins takes a moment to sit outside on the patio with Kathy, looking at the ocean and talking about the journey and what happened with the trailer. When the girls get restless from coloring, they get to play dress up with the clothing for Dahlia. Once they are back in their own clothes, it is time to go to the playground and soak in the warm, sunny California day. Finally, a day of California dreaming is realized. The irony is that it's tinged with yesterday's loss.

It takes Mike and me several hours of travel and shopping to get the trailer and the parts for the modifications. In his workshop we piece our third trailer together, now with the modifications we've come accustomed to. The arm that reaches from trailer to the rear tire of the bicycle gets shortened several inches by Mike. I add an extra axle point that I managed to save from our old trailer. The top rack sits outside in the sun, drying off from its thorough *soot cleaning*. It'll have to do for now, because no one nearby has a new Burley rack. It takes us all afternoon, but by the end of the day we have a new trailer, raring to go. Mike found a set of camping pots in his garage that he lets us have. Most of the other items we were able to pick up on our shopping spree.

We are again thankful for new friends. The help we receive to get us back

Mike and Kathy's help has been incredible
in getting us back on the road again.
March of 2010

on the road has been incredible. We thought it would take us several days to pick up the pieces and put them back together again. With the help and friendship of Mike and Kathy, and many others, we are only down for one day. With the pressure on to get to Fairbanks by the end of August, each day takes on new importance in reaching our goal. We ride away humbled, under the weight of loss. We didn't plan this lesson, but we realize its importance as well.

From Todd in San Diego we head
north: North to Alaska.
February of 2010

Beach bums: Mae, Amarins, Robin, Cheyenne,
Sullivan, Kai and Jasmine.
February of 2010

Sunset at Huntington Beach, California.
February of 2010

We're following the
California One for
many miles.
March of 2010

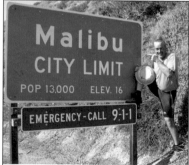

Bill made it to Malibu in his Red Wing
work boots with his porcelain wash pan.
February of 2010

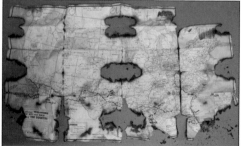

All that's left of the master map.
March of 2010

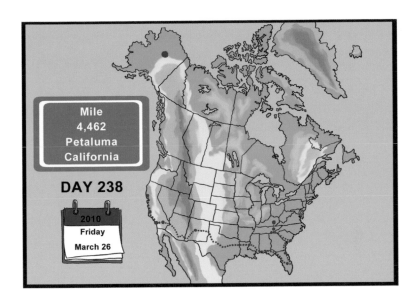

Mile
4,462
Petaluma
California

DAY 238

2010
Friday
March 26

CHAPTER 15

IT IS LATE MARCH. We just woke up from the whirlwind of yesterday's events. The Petaluma Wheelmen rode with us from San Rafael, above the San Francisco Bay area. They treated us to a picnic at a local cheese factory situated in the picturesque landscape that frames this part of California. Our day's ride concluded at Pizzicato's, where the specialty of the day, The Pedouin Pizza, caught our eyes. Our host had warned the town about our impending arrival. The people responded, treating us like heroes.

"YOU DON'T KNOW THE SONG *My Old Kentucky Home*?" The girls shake their heads "No," making me feel like a derelict father. Who would have guessed? We travel over four thousand miles on a peculiar bicycle, through all kinds of weather, meeting all manner of people and I get harassed because my girls do not know how to sing a Stephen Foster classic. I knew we were destined to become friends with people who ask questions like that. These are the Maloneys. They welcome us like family: long lost family that has come home. Tom, a physician, married a Kentucky girl named Carolyn over forty years ago. She grew up only fifteen miles from my hometown of Fern Creek. In this charming sleepy California town dotted with turn of the century cottage homes, hills, and lush foliage, watered by ample rain and mysterious fog banks, they raised their twelve children. All but the youngest learned to drive in a red Volkswagen bus they bought new in 1970 when they settled here. They lovingly call it Gus the Bus. Gus shows all the wear that one might imagine, and Carolyn still drives it. Since the Maloney's nest has long been emptied, we fit quite well in their modest home that sits on top of a knoll.

Carolyn's sister in Louisville put the Maloneys onto us. "I saw this in the local news and decided to forward it to you, Carolyn. Best be on the lookout for these crazy hillbillies on a bike," wrote Norah Kute. We had planned to keep to the coast, but Carolyn's enthusiasm leapt out from her emails and through phone calls. It caused us to change course once we crossed the Golden Gate Bridge.

Carolyn's loving arms scoop up our three girls like one might scoop up a pile of kindling needed to start a fire on a cold evening. She treats them like they are her own grandchildren. By midday of our first full day at Maloneyville, the girls are having tea time under some tall bushes in the front yard in a spot called "The Fort" which was a hideout for their twelve kids. In a setting speckled with sunshine radiating through the bottle brush plants, they spread a blue cloth with white lines across the ground. A tall white tea pot with blue hearts sits in the middle of the cloth. Cheyenne is in shorts and barefoot; Jas-

Ms Carolyn shows the girls how to eat an artichoke.
March of 2010

mine is in her pink dress; and Robin kneels down in her blue jeans. They eat apples and bananas from a plate and let their imaginations take flight. From the looks of it, one might think the girls have always lived here.

After forty years of living in Petaluma, the Maloneys seem to know everyone, including the local newspaper personalities. Bob Padecky from the *Press Democrat* in Santa Rosa comes by to see us. Amarins suggests I deal with the interview while she updates the website. Wanting some privacy from the unbridled energy unleashed by not having the girls tethered to the quint, I invite him into "my office." Opening the side door of Gus the Bus, we climb in and sit on the well-worn white bench seat just behind the driver's seat. Bob is determined to find some deeper motive for our journey. We spend nearly three hours bantering back and forth, chasing and eluding. Halfway through our experience, J.J. Jackson of the local *Argus-Courier* joins us. Perched in the front seat, he sees our story from a sports angle. When Mrs. Maloney pokes her head out to make sure we are fine, she shakes her head when she sees us huddled up in her old bus.

"Of all the places," she exclaims.

"It's okay," I assure her. "The scent of aged horsehair stuffed seats, old plastic, and a well used engine are like the perfume of my childhood. It's a comfortable place for an interview, Mrs. Maloney."

Laughing, she just turns and retreats back inside.

Saturated with well worn dialogue, we exit Gus when the girls come out bearing flowers. Jasmine, on Carolyn's invitation, led a posse of her sisters to recycle some old flower arrangements, transforming them into bouquets for the journalists. As each reporter receives his, Cheyenne thanks them for putting our story in their newspapers.

It's only fitting that we should feel like stars in the Golden State, home to Hollywood. The press follows us heartily on our journey up the coast and delights in interacting with us and spinning our story in a positive way. Channel 8, the NBC affiliate out of San Diego, got some aerial shots of us at Torrey Pines. Then the road crew allowed Cheyenne to hold the camera and shoot some footage. At the bottom of Devil's Slide, south of San Francisco, Mike Sugarman of CBS5 had us all enjoying his portrayal of the Pedouins as he took a spin on our bike. Mike entered our world by sitting on our quint, and it showed in his presentation of our journey to his followers in the Bay area.

WE, TOO, TAKE PART IN documenting our Pedouin days. In Yosemite, I frame the girls in Amarins' camera display. On the screen, Ama stands on the downhill slope with her left hand on the face of El Capitan. Cheyenne's left hand fingers graze the stone while she stands perched on one leg like a flamingo she saw in the Florida Panhandle. Jasmine is in the corner with her back against the massive wall, and Robin is between them all, leaning against the granite surface with her head turned toward the east.

The nature that surrounds us wouldn't be preserved in this same way if not for a four day outing John Muir and President Roosevelt took through here in the spring of 1903. Because the two men set this cherished land aside, we get to enjoy this national treasure. Long after we leave and continue our ride, the palpable beauty and vastness of our world, as depicted so sensually here in the wilderness, stays with us.

Our images digitally frozen, we sit down for a noontime snack under the watchful care of El Capitan's 3,000 foot face warmed by the sun as it hits us directly and reflects off of the massive stone face. The blue sky is our cover. Starting at daylight when the temperature was around freezing, Amarins had corralled Cheyenne and Jasmine up the rubble base like a sheep dog herding her sheep. I had Robin in a back carrier, and it tested my strength to tote my little chipmunk for almost four hours, straight up.

The girls have their places staked out under various plants and small trees where the face's rubble tapers off precipitously towards the valley below. I feel a kinship to these hardy plants. As they attempt to be rooted in the mountain's rubble, we too try daily to stay atop our medium, legs like roots, planted amongst the lower part of Yeller's elements.

Like little squirrels scrunched up in the fork of a tree, the girls gnaw on white Gouda cheese, hunks of beef salami, and peanuts. The view of the canyon floor below us paints us in a fairytale scene. Fulfilled with snacks, scenery, and chattering amongst sisters, we feel centered in this world and connected to each other. Perched on the edge of our wide earth, our girls find a home here, which they will pack up and unpack again and again in other distant, unknown locations. This will always be a part of them—and us.

Ama and I lie on our backs, gazing into the seamless blue sky. We feel the heat radiating from El Capitan. "What are the chances of being greeted by David McPherson in Sausalito, after rolling over the iconic Golden Gate

Bridge with a police escort, then down a steep windy road into the little bay town?" I wonder out loud.

"A hundred percent," Amarins replies. "With the way we have been blessed with wonderful encounters of the unexpected, we were bound to find him on our path."

David, in his older BMW, handed me his business card with eighty dollars stapled to it as we slowed down for a stoplight. "Call me and I will lend you my van so you can take your family to Yosemite!" He yelled. We took him up on his offer, thus here we are lying at the base of this marvelous chunk of rock.

It becomes a time to relax and a time to reflect. Why do we keep going on? I feel tired and the enormity of the journey has taken its toll. Broken bike parts, the grind of constant road awareness, unending rain and cool temperatures, our own fatigue of mind and body—why not end it here with this crescendo of majesty and hospitality?

Leaving my thoughts, I turn to face Amarins, "Ama, what keeps us going?"

"What do you mean?"

"I have been thinking of all the struggles and sometimes it feels like we're just logging miles."

"I know what you're saying. It was a magic moment hitting the ocean in Charleston and now here. I have also wondered about our purpose. We have already completed something fantastic. It seems like there can't be anything new beyond this. But then a chance meeting like with David happens and here we are."

"I know it is hard for you to keep the website up and the girls have been talking about our home and their friends. I think the last few days at Maloneyville have made them a bit homesick."

"Bill, we have to keep going. There is a finish line, and it is still over two thousand miles away. There is still a lot of country to see and our stop here in Petaluma should give us some much needed rest. Besides, think about all the people that are following us. We are affecting so many people in ways we can't even imagine."

"Babe, I have thought about that a lot. Before I met you, most of my working years were spent in the helping professions and now that we are living out

Jasmine and Cheyenne are in awe of Half Dome in
Yosemite National Park.
March of 2010

one of our dreams, we are inadvertently bringing a lot of good stuff to a lot of people. It is so ironic. As you have said many times, we don't need a reason to be on this journey. We just are. There really isn't a reason to stop now is there?"

"No, there isn't," she says.

WHEN WE GET BACK TO Petaluma, we're back on the ball. Mrs. Maloney seems to have spoken to the whole town on our behalf. We visit Grant Elementary School to give a talk about our journey. Amarins looks at maps with Papa John, one of the folks from Petaluma following our journey, considering the different routes that take us north. I meet two more Bill Harrisons who live in the area. The girls go swimming with Mrs. Maloney. Amarins runs errands with Susan, who, like John, is intrigued with our story and wants to be a part of its forward progress. Together they exchange our tent and apply for a new passport for Jasmine. I meet with Greg and Yuri of The Bike Monkeys while Amarins enjoys a massage at Quintessence which was arranged by Jean of Petaluma.

The day ends with supper made by the Pasta King. The Maloneys are determined to send us off with full bellies. We've fed the girls a little earlier so we can have a grown-up night. They are winding down after a full day.

A bit after six, the Pasta King pulls up in his white van. His picture sits smack dab on the side where the words "Certified Delicious" sprawl out from his monogrammed red chef's apron and also on the one he is wearing. Aluminum foil containers of many shapes and sizes are carried inside. In the formal dining room is a table big enough for an army, an army that consisted of twelve kids, two parents, and, many times, kids from the neighborhood.

Art Ibleto, The Pasta King, is an eighty-four year old World War II veteran. At only five foot nine with a barrel chest, his affable smile commands attention when he enters the room. Having emigrated from Italy in his teens, he's in love with this country and the opportunities it has afforded him and his brother. Pro-business, even in his later years, he's here to give back, something we

Thanks for a fantastic meal Pasta King.
March of 2010

understand he does quite a lot. His dishes have won numerous gold awards in this part of the world. He has served food to the California Chambers, including the likes of Nancy Pelosi, and was congratulated by George Bush in Washington D.C. because of his entrepreneurial spirit and life. Around the table are Tom and Carolyn Maloney, Amarins and myself, the reporter Chris Smith, and of course the Pasta King, who sits at the head of the table. In front of us are an abundance of dishes, some of which Ama and I had never tasted, like the pesto and polenta dishes. Pasta with a light green pesto, lasagna, polenta, meatballs covered in red sauce sprinkled with herbs, and garlic bread adorn our plates. We raise our glasses to offer hardy cheers to Art Ibleto the Pasta King, the Petaluma people, and to the Pedouins on a journey to remember.

The Big Sur awaits our arrival.
March of 2010

A field of artichokes.
March of 2010

We biked across the Golden Gate Bridge.
March of 2010

At the face of El Capitan.
March of 2010

Pile-O-Girls in Yosemite National Park.
March of 2010

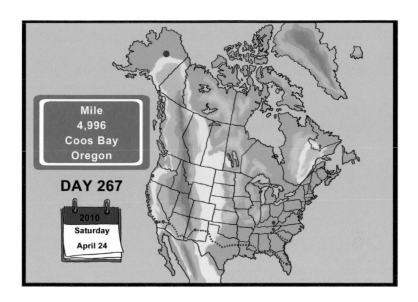

Mile
4,996
Coos Bay
Oregon

DAY 267

2010
Saturday
April 24

CHAPTER 16

THE 1970S WAS A TIME of innovation. To my neighbors (Mrs. Seabolt, the Aldridges, and Neanderthal Bob) the world was spinning too fast. With the advent of color television, rock & roll music, and spaceships to the moon, their country was becoming strange and foreign. Through my nine-year-old eyes, these folks appeared ancient. What they saw as offensive was just plain normal to me.

Half a mile up the road from our orange brick tri-level home, on the other side of an S-curve, was a man who lived with the aid of an iron lung. Though none of us kids ever saw him, the stories of this giant iron machine breathing for him kept the fear of God alive. Down the hill from him was an old homestead with a coal mound. Behind this pile of blackness, undisturbed for many years, was the small Fern Creek. This creek was the route to our private dig area.

A typical spring day consisted of feeding our family's chickens and then walking to the Johnson's house. Hanging outside until my friends Raymond and William could go, I would then head with them down to the creek and up the water's edge before finally peeling off to the right and up to the coal pile. Over time we dug a trench like those we saw in war movies. In this trench the outside world that so many fretted over disappeared. Raymond, William, and I spent ample hours uncovering pieces of discarded household items. We each claimed our lucky spot and pecked away with our dirt covered fingers, pieces of sticks, or rusted pieces of metal we uncovered. It was common to find whole glass milk jugs embossed with brand names like Sealtest and Borden's Dairy and cork top medicine bottles. From time to time we unearthed metal items and bits of earthenware that were mysterious to us. Special finds were whole, old, clay crocks and soft drink bottles that still had the paint left, like the early 1930s RC Cola bottles with the red pyramids still visible. We may not have been able to go to Egypt, but in our hideout, we explored the world through trash. When one of us found the lip, bottom, or handle of something unusual, we would all gather around as the finder worked. Skilled with a stick or file point, we scraped years of dirt and rubbish away. Sometimes our hearts would beat fast in anticipation of what the ground was about to give up. I wondered many times what the story of the person who last held this object was. At what point did they decide to throw it into this pile of rubbish? Often we held our breath as a larger portion of the glassware became visible, waiting to determine if the object remained intact or if time had left the piece in fragments. Like archeologists discussing the position of some artifact at a dig and the best way to discover without destroying, we would each offer advice on how to unearth the relic. If it turned out to be whole and unrecognizable, we celebrated by handling it and trying to guess its purpose or function.

Amarins and I propel our girls along on a similar hunt as we cross from Northern California into Oregon. Instead of glass and clay buried in the earth or mysteries described in western novels written by Dutch authors, we seek the intangibles around the next corner and beyond the next hill. Each turn, each ascent has the potential to reveal some sublime panoramic landscape: a flutter of soaring monarch butterflies, the soft blush of wind tangling with the endless conifer needles almost muted because its sound is being absorbed by the plated trunk bark, or the transcendent smile of some other travelers who find their own meaning in our affair.

Cheyenne, Jasmine, and Robin enter this part of the world with the same open minds with which they passed through the previous states. Their understanding deepens and expands with each new experience, as they learn from the present and measure every new environment against what they remember from home. Amarins is tickled to be in each state, mentally marking another one off her list; she wants to visit all fifty of them. Like the girls, her mind is an open book being filled with each new thing. As I reflect, I am content to be moving, pushing ever forward toward our goal while enjoying each and every day. My mind is focused on living in the now and hoping it unfolds in safety. We all are excited about the thoughts of reaching Cape Disappointment. It's just across the Columbia River in Washington and is where the Corps of Discovery (the official name of the Lewis and Clark Expedition) finished their westward trek. But before we reach the northwest corner of Oregon, there are still 500 miles of Oregon and its inhabitants to experience.

THROUGH THE INTERNET WE'VE BEEN contacted by Bill, owner of Gib's RV in Coos Bay. He had caught our story in the media. He wrote, "I want to provide you with one of your top ten experiences of your journey."

After several rainy days along the coast of Oregon, we pull into the West Coast Game Park, between the towns of Langlois and Bandon, under a mild blue sky. Entry tickets are waiting for us. Remembering our time at Safari West in Santa Rosa, California, the girls

Cheyenne pets a leopard cub.
April of 2010

get to pet the animals and let their imaginations run wild. Mouth dropped open in awe, Robin pets a leopard cub. Cheyenne did just that right before her and this gives Robin the courage to stretch her arm out to this beautiful and wild creature. After the leopard, the smaller animals are brought out to be petted. Jasmine cautiously rubs the fur of a ferret that Cheyenne holds. A skunk causes giggles among the girls when it lifts its tail. The girls are glad to hear it can no longer spray them.

I sit outside the petting zoo next to Yeller when Bill pulls up. After I show him our ride, we sit on the tailgate of his full-sized, heavy duty Chevy truck. I soon find out that he was in Vietnam in some heavy action. When he got out, he married his sweetheart and has become a successful businessman. He has been "blessed" as he calls it. With the same excitement I show in meeting a fellow entrepreneur, he is amazed with our story and wants to treat us to some good lodging and entertainment. I thank him for the animal park tickets while he gives me directions to our camp spot for tonight.

Up the road in Bandon we stop on some roadside scales. We register 650 pounds with our bike alone. Combined with our trailer, we are about 800 pounds. As we sit and contemplate the weight we have been lugging across the continent, our host and the local TV crew pull up.

As usual the girls are the center of attention. No matter how long and far we travel, the girls are what garner the most interest in our unique story. When Cheyenne isn't playing coy, she rattles off the states we have been through and tries to get the camera in her hands. Jasmine shares her feelings about the latest experience. Robin spends her words telling everyone "I'm a chipmunk." She loves this animal and has expressed this since before we left home.

We move on, knowing the name of today's destination, Charleston, but are not quite sure where it is. The town lies somewhere on the coast, but it isn't on our map. It is one of the few times that we do not have at least a portion of a map showing us what lies ahead. We ride more miles and over more hills, some of which feel like mountains.

It has been a strenuous day with weather and breakdowns. The wind batters our faces constantly, trying to blow us back to California. The chain keeps falling off because it is badly stretched. We endure a constant drip of other challenges as well. We stopped once because Amarins' shoe lace got tied around the pedal, another time to pick up Cheyenne's gloves that fell, and once more because Jasmine's mirror dropped to the road surface and somehow survived the fall. We can't seem to get into a pattern of riding today. With thirty miles behind us, we cannot wait to prop our bike up and settle for the evening.

We keep on highway 101 past the Seven Devils turn-off. The next exit is the one we'll take to the ocean. There we see the sign for Charleston: fourteen more miles to go. It might as well be 140 miles; it's just too much.

The girls pose in Pedouins-Gib's RV sweat shirts.
April of 2010

The Oregon terrain kicks our butts. As Amarins and I bemoan our situation, we see Bill up ahead in his truck. He's been with us off and on throughout the day. We decide that Amarins and the girls should ride with him to our final destination for the evening. I will have to finish alone.

Leaving highway 101, I cut toward the ocean. The climbs are rugged as I continue to roll along the evergreen laden countryside. This stretch of road rides like a roller coaster. Midway up a hill Jasmine's stoker chain, the chain that connects her remote pedals to the main crank assembly, shatters. One of the links fails, sending metal projectiles against my jacket. At least it does not affect the main chains.

By the time I get to the campground, the evening is full on. The shadows of night are beginning to come out. Our lodging is a huge fifth wheel camper. It has an artificial fire place which creates a great atmosphere. After a meal at a local dive with Bill and his family, my family and I lie around the gas flames, revisiting the adventures of a challenging day and the rewarding evening.

Bill provides us with lodging for three nights. Each time the fifth wheel gets moved to our next location by his wife, Barb. Bill is also instrumental in getting our quint going again. Moe, from the local bike shop, gives it a good tune-up with new chains and a new rim. Coos Bay definitely makes our top ten. Gratitude, well-rested bodies, and joy-filled memories guide us on.

A COUPLE OF DAYS AFTER we leave Bill's hospitality, we cut inland to come up the middle of the state in order to avoid the coastal winds and hills. Since somewhere in mid-California we were wrestling with the idea of avoiding part of the rugged Oregon coast and the desire to visit the Burley trailer company in Eugene. The Co-Motion factory, where our bicycle was built, is in this town too. After a tepid reception there, we head to Burley. The folks here have helped us tremendously in our travels and receive us like family. We finally put faces to the voices from our many phone conversations.

It IS THE MIDDLE OF a sunny afternoon when we arrive at Craig and Angela's Portland home. They live in a cute, early American, white, wood frame house sitting up on a small hillside. They had seen our story in a bike publication they read as avid bikers. The girls play in the small patches of grass in the front and rear of the house. They pluck bloomed out hydrangea flowers and cover the ground with the white petals, making it look like snow. Visitors from all over Portland arrive for a potluck dinner with us, arranged by Angela. It is an eclectic group of people dedicated to bike travel and common sense green living. By evening our host's driveway looks like the bicycle stalls at the Central Train Station in Amsterdam, the Netherlands.

During our stay in Portland, we are invited to visit the KEEN shoe company. As we ride into downtown Portland, the traffic is aware of our presence and gives us plenty of room, not because we're the Pedouins, but I think because of the town's bike awareness. Portland has the reputation as one of the most bike friendly places in America. As we biked in, we noticed many streets marked with bike lanes and bike directional signs. We passed bikes ridden by people wearing everything from biking gear to business attire. Today is no different.

Yeller gets locked to a piece of railing next to the street in front of the local company. Inside the warehouse loft of this company, with its family-friendly values, we enjoy pizza and play time. KEEN provides cutting edge footwear for active feet and we certainly fit their genre. Visiting a company with a flexible work environment and a shared business model that includes its employ-

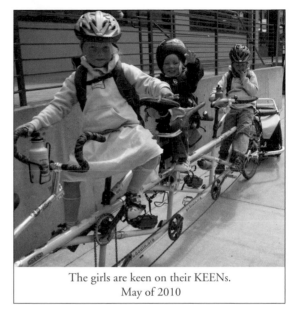

The girls are keen on their KEENs.
May of 2010

ees, Amarins and I are tickled to show our girls another working model of American innovation in industry. The girls pedal away with happy feet in their new sandals and a KEEN backpack on each back.

We leave Portland a little inland from the Columbia River. Moving awfully slow up a slight grade, with sweat dripping down our backs, as the days have warmed a bit, we stop. Yeller is barely moving despite our efforts to the contrary. I am beside myself to solve the problem. Ama thinks we have a flat tire, and Cheyenne thinks I have the brakes on. In my exasperation, I lean over the handlebars to catch my breath and zone out for a minute. As I do, I see something out of place with the front brake caliper. "Hey Ama, come up here and take a look at this!"

"Look at what?"

"Take a look at this brake caliper."

She walks to the front of the bike and bends over to look. "It looks like a rock is wedged in this thing. I think you are going to have to get this out of here."

Amarins holds the bike up so that I can pick out the piece of pea gravel with a piece of wire I pick up off the roadside. The rock probably flicked off the tire and landed in between the caliper and cable lever that activates the brake pads.

When we take off, it feels like someone is pushing us forward. Cheyenne was right. "Nice guess girl," I compliment her as we continue.

Toward the top of the mountain, the Columbia River comes into sharp focus. We find a spot to pull over. The girls delight in getting so close to the famous river. Jasmine even wonders if one of the boats belonged to Lewis and Clark. This brief stop turns into an event that addresses past, present, and future.

Around fifteen miles on, we crest a hill and roll into Astoria, located on the Columbia estuary. In calm, partly cloudy weather, we make our way to the Fort George Brewery. Here we are treated to a feast and friendship. Scott, a biker we met in Malibu, contacted his son, who is the brewer here, and asked him to pull out all the stops for us. Their menu is all ours. The girls have the usual root beer and fries. Amarins fills up on vegetables, and I enjoy the fish, which I share with Jasmine. Sitting just inside the wall of windows, we watch people stop and enjoy our bike that is parked on the sidewalk. Folks come in and out to greet us and cheer us on. One of them is Vern, a hardworking laborer, who invites us to see the Astoria Column on the mountaintop above town.

Robin and Vern at the Astoria Column.
May of 2010

Just Robin and I take Vern up on his offer, because of the limited truck seating. He parks near a 125 foot column modeled after Trajan's Column in Rome, Italy. Completed in 1926, it depicts the history of the area, home of the oldest American settlement west of the Rockies and the highest point in Oregon. With Robin on my back, we climb the 164 steps to the top. From here, we can see the mountains to the north in Washington

State and the ocean to our west as far as the eye can see. Looking south, we see waterways that the Corps of Discovery wintered along, and to the east, rolling landscapes line both sides of the Columbia River. To Robin's surprise, Vern brought some balsa wood planes with him. I hold her as she launches plane after plane, watching them coast down and sail beyond the parking lot into the wooded surroundings. I look and wonder where the end of this journey will land us.

Behind the scene at Safari West, California.
April of 2010

The Drive Thru Tree in Leggett, California.
April of 2010

Cheyenne has found a giant pine cone in
Northern California.
April of 2010

Waiting for the rain to pas in Oregon.
April of 2010

The Willamette Valley, Oregon.
May of 2010

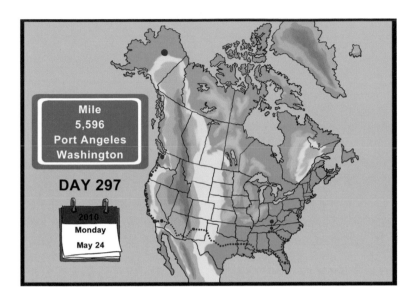

Mile
5,596
Port Angeles
Washington

DAY 297

2010
Monday
May 24

CHAPTER 17

A SUNNY, WIND-FREE MORNING WELCOMES our departure from Astoria,
Oregon. In a pedal and stop rhythm we climb higher up the ramp to the
Astoria-Megler Bridge. The bridge spans the Columbia River and completes
highway 101 that runs from Los Angeles, California, to Olympia, Washington. The bridge, with the longest continuous truss span in North America,
took almost four years to build in the 1960s. We are still a ways from the
highest point when we stop to enjoy the view once more. Down below, we see
Vern and his buddies waving at us. From here, Robin recognizes the Astoria
Column up on the hill. Cheyenne and Jasmine now feel a little jealous that
Robin went and they couldn't come. We wave to our friends and pedal away
from Oregon, ready to traverse the steel and concrete.

Astoria reminds me of pictures Grandpa Byers showed me of Louisville,
Kentucky. He worked there from the 1930s til the 1960s. Perched on two dif-

ferent waterways, located more than half the country apart from each other, the two cities appear to be kindred in spirit. In both, many of the working trades are active: logging, shipping, tradesmen related to each industry of sea and land, and townspeople supporting these trades with small businesses. I think Astoria is by far the most deeply blue collar town we have been through, and the people we meet prove it with their worn hands, matched with proud, yet humble, smiles. So far from home and yet I feel connected with hard working folks in a way I was not expecting.

We cannot see the end of the four-mile bridge from its crest of about 200 feet above the Columbia waters. We are even higher than we were on the Sidney Lanier Bridge near Brunswick, Georgia. As we move along, the river life below comes into focus. Boats, fish moving about, churning water from where the ocean meets the river, and shore activity abound. The girls nervously take it all in. Even Ama and I can feel our bellies churn like the water down below us.

View from the Astoria-Megler Bridge.
May of 2010

Traffic is heavy at times on the bridge. Construction points let the traffic loose at regular intervals. We reach the top and see a steep descent in front of us. The grade levels out halfway across the river before it skims across the top of the water for the final two miles. I feel a flutter of apprehension that comes over me when the brakes need to be tested again. I tell Amarins to hold onto her brake as well.

During our cautious descent, the girls notice bald eagles standing on some sandbars to our west. When we reach the flat part of the bridge, we pull over to look. I do not see them until Cheyenne says, "Dad, they are at the water's edge on the sand bar." Sure enough, they are eagles. Cheyenne recognizes them as our national bird by their white head feathers and their proud pose. Amarins snaps pictures for our website before they fly away.

CHEYENNE IS ALWAYS THE FIRST to spot the state highway signs. Even though she sits all the way at the back of the bike, her eyes are sharp as an eagle's and explore their surroundings for new discoveries. When we come off the bridge onto the solid ground of Washington, she sees a sign with a white head on a black background. The head looks like George Washington's. The road number 101 is in black inside Washington's head. She finds it quite comical. Robin is confused and thinks it is my Grandpa George Washington Byers on the sign.

Cape Disappointment was named by a sea captain who had hoped to find shelter beyond the point. A disappointment to him, it is a splendid experience for us—no gaudy monuments or high-rise hotels. With the exception of roads and ornamental trees, this is probably what Lewis and Clark and their men saw when they scouted this area for food and shelter. Cliff-like hills, scrawny, windswept trees, and a constant breeze are part of the challenge of making camp here. Upon realizing that there was not any protection from the ocean weather, the expedition headed up the Netul River, a side river of the Columbia River, to make a winter camp.

Leeward of the cliffs is a campground. We find a fluffy piece of grass near a small creek to make our camp. A picnic table and bear box sit between us and the creek. The bear box is used to put our food in, not just to keep the bears out, but more likely to keep the raccoons from feasting on our supper. Across from our campsite, the raccoons have a picnic with someone else's food.

Cheyenne asks, "Don't they only come out at night?"

Amarins says, "I thought so, too, but I guess they can't pass up a free meal."

"Maybe it is our failure to keep our food from them that has made them get out of their habits. If campers kept their food secure, the raccoons would not be scavenging like this. What is easier, getting something for free or working for it?" I say.

Jasmine and Cheyenne are ready for a hike.
May of 2010

The girls roll their eyes at this.

Cheyenne is ready for a hike. A long hike! She has her KEEN sandals on and a stick over her shoulder. On the stick hangs a green rag tied on four corners with snacks tucked inside. With Robin hoisted on my shoulders, we bring up the rear as Cheyenne leads and Jasmine and Amarins fall in the middle. When we get several thousand feet up the trail, Cheyenne halts at some crumbling concrete steps. Leading up to a level place the size of two old Volkswagen buses are twenty or so steps covered in vegetation.

"Mom, I saw a snake!" she exclaims.

"Cheyenne, maybe you just saw some grass moving in the breeze," I suggest.

"No, Dad. It was a snake. I'm sure. It was near the top."

I put Robin in Amarins' arms and climb up. They stay frozen at the bottom, their feet fused to the ground in the same way the ghosts of the Corps of Discovery's stories are trapped in this piece of landscape on the edge of our continent. Near the top, I rustle up a snake by poking in the ground cover with a stick I picked up at the bottom of the incline. I watch it slither away.

"Girls, it's a harmless black snake. She was just here warming herself on the concrete." It still is not enough. I have to carry Cheyenne and Jasmine up one at a time in my arms.

At the top, we have a wide open view of the Pacific. It is a beautiful sight to see the waves crashing upon the rocks below the cliff we're standing on. The wind blows strongly from the west. Amarins tells the girls to look at the trees that have grown leaning toward the east and adds that this is the result of nature bending to the prevailing winds.

I decide that this is as far as I want to go. The ladies are not done exploring yet. They walk the rest of the way to the interpretive center as I enjoy some alone time surrounded by the ocean's voice, walking back to the camp site try-

Robin eyes the Pacific Ocean.
May of 2010

ing to imagine how the early explorers must have felt when their feet trod this same piece of earth.

The girls arrive back at camp a couple of hours later with huge grins on their faces. "Dad, we found the interpretive center and decided to explore the inside. We all got a card with the Lewis and Clark Trail on it. Throughout the center we found secret rocks to stamp our cards with." Cheyenne fills me in.

"We found them all, Daddy," Jasmine proudly shows her card.

"Too bad you didn't go with us. They had a miniature canoe that you had to fill with blocks. It was set up as if it was in water," Amarins explains. "Robin had a blast loading it. It would tilt when it was overloaded, but then she'd just try again. She never gave up. I literally had to pull her away from the canoe so we could go on discovering."

Robin lights up when I applaud her persistence.

Amarins goes on, "They even had a sextant that we could touch and move. I finally have a slight understanding of the workings of it. You can measure the distance of the sun or a star above the horizon. And this helps you find your position north or south of the equator."

"We ate the snack at the lighthouse, Dad," Cheyenne says.

"Was the lighthouse at the interpretive center?" I question.

"No Bill, I wished it was. It was still over a mile walk to the lighthouse. The trail started at the center, into the trees, and went up and down the hills, similar to the part you walked with us. I thought I would need to carry the girls there and back, but my concern was not necessary. They loved the secrecy of the windy, hilly trail. Walking on a real road would have been much less fun." Amarins tells me.

In spring-like temperatures, our dreams mingle with those who camped here in the early 1800s. The girls, each in her own way, know a little more about what the early Americans' westward expansion was about and savor adding their own story to the past.

Amarins and Bill at Lake Crescent, Washington.
May of 2010

THE LANDSCAPE CHANGES EVERY TWO hundred miles or so. For days we have traveled through some of the most beautiful, wild, untamed land of the journey. Endless hills, loaded with vegetation fueled by ample rains and moderate temperatures, make for exhausting pedaling and enchanted views. Rain forests dot the landscape. We ride through one forest and into another. With the exception of an occasional tiny town and the constant drone of roadway, our environment appears primitive. Mile after mile we ride Yeller in silence. Amarins and I do not have to remind our crew to keep quiet when we climb another mountain or hill.

Either we are numb to the elements, awed by the surreal surroundings, or just plain ready to reach the ferry port, we are a pedaling machine. In the past I would moan when there was a flat tire, fuss sometimes when the girls were being children, grumble at too many hills and the never-ending rain. Now we seem to be one with the bike, having been whipped by the elements and forced to submit to whatever comes our way. Cheyenne, despite the loss of her Dogge in California, presses on. Robin climbs onto Yeller of her own accord in order to show her ability to be a functioning, independent part of the team.

Jasmine keeps us all in tune with the songs she presents us from within her soul. We are purposefully pushing toward our goal.

Drive is a wonderful thing. I don't know if it is innate or learned, but we have it. It is something we want to pass on to our girls. We can already see a bit in their persistence.

My Grandpa Byers instilled a strong sense of drive in me. There were many mornings in the early 1970s that we went on the paper route with my tummy crying for food. We had one of the longest car routes for the Courier Journal and Louisville Times newspapers. Led by his drive to support his family, Grandpa needed something to keep himself busy after retirement. His nature dictated that you can't just quit working because you're old. I am also convinced that he was a product of his environment, which included the Great Depression. His lessons became my instruction, and this in turn supported my desire to succeed in my own struggles.

At the age of ten or eleven, I was old enough to sit on a bundle of papers held together with a metal band. I'd shove rolled up morning and evening newspapers into round aluminum paper boxes strung out along our rural route. Before we'd leave the house, he would wake me up at ten after four in the morning and then go down for some oatmeal with raisins, milk, sugar, and buttered toast. If I did not get up and get at it, he would finally get me after he had his breakfast. I would go to the '64 Ford Falcon and put papers in the boxes, hungry! Tough love, but I eventually got the lesson and learned to roll out of bed and eat when the food was ready.

As I force myself to make the pedals go round and round, I realize that his lessons in many ways prepared me for this very journey. I am also wise enough to listen to my fantastic partner, knowing when to back off after I act too much like Grandpa did on those early morning wake-up calls. Yes we need to get rolling, but some mornings do not facilitate a quick getaway, and that is okay too. The Pedouin ride is the journey and it's not necessarily dictated by when we arrive like the papers had to.

Amarins tells me that drive is definitely something she had to learn. For her it goes hand in hand with purpose. As long as the purpose is clear, the drive will follow. The key is to find a purpose.

AFTER MORE DAYS IN THE rainforest than we care for, we pull into Forks, located in the northwest corner of Olympic National Park. Dodging the rain for over a week has taken its toll. We pull over at the first inhabited restaurant, a pizzeria.

Our clan wearily heads in and grabs a booth along a partition with the salad bar. As we do this, all eyes are on us, like they have just seen the elusive "Spotted Owl" of the Washington woods. In the middle of this dining space is a large table. Four guys and one gal, all seemingly in their thirties, sit there together enjoying themselves. They have finished all but one piece of pizza on the two pans at their table. Only small dribbles of beer are left in the bottoms of their glasses. Wadded napkins are strewn over the table. As we get ready to order, Jasmine wants to give them some of our Pedouin cards. I slip her a few and she walks over and hands each person a card. She then pulls up a chair at the end of their table and starts to talk. As she begins to share some of our story, they look our way as if to ask, "Is she for real?"

Through the long lunch they reveal that they are all college buddies who work in Seattle, Washington. They've come to the National Forest for a day hike. One of the guys says, "We were laughing among ourselves, and stating how we were entertained the moment we saw you all pull up on that bike. Now we realize that our little hike is nothing compared to what you guys are doing. You also have these girls with you. How do you do it?"

"We do it by taking one stroke, one mile, one day, one state at a time. Kids are much hardier than we give them credit for. Our girls are especially strong because they have lived most of their lives out in the fresh air at our home in the mountains of Eastern Kentucky. By the end of most days, Amarins and I are tired to the bone. Yet, the girls get off the bike and they are ready to tackle their newest environment. We usually fall asleep before they do. It is the parents you guys need to be feeling for."

When we eventually get up to leave, we find out that a couple behind our booth has paid for our lunch. That and the money the five friends kicked in will go a long way to help us pay for the ferry to Victoria, Canada in a few days.

ON MAY THE 24TH, 2010, we crest our final peak in the lower forty-eight states. Canada's snowcapped mountains beckon to us on and over Vancouver Island.

Cotton clouds hang on the horizon to our north, in contrast to the glassy surface of the water in the Strait of Juan de Fuca. Ferry horns and braying seagulls welcome us along the last miles we will pedal in the contiguous United States of America.

Robin looks for the ferry in the Strait of Juan de Fuca.
May of 2010

Washington – our fifteenth state.
May of 2010

The road to Cape
Disappointment.
May of 2010

Spotted Owl Helper.
May of 2010

Lake Quinault, Washington.
May of 2010

Amarins and Jasmine in
Olympic National Park.
May of 2010

Creative Jasmine in
Port Angeles, Washington.
May of 2010

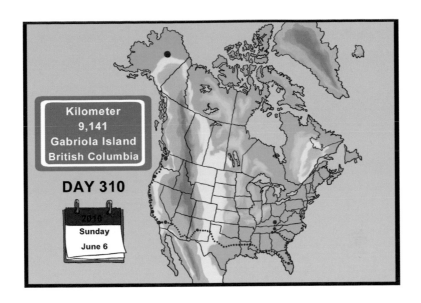

Kilometer
9,141
Gabriola Island
British Columbia

DAY 310

2010
Sunday
June 6

CHAPTER 18

O<small>UR PERSPECTIVE SHIFTS.</small> Instead of the relentless asphalt beneath our wheels, we feel the gentle sway of water as Yeller stands stationary and various ferries cart us farther toward our goal. We get to know this odd sensation of moving forward while standing still. We entered Canada by ferry and will use the waterway system several times on our journey north.

Ferry decks shift our vantage point from up close to distant. We get the chance to observe one another more often than we do on land. On one ferry ride, Robin shows us the world through her eyes. While the three girls sit against the steel side of the ferry, Robin leans over to look through one of the small rectangular shaped holes cut out in the ship's side near the deck floor which lets water run back into the bay. On this gigantic machine with sounds and structures beyond her comprehension, she is totally engrossed in her

We're ready to roll onto the ferry to Gabriola Island.
June of 2010

small piece of this world. The two braids on the left side of her head lie across her face. Her head rests on her little hands that lie on the ship's deck. Robin's pink rubber-covered legs are tucked close to her stomach, and the flowers of her pink rain jacket peer up at the cloudy sky. Her self-made window to the world is framed in white metal with bubbles of brown rust along its top edge. Half of the view is of water, and above it are several layers of rolling hills covered in trees with occasional gray rock cliffs meeting the water's edge. In a sliver of space above the tree line are clouds of white and gray blues. Amarins has the foresight to snap a picture of our three-year-old in her process of growing up.

On the ferry from Vancouver Island to Gabriola Island, the indoor passenger seating allows the family to ride in dry comfort while I get the pleasure of standing next to Yeller on the deck during a downpour to keep her from falling over. By the time we arrive on the island, the rain is moving out.

Gabriola Island is like a big hill that rises steeply up from the water. We manage to overcome the incredible climb up from the water's edge to the upper reaches of the island. The road takes us up and down across the island with a big loop, first going north, then east, then south, before we head a little west again. Our host Paul comes out to meet us on a little bicycle without a seat and rides about two kilometers with us. His calves are huge compared to mine. Who knew I would be one to succumb to "calf envy."

As we climb the last hill and near the turnoff to the house, we let the girls off to stretch their legs. The sun makes a welcome yet feeble appearance. Cheyenne and Jasmine are about half a football field ahead. They admire the green vegetation along the roadside. In the middle, Robin looks up at Paul as he pushes his bike along and walks with her. Robin, looking like an Ewok out of Star Wars in her pink rain outfit, and Paul appear to be engaged in deep conversation. It never ceases to amaze us how the girls don't miss a beat with each new host and their ever changing surroundings.

Robin talks to Paul on the way to the Slow Rise Bakery. June of 2010

Paul and his wife Michelle invited us to stay for several days. They contacted us before we left Kentucky. They were among the first folks to reach us through the web. It has been such a long time since the first contact was made that neither of us remembers how they found out about this impending journey. They have two daughters, Thea and Rosie, who are a little older than Cheyenne and Jasmine, respectively. Wanting to see some of the less trodden pathways and be out of the public eye for a short while, we agreed to take them up on their offer of hospitality.

From the emails, they appear to be folks who are self-reliant like us. It proves to be true. They live in an old wood framed, single story house, with some sleeping space in the attic. They've put a lot of elbow grease into fixing the old farm house to make it livable. Their rolling piece of property contains a bakery and a greenhouse which they built themselves from scratch. The greenhouse is in its final stages of completion behind their home. Paul is fabricating raised plant beds in it. Down below the house is a beautiful, simple log building that contains their bread bakery business, the Slow Rise Bakery. The oven is a huge clay oven that is wood fired. The building has a simple shed roof and plenty of glass on the tall front side. They have a dream of becoming more self-sufficient, which includes living off their land. We delight in meeting Canadian small business owners. Our plans for our stay here include rest, play, and the availability of my services as a handyman. We savor the opportunities we get to give back. Being here in this peaceful cul-de-sac turns out to be a great unexpected opportunity in the way we once described to a reporter.

As we stopped for a newspaper interview in Destin, Florida, the reporter asked, "Why are you doing this?"

"We are turning upside down the Puritan work ethic in order to bring joy and laughter," I blurted out.

Mulling it over after the interview, I realized it is what I really believe. I grew up learning to work from sun up to sun down. There was not a whole lot of elation in it. Now, we are working our bums off, not for money, but for the pure pleasure of it. Through the process we notice that we've inspired a lot of folks along the way and, also through our website, encouraged them to reexamine their work-life situation—not to inspire them to quit working, but to find their purpose and meaning in the work they do and the lives they lead. Work can be fun and should be. It is not our enemy, and our three impressionable girls are living this lesson with us.

In the front yard is a dump truck load of planting soil. Amarins and the girls spend hours shoveling and then wheel barrowing a large portion of it into the raised beds in the greenhouse. In between work and eating, the girls play with Thea and Rosie, moving from the homemade rope swing to the trampoline, then into the house to create with the art supplies. It is hard to tell what our girls enjoy more, moving dirt or moving toys.

Amarins and Jasmine also find time to help in the bakery. Jasmine has always enjoyed being in the kitchen, so she loves the opportunity to see the bread being made and the chance to get flour on her clothes. The products that are baked by Paul and his business partner are organic. They include several kinds of breads: nut breads, baguettes, scones, and Paninis. Since the bakery is not on a through road and does not have a storefront, they take their produce to town and to Vancouver Island.

Before any of these products get to have their dose of roasted almonds, walnuts, and oats, Jasmine gets to be

Before sunrise, Paul is already at work in the bakery.
June of 2010

the official taste tester of the roasted nuts. Amarins enjoys the business side of their operation. She thinks we can do something similar when we get back to Kentucky. Maybe there is room for an organic bread shop in our neck of the woods. This dovetails with one of the threads of our Pedouin journey: opening ourselves up to new possibilities by being fully present on this journey, always embracing the chance to learn and experience something novel and heretofore, unknown. Amarins' wheels are already turning.

While all this goes on, I get busy on a door for the upstairs bedroom. Between the business, greenhouse, and family matters, Paul hasn't pieced together the time or the patience to get it hung. The primary challenge is that the walls leading to their bedroom are not square. Finding studs in the old structure proves to be problematic too. With the help of a neighbor and his power tools, we are able to shape some rough lumber into usable finished material and construct a frame that will house the bedroom door. With the door hung and latched, I go to repay the neighbor for surfacing the lumber with his machines. I agreed to take a peek at his 1968 Dodge van. This thing is in pretty good shape. It has a 318 V-8 engine which looks out of place in Canada.

"One of the stereotypes of Canadians," I jokingly broach, "is that you are so environmentally conscious. How can you have a gas guzzling Detroit-made eight cylinder engine?"

He says, "The price was right and it matches my persona."

After some testing, we decide that the head gasket is probably leaking coolant in the combustion chamber, and that is where his coolant is disappearing. Once we install some new parts it runs much smoother.

RANDOM ACTS OF KINDNESS HAVE followed us our entire journey. It brings great delight when we get to give something back. Besides being mentally thankful, we delight in getting to demonstrate our gratitude even more.

Not even three weeks into our journey, we relished the chance to help. We stayed for several days with Scott and Katie Magley in South Carolina. Jasmine had had a bad fall on a section of the Appalachian Trail, trying to outrun some bees. That same evening we decided to have some treats. While eating at a local dive in Clayton, Georgia, we met the Magleys, and the invitation flowed once they heard our story. Eight kids, including ours, filled their home. Their ranch house looked like an ant farm. When we first pulled up, I

noticed the roof over the garage sagged several inches. Upon inspection, the triangle-shaped wooden roof trusses were not properly built. They were weak and not close enough together. Scott and I discovered many nails lifting through the asphalt shingles. These openings contributed to water spots on ceilings inside the home. Scott was not sure how to go about fixing the defects, and money was tight. We agreed to help. Over the next couple of days, we worked in the broiling sun to solve the problems.

We worked together on setting new support structures in the garage and patching more holes in the roof than can be found on several golf courses combined. In between, Scott gave our girls safety lessons in class two and three rapids of the Chattooga River. While all this went on, there was the constant buzz of two home school families' activities, home cooked meals, and the steady, joyous hum of eight engaged and curious children.

Our visit to Portland, Oregon, concluded with a stay at Joe Kurmaskie's home. Also known as the Metal Cowboy, Joe and his wife Beth are central folks in the long line of the Portland bike riding community. Besides being a part of the Portland bike community, Joe has written several humorous books about his family's long distance bicycle trips. He also travels the country giving motivational speeches. Because of our common interest in family biking, we got together after meeting at a party in our honor several days earlier.

Speaking, writing, riding, and a new baby have all taken Joe's time away from his honey-do list. His patient wife has wanted a tub in the upstairs bathroom for years. The antique, claw-foot, cast iron bathtub sat in the garage behind their house waiting to be installed.

After some sales-
manship on my part,
we got them to agree
to let me put in the
tub. On Mother's
Day we hoisted the
beast up one flight
of stairs. We wrestled
it into the bathroom
without breaking our
backs. We ripped out

the old plumbing fixtures and ran new PVC drain and copper water supply
lines. By the end of the day, the new plumbing lines were capped off and the
water was turned back on.

MORE TIMES THAN NOT, A catalyst is all that is needed to get something going or even finished. Like a match to a campfire, one small action can create
something greater than itself. Our girls see others give to us, but they also see
us give to others. As a result, Cheyenne, Jasmine, and Robin gladly join in
when it is time to help, whether it is moving dirt, pitching the tent, or helping
set the table.

Arrival in Victoria, Canada!
May of 2010

The Canadian Flag stands out
in a strong wind.
May of 2010

Robin is snuggled
deep in her sleeping bag.
May of 2010

Worn cogs,
once again.
June of 2010

Angela and Cheyenne are being silly.
June of 2010

Shell Beach, British Columbia, Canada.
June of 2010

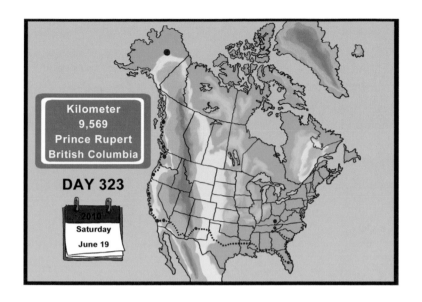

Kilometer
9,569
Prince Rupert
British Columbia

DAY 323

2010
Saturday
June 19

CHAPTER 19

PARENTING IS WROUGHT WITH REWARDS and agonies. Of all the questions a parent might have, how we prepare our children now in order to let go with confidence in the future is perhaps the most important one. You teach your children your beliefs, beliefs based on your own upbringing and the life lessons you've had since coming of age yourselves. That is not different from us.

Amarins and I realize that it is our responsibility to teach our children, whether through the public school system or by choosing to have more control in what is learned and when it is learned by using a home schooling network. Of our children, only Cheyenne has participated in the public school system. She loved Pre-School because her teacher understood each child's individuality and offered students opportunities to grow in any direction they needed. The confines of Kindergarten were not beneficial to Cheyenne's growth. Cheyenne already knew how to read and learning the letters "T," "B," and "E" were not interesting subjects to her. As a result, her joy in learning decreased.

When the idea of our bicycle journey came up, it was an easy decision to switch Cheyenne from the public school to home schooling system during Christmas break. After all, that's what we were going to do anyway while we were on the road.

Although the decision was a relatively easy one for us to make and implement, as it is for countless families who choose this every year in the United States, our choice caused a stir in the Netherlands with Amarins' family. Home schooling is not readily accepted there, which made it particularly hard for Amarins' parents to appreciate our actions. In the Netherlands, unless you have a solid health or religion-founded reason and can back that up with lots of paperwork, you are not allowed to take the education of your child into your own hands. School time belongs to the local municipality. Outside of school hours, you are of course free to do as you please.

With a child's first breath, the process toward independence and eventual separation from Mom and Dad begins. Our country considers eighteen-year-olds to be adults. The true cutoff age when parents and children separate might come sooner, later, or, in some cases, not at all. My parents let go of me when I was fourteen. Amarins and her parents are still trying to figure it out. They want the best for her and want her to be happy, but it would be easier for them if we chose to live life according to their beliefs. It was hard on them to see their daughter leave for the United States and find happiness in Kentucky. Our uncommon lifestyle does not help any either. Neither one of us has a regular nine to five job. We're not building a normal retirement fund. We've had several misses when it comes to being a business partner without an underlying contract or being a business owner with a product that we enjoyed using but didn't enjoy selling. Ama and I look at these experiences as great learning opportunities. Her parents might have a different take.

Communication strained even more once we decided to go on this bicycle journey. Chances for a regular job went out the window. We gave away our vehicle. We gave up our house for the next two years. Our girls might miss out on social skills gained through being with peers on a regular basis. And we put ourselves in a risky situation by becoming a constant part of traffic. What if it didn't work out?

Two months and 1,500 miles into the journey, we received our first phone call from Amarins' parents. Amarins lit up when she heard her parents' voices. Some of the concerns were finally discussed. They didn't think the bicycle would make it 500 miles, let alone the 7,000 we'd planned for. And when the bicycle would break down, then where would we live and how would we get around? Since the bicycle made it that far, they were a bit more positive that it will make it farther. "Keep on pedaling and we'll be in touch again." That surely put heart in the matter.

ALMOST 10,000 KILOMETERS INTO THE journey, we ride through the tree covered hills in northern Vancouver Island. Traffic is an alternation of logging trucks and RVs, big and small. Amarins straightens in her seat at every approaching RV, whether coming from the north or the south. Her parents are vacationing in British Columbia. We've been biking hard to make it to this area and catch them at the end of their visit to this island. We hope to ride the ferry together from Port Hardy to Prince Rupert.

We eat our lunch sheltered from the wind in the tall grass between young evergreens. There is something for each of us: sandwiches with chocolate spread, cheese, summer sausage, and water. When we've all had our fill, we load up again. We are about thirty kilometers south of Port McNeill, our destination for the night. As Ama secures the girls in their seats, a camper van comes up from behind with blinking headlights, while an apron with the colors of the Frysian flag is being pushed out the window. This can be no one else but Amarins' parents.

The girls are instructed to stay seated on the bicycle so we can figure out where to go to have a proper greeting. We relocate to a lot across the street where we are out of traffic. The girls swarm around their grandparents with the sounds of "Pake" and "Beppe" filling the air. These are the Frysian words for grandpa and grandma. We can't get a word in edgewise.

Even though we just finished lunch, there is always room for special treats from the Netherlands. To eager cheers from the girls, Pake pulls out the "muisjes." These are fruit flavored sprinkles that are delicious on bread. This silences the girls a little.

Pake and Beppe have arrived!
June of 2010

Pake admires Yeller and approves of the strong construction. Seeing the design in person makes him understand better how it is possible that a long stretched out bicycle like ours can make it so many kilometers.

Here we sit in rural British Columbia; a family from the Netherlands and a family from Kentucky. The last time we were together was over three years ago in Fort Pierce, Florida, when Robin was born. Still, it feels normal too.

After the extended lunch there is no chance we're getting the girls back on the bicycle. They will ride in the van and go ahead to find a campground in Port McNeill for the night. Amarins and I are on our own. It is rather strange to ride without the girls. The bicycle flexes more. When we both stand on the pedals it almost feels as if it's going to fall apart. Shaken, we quickly put our bums back in the saddle. At a little pond, closed off by a beaver dam, we take a break. We enjoy a game of throwing rocks into a partially sunken bath tub. This proves to be hard, yet fun. After only one direct hit, we ride on.

To our surprise we see the van appear again. The campground was quickly found. So was a store where ice cream is sold. We're going to be spoiled once again having family riding with us.

THE NEXT DAY WE PLAY tag between bike and van, alternating who and how many are riding on Yeller. Pake and Beppe went ahead to find the campground and to see if there was space available on the ferry to Prince Rupert tomorrow. They come back with good news. There is space for all of us and the van too.

Beppe rides the bike the last fifteen kilometers to the campground near Port Hardy. The terrain is gently hilly, but nonetheless she realizes how much effort goes into riding the bike. A red face and a sweaty back are hers to prove

Beppe gets to ride on Yeller.
June of 2010

it. And we weren't even fully loaded. It is always nice to let someone else ride for a little while. Nothing compares to the involved experience. Having Beppe on the bike brings back memories of when Amarins' brother, Wâtte, was with us during some heavy weather this past winter.

BY CHANCE OR SUPERNATURAL DESIGN, Wâtte had decided to come visit us for a week beginning December the 28th of last year. His arrival corresponded with a heart wrenching decision to port us, our gear, and Yeller from Socorro, New Mexico, to Tucson, Arizona. The last week of December, 2009, we were assaulted by the winter weather in New Mexico. Never ending snow storms thrown at us from all directions, an unceasing wind and temperatures in the twenties and thirties made us decide to head for warmer weather sooner than we had planned. We worked hard to make it a nonstop bicycle journey across the country, but here we had to put a stop to it. Riding in that kind of weather was unsustainable, and we had to make wiser choices.

Amarins and our hostess, Catherine, took the girls sledding in a fresh coating of snow on the golf course. Wâtte and I put our noses into the phone books to find some transportation, whether it was renting a pickup truck or even a U-haul. Determined not to overburden our hosts by staying longer then anticipated, we quickly tried to finalize a plan. We had no luck though. At the

U-haul rental store, we were told they didn't have a truck after all, even though they had told us over the phone that they had one. I still had my hands in the air, wondering what the universe was up to, when the phone rang. An Albuquerque cycling couple came to our rescue. They heard we were in the area and were wondering whether they could see our ride. They happened to be on their way to Tucson in their pickup truck and would have no problem taking our quint with them. By evening we were all loaded in Wâtte's vehicle.

In an unfamiliar concoction of gratitude and loss, we stared at the frigid shifting landscapes. The miles rolled by and never-to-be-had biking memories faded into the almost touchable, cold, Rocky Mountain peaks. Having Wâtte with us helped us keep perspective. His encouragement and support of our decision helped us cope with this feeling of defeat.

The dry desert Tucson air soothed our wounds and helped us forget the brutal weather we left behind. Wâtte had a chance to ride our quint, and the girls alternately giggled and chattered, thrilled to have a new rider aboard, just as they would later with Beppe.

BEFORE PAKE AND BEPPE CONTINUE their vacation, we get to experience another spectacular event together. At least that is what the brochure says. The Inside Passage is one of the items you might find on a person's "must do" list. That we get to do it together makes it even more special.

As the sun increases in strength, the sky gets clearer by the minute. An entire day we spend on the ferry running from side to side chasing the changing scenery. We see a humpback whale breach and killer whales swim by. Waterfalls of every stature and strength cascade around us. Abandoned villages sit with snowcapped mountains to their backs. It is exactly what you hope to see when you take this route.

A peek into the Inside Passage.
June of 2010

We're getting a reprieve from the weather, as well as an incredible gift from Pake and Beppe who made it possible to experience this part of our journey with us. Whether they understand our choices or not, at least they've gotten a glimpse into our current lifestyle. We are still family, no matter how far away from each other we may roam.

Art by Jasmine.
June of 2010

Updating the website takes about
two hours per riding day.
June of 2010

The home
school parents
of Nanaimo.
June of 2010

Crossing the 50th Parallel in
Campbell River.
June of 2010

Camp Pedouin in Royston, Canada.
June of 2010

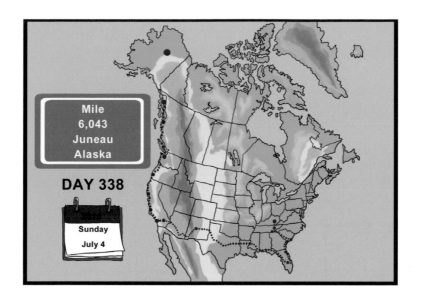

Mile
6,043
Juneau
Alaska

DAY 338

Sunday
July 4

CHAPTER 20

A SOGGY DAY GREETS JUNEAU's Fourth of July festivities. The town was born in the 1880s when two prospectors found gold here. Now it has about 30,000 residents. Life in the capitol of Alaska is sustained by its overwhelming government and civil servant job core. This picturesque town, surrounded by mountains, glaciers, and sea, is accessible only by air or water. We arrived by ferry from Prince Rupert a little over a week ago.

WE ARE STAYING AT JAMES and Anji's house this weekend. Anji contacted us via our website a couple of weeks ago with an invitation to stay with them in Juneau. She'd been told about us by Carolyn who rode into Portland with us on May the 5th, 2010. All the connections we're making are like a game of dominos when you stand them on end. When one falls over, it taps another, then another.

Their home sits high on the side of Mt. Rogers in the middle of a mountainside neighborhood. Far below we can see downtown and the Gastineau channel where the cruise ships sail into Juneau's harbor. On a clear day we'd be able to see Douglas Island across the channel, but we've yet to have a clear day here. Rain is a part of life if you live in a temperate rainforest.

On this Independence Day we have been invited to participate in the parade by George, a local war veteran, whom we met on one of our visits to Donna's Restaurant. James rides with me to the parade grounds. Amarins refuses to ride. She's had enough of the rain and wants no part of it. I tease her that it is her "patriotic duty."

Pulling into the staging area, it looks like a carnival. There are tons of people in the large parking area. Floats, walkers, bikes, and cars are decorated with all sorts of red, blue, and white paraphernalia. From jump rope jumpers in matching outfits to roller skaters with skirts and silly hats, people are oblivious to the falling drizzle. The crowd is intoxicated with the need to be outside, be together, and celebrate. Kids and adults in rubber rain boots walk among the parade participants, taking it all in. Rain jackets are optional.

Our quint stands proud in a marked-off parking spot. A fat white number 80 is painted on the ground next to her front wheel. Yeller is so long that her delicate front rim and tire stick out of our spot and almost tickles passing pedestrians' legs. James disappears into the crowd, talking to his friends in this close knit community.

I am so pumped, I give Ama a call. "Honey, you have to bring the girls down here. I don't want to ride alone. There are kids here, lots of them. They are playing in the rain. This is the total opposite of Polk County, Tennessee. How about getting them dressed and come on down?" Ama starts to crack and finally agrees to come.

Anji drives them down the mountain. Soon the girls and Amarins are excited by the goings on too. Amarins looks at me and says, "Wow, you are right. The people embrace the weather here for what it is. I could have known. We've seen their acceptance of what weather has to give since we've come off the ferry."

The girls hand out cards as we wait for the parade to begin. Cheyenne, Jasmine, and Robin collect balloons and American flags from various participants. Cheyenne and Jasmine are in their element as they socialize with the crowd, young and old. They never tire explaining our story of embracing the freedom to choose and taking responsibility for those choices. Robin stays close to us absorbing the buzzing sounds of the festivities.

At noon we can see the front of the parade start to move. One's number doesn't seem to matter. There is a structure to the madness of movement and eventually we're riding too. Leaving the parade grounds, we see hundreds of people lining the streets. Sometimes people stand two and three deep and always shoulder to shoulder. Those who dressed for the weather wear raingear of every conceivable color and style. They've brought out their arm chairs and some souls even have umbrellas. While surveying the multitude of people, I hear Ama yell to me, "This is the energy you expect in a capital city. Incredible."

Glancing in my mirror, I see Robin suck her thumb and wave her other hand to the crowds. Cheyenne soaks up the attention and peers through the crowd to see if she can find Mason and Max, James and Anji's sons. Jasmine as always represents herself as the de-facto princess. We are a crowd pleaser, home-grown, earthy, real, and from Kentucky. We are in

We're on a roll in the parade.
July of 2010

the Juneau Empire today and get a lot of recognition because of it. We enjoy the coverage we get from the local papers. Our route takes us through the old town with its string of shops that cater to the multitudes of cruise ships that dock here. When we circle around where the tourist boats dock, scores of people wave from the upper decks. Before we know it, we're almost back to the parade's beginning, invigorated and glad that we were a part of the celebration of our freedom.

OUR STAY IN JUNEAU IS rewarding. We have a warm, dry place to stay. Our girls have the boys to play with. Amarins gets full use of a real kitchen and lives out all sorts of baking fantasies. And I get a chance to give something back.

Several families, including our hosts, have bought the old mansion overlooking the bay below together, making home ownership affordable for everyone involved. Each of the four families has its own home within the outer walls. One owns the basement; another family owns a first floor apartment. The second floor apartment has a staircase to the attic. James and Anji have half of the first floor and a staircase to the bedrooms on the second floor. It's quite well puzzled together.

On their side of the home, James is working on a patio area. The challenge is to carve it from the mountain slope and have something visually stimulating and functionally appropriate on their postage stamp size section of yard space. Because of the liquid sunshine, we erect a green tarp to work under. At one point, it looks like a canopy for a Jewish wedding; all we need is a Rabbi. But it keeps us dry and working. After moving the boulders along the property line out of the way by using sheer muscle power, we dig out a spot for the pressure treated stair step stringers. The girls have a blast playing in the saw dust and chunks of wood. Toward the end of our stay, the step treads are in place and several posts are fused to the landscape. The project is well on its way to completion.

Anji remarks that our little travelers have become true "Juneaunians." The girls slip on their rubber gear and attack the park, walks, and outdoor games without complaint, that is to say, except for a walk through the ruins of the Treadwell mines. Jasmine lets us know she is tired of being drenched by rain. Her wailing doesn't stop until we're on the way back to the car across the beach of Douglas Island. If there are any ghosts in the ruins, they are scared off for sure now.

We've come to understand that if people waited for dry weather, very little would get accomplished. It is freeing to be in a place where folks let other folks live and play with little meddling. We have zero fear that we are going to be challenged for riding in the rain. In fact, people appear to be greatly entertained seeing us out in the elements, plowing forward.

This freedom from fear was not how we arrived in Juneau. Our sea legs were a bit wobbly when we hit the mainland. It was eleven o'clock p.m. and dusk was setting in fast. The ice of the Mendenhall Glacier was still visible on the northern horizon. The surroundings had a soft blue to them, like a fuzzy dream you can't quite remember. To sleepy eyes of three, five, and seven-year-old girls, it was meaningless.

While other patrons took their cars and trucks, we rode our well worn quint. The rain we experienced throughout the day on the water was still by our side as we rode off the ferry. Instead of turning right into the direction of Juneau, we'd decided to take a left to head for the Auke Bay campground three miles up the road. Between the rain and the descending darkness, we were apprehensive about this ride. And for good reason. This was our first night ride. Yeller possesses no light, since one of our road rules was not to ride in the dark. Making do with a flashlight was our only option. In our state of fear, we anticipated bear and moose everywhere. With every approaching car, our bodies tensed as we braced ourselves. With the turn to the campground, the traffic disappeared but the roadside lighting did too. When we finally arrived at the campground, we were relieved to find it open on weekdays. We pitched the tent at the first available spot while the girls stayed out of the rain under the tarp. As soon as we crawled in our sleeping bags, we sank into a deep sleep, weary from our travels and drained from the perils of a midnight ride.

A feeble attempt at daylight woke us. Coming to alertness, Amarins and I heard the rain and we went back to sleep. It is not necessary to guess, ponder, or scheme on rainy days. We were going to be in the Juneau area for the next ten days, awaiting the Cross Gulf ferry ride to Whittier which goes only once a month during the summer. In Whittier we would disembark for the interior of Alaska.

The hunger for real food led us to break up our camp the next day. We made it halfway to Juneau, to Donna's Restaurant, where a warm atmosphere and rich smells greeted us on our way in. Our waitress, Mary, loved our story. She shared it with her fellow workers and the owner of the restaurant. He invited us back and even gave us a gift certificate to eat at their place for several

We've enjoyed eating at Donna's.
June of 2010

meals. This was on top of having our first meal taken care of by some unknown stranger who overheard our story.

What a warm welcome to Alaska. Then, when we left Donna's, a driver and owner of a local cab company gave us a monetary gift. She'd waited outside the restaurant after spotting our bicycle, curious about its riders. It helped offset our charge of $71.09 for seventeen grocery items. This proved to be a great economics lesson for Cheyenne and Jasmine. After the grocery cart had been emptied into the panniers and into the front section of the Burley, Cheyenne asked, "Mom, why does the food cost so much here?"

The girls had fifteen states, three countries and almost 6,000 miles over 329 days to watch, observe, and participate in our buying habits.

"Transportation costs, I'd say. The only way to get supplies here is by boat or plane. Transportation, or moving things by car, train, or plane uses fuel. Fuel is expensive and the transports have to pass this cost on to the buyers of these items. When we buy our supplies from the stores, they include these costs in our price. Alaska is a long way from the factories that make cereal and the farms that produce the milk."

"What about Canada? It cost a lot to eat at McDonald's there."

"Vancouver Island is part of Canada. Their government puts higher taxes on their items than the United States government does."

Jasmine interrupts, "What are taxes?"

"Jasmine, you know when Dad takes a bite out of your cookie or sandwich sometimes? That is an example of a tax. He takes a portion of your food before he gives it to you."

This is one of many conversations in the same vein. Learning is never final—it's a process. On the road together, I'm thankful we're here every step of the way to field their questions and encourage them to reflect and discover their own answers.

In the following days, they would continue to discover, probe, and comment. We witnessed the beauty of three girls actively engaged in the discovery of their world and of themselves. Our six thousandth mile was logged crossing the Mendenhall River. This river is fed by the glacier and the incredible amounts of rain that Juneau

The Mendenhall Glacier in the distance.
June of 2010

receives. Cheyenne asks all kinds of questions about volume and color and if fish can live in the murky waters. Some questions remain unanswered for the moment. In the days ahead, we'd take the time to find answers in local libraries and visitor centers or through interactions with the locals. In windows of dryness, we spent time around the glacier. Amarins and I had touched some small glacial remains near the top of Longs Peak, a 14,259 feet tall mountain in Colorado, in 2001. But that does not compare to the massiveness of this place. The girls touched ice that is hundreds of years old. Playing around the lake directly fed by the icy runoff, they hiked, ran, observed, and marveled at the countless wonders in their outdoor classroom.

The Alaskan Flag.
June of 2010

Amarins has the ferry tickets to Alaska!
June of 2010

Our first
Alaskan road.
June of 2010

Our 6,000[th] mile on the bridge across the Mendenhall River.
June of 2010

James is putting down the
steps of the new patio.
July of 2010

Jasmine touches ice that's hundreds of
years old at the Mendenhall Glacier.
June of 2010

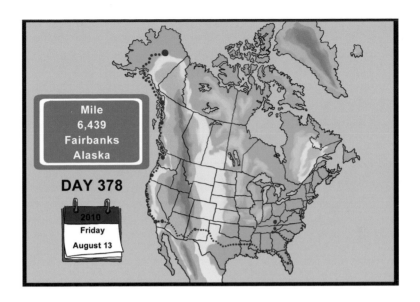

Mile
6,439
Fairbanks
Alaska

DAY 378

2010
Friday
August 13

CHAPTER 21

AMARINS AND I LIE SNUGGLED up in our double sleeping bag. We are restless in anticipation of reaching Fairbanks today. Yesterday we stopped six miles short of the town in the small community of Ester, not wanting to arrive at the city limits of our final destination while tired from climbing the hills between Nenana and here. We wanted one last night to soak up this final leg of our journey. Even though our emotions have played themselves out with every vista, breakdown, and act of kindness, we want to be alert and open when we reach our goal today. There is also something special about a Friday the 13th for us. It was on Friday the 13th when we climbed out of the Grand Canyon and where our journey together began, so it seems a fitting end day to our present journey.

We look at each other, listening to the sounds of our sleeping girls, reminiscing in whispered voices to each other of the journey that is almost coming to an end and the one that lies ahead.

"Hey Buddy," Amarins says. "Can you believe it? That we are almost here? It is such a funny feeling. In my mind I had us pictured on top of a mountain ridge, overlooking the valley in which Fairbanks is located. I know from the map that we are within miles of town, but with our being in the valley between these hills and no sign of a big town anywhere, it could easily be another hundred miles."

"You know what; I think I would be fine if it had been that," I say. "Life on the road has been so rewarding. We have met so many wonderful people. We have overcome obstacles. Another hundred miles would mean more experiences."

"I don't want the journey to end yet. We can always go on to the Arctic Circle. That's only two hundred miles or so." Amarins adds with a grin.

I know she is being melancholy, not wanting this chapter of our lives to end. "Well, Ama, you know just as well as I do that this is not the end of our adventures together. Can you imagine spending the winter here—snow and ice and temperatures that drop far below zero?"

"You're right, Billy," she says. "I've heard that it is going to be thirty or forty below for months on end."

"We'll find out soon, I reckon. First, we still have today. Let's focus on that. It's nice to spend our last night on the road in the tent together, to end the way we started at the Renfro Valley KOA in Kentucky. It is probably the last time for a while. The next two nights we get to spend at the Hampton Inn. What a luxury that will be again."

"I'm so thankful that Erin was able to arrange that for us. It's stunning how many connections we've made across the country. It was so nice of her and James to invite us into their home in Anchorage." She grins when she adds, "Did you see the confusion on Robin's face when she found out our host's name was James, like James in Juneau? I guess she's figured out that one name can belong to many." She continues, "We were lucky with the weather there, too. Remember when we went to Kincaid Park near the Cook Inlet? It is where we saw Denali for the very first time in all its glory."

"Yes, that was beautiful. It was all snow covered, as was the rest of the

Alaska Range as far as we could see. I think Erin told me the range was still two hundred miles from Anchorage. That tells you something about the height of the mountain."

"It sure does. It was a magnificent feeling to be within sight of the highest mountain on the North American continent. It still is, every time I see it. Do you think we can see it from Fairbanks?"

"I believe so, Ama."

I wrap my arms around her a little firmer, not wanting to let go.

THE BIRDS ARE STARTING TO wake up outside. The chirping and fluttering of wings serenade us and offer hope for a dry riding day. Last night's rain has stopped and that adds to my hope. We camped under a pavilion next to a playground in an effort to keep the tent dry. Although dry from rain, it is not dry from dew. I'm glad we're not in a hurry. We aim to be at the Fairbanks city limits sign at two o'clock this afternoon. This will allow the tent to dry before we pack it up.

We quietly crawl out of our sleeping bag, not yet ready to wake up the girls. A fog lies across the area. It is hard to tell what the weather will do today. Hand in hand we walk to the outhouses. In the parking lot across from the playground we see local farmers setting up for the weekly farmer's market. We recognize a couple of them. They had a get together here yesterday evening with their families so their children could enjoy the playground. We got to be part of the fun too.

As we root around outside the tent, the girls begin to stir and come out one at a time. They head straight for the playground, picking up where they left off last night.

Amarins gets back in the tent to clear it out for the last time. "Billy," she yells from inside, "We're going to miss this cozy home of ours. If it could stand the winter, I'd love to keep it as our home."

I laugh, "I bet we'll find a snug cabin for the winter. I think you are going to enjoy a little extra space and the heat of a wood stove."

"This is going to be a busy week trying to figure out where we'll stay. I'm glad we have several options. I guess we can't be too picky, but there seems to be a challenge with each one. The eight foot by ten foot cabin in town seems a little too small. The house with electric and running water outside of town almost sounds too easy. Then the cabin off the grid seems to be too far from town." She goes on, "It is hard to focus on today when there is so much to do to get ready for winter."

When she is finished inside and the trailer is loaded with our belongings once more, it is time to pull down the tent. Together we walk the outer fly to the grassy field next to the pavilion. The sun starts to break through the fog and will help dry our tent. Then it is time to take down the inside.

Robin helps take the tent down one last time.
August of 2010

While I focus on that with some help from Robin, Amarins gets breakfast ready. Leftovers of all kind are pulled out of the panniers: a loaf of plain bread, some raisin bread, Nutella and jam, some applesauce, crackers, cheese, a handful of granola bars and a Ziploc bag with some raw broccoli. It is not a real feast, but it will do, like it has for so many mornings along the roadside.

As the breakfast table is set, Tom from Calypso Farm comes over with a pail. In the pail is a fresh loaf of bread, a box of boiled eggs, some cheese, and fresh goat's milk. Breakfast is starting to look like a feast now. Amarins hollers for the girls to come on over. Each of them gets a cup with goat's milk. They hesitantly drink it. Even though they've been all over the country for the past year and thirteen days, this is their first taste of goat's milk. The more we travel, the more we realize that there is always something new to experience.

AFTER BREAKFAST IS FINISHED, I push Yeller to the gravel between the playground and the grassy field. It is hard to get over the fact that this is the last time I will go through these motions for now. Where did the time go?

It took almost eleven months to bike from Kentucky to Alaska. For the past month and a half, we've been in Alaska, first with our stay in Juneau, then on the road from Anchorage across the Alaska Range to right here -three hundred and fifty miles of wilderness. Tiny communities were scattered along the way at roughly thirty mile intervals. This was ideal for us, yet strenuous, too, since we were climbing our way up to the Broad Pass, where the Parks Highway crosses the Alaska Range. Leaving Anchorage at about sea level, it was a 2,400 foot climb stretched over two hundred miles. A breakdown with two cracked rims in Trapper Creek, a blown out trailer tire at Honolulu Creek, and an abundance of rain on the south side of the range gave us ample time to soak up the area.

Once we were on the north side of the range, the weather finally gave us the break we were waiting for. It was as if we'd at last arrived in summer. The girls and Amarins stayed for over a week in Denali National Park and Preserve, while I flew back east to Tennessee to see Adam finish his Advanced Infantry Training at Fort Benning, Georgia. When I got back to the park, the girls almost talked my ears off with all the great experiences they'd had there.

Special shuttle buses took them from Campground to Visitor Center, to the dog kennels and to Savage Rock at mile 15 of the park road. Ranger programs at the campground where they learned about bears and scavenger birds alternated with learning experiences at the Visitor Center which is filled with animal expositions and information about what nature the park has to offer. Hiking trails alongside Savage River, a picnic at the top of Savage Rock with a view of Mount McKinley, and learning about dog sledding fueled their imaginations. Meanwhile, moose and caribou roamed the taiga, while Dahl sheep could be seen at the rocks above the tundra. A lone wolf, a fox, and a sprinkling of bears added the wild to this wilderness experience. I missed out on it physically, but was filled in on every detail by my girls.

Life is about choices. Whether we choose or not, something will happen. If we choose, we have more say so in what happens. I chose not to share this time with my girls. Instead I chose to be with my other children, to share a once in a lifetime event with Adam, surrounded by the love of Jesse, Sara and Chris, and my grandchildren Christopher and Lindsay.

I SNAP OUT OF MY trance when Amarins points to some people walking directly toward us. We head their way to greet them.

"Hi, I am Laurie, and this is my dad, Puz, with his wife and my friend Barbara."

"Yes, you are the one we have been communicating with on the website, correct?"

"Sure am. It is good to finally meet you all. We have been following your journey since you crossed into Oregon."

"How did you find out about us?"

"A friend of mine, Tracy Ann, contacted me through Facebook and said I needed to check out the link to you guys. I did and here we are."

"Sorry Amarins and I have not been in touch lately, we have been in a dead zone since we left Nenana, several days ago. How did you know we were here?"

"We have been watching your tracker, the one you were given by Brian at the REI store in Marina, California."

Amarins grins, "You really have been tracking us."

"We wanted to give you a hearty welcome to Fairbanks and ride with you this day," Laurie says.

"We would love to have guests. It is always nice to have local bikers ride with us. Beware though, the girls have many stories to share and won't stop until they are through with each and every one of them."

WE TALK AS WE FINISH packing up. The sun has won the battle with the fog and has dried our tent out nicely. Packing up is such a routine; we can do it with our eyes closed. Once the trailer is completely loaded, I pull it to the quint and connect the two.

I notice that a news van has pulled up in the parking lot. The news anchor from a local Fairbanks television station is here to witness our final takeoff.

The moment is here. We are about to embark on our last ride of this journey. I straddle Yeller, holding on tight to the handle bars, not only to keep her steady while Amarins loads the girls on the bicycle like she has done so many hundreds of times over these thousands of miles, but also to try to hold within what needs to come out.

I thought that all the emotions had played themselves out, but I could not be more wrong. Amarins works her way from girl to girl, from shoe strap to shoe strap. She knows me so well. I cannot hide my feelings from her. By the time she gets to me, she's read the book that is written all over me. Once again there is no need to say anything, just as there was no need to say anything when we were getting ready to leave our front yard on July the 31ˢᵗ of 2009.

Her welcoming arms surround my shoulders, her forehead touches mine. In the comfort of her presence, I can let myself go. Tears stream down my cheeks to the tip of my nose before they drip on Yeller's wheel. Ama's emotions reflect mine when she, too, cries. With all we've done and overcome, this is probably the hardest moment of the entire journey: to start the last day.

As the camera peers in, we allow ourselves our feelings: feelings of loss, feelings of gratitude, and feelings of happiness for having accomplished what hardly anyone believed could be done.

When we are eventually ready to ride, we see that Barbara and Laurie are waiting patiently with their bikes, allowing us this space. We give a smile of gratitude for their understanding.

WE RIDE YELLER OFF THE gravel to yet another new road surface to travel. She has carried us over sand, gravel, concrete, and asphalt, up dry gravel washes and on the shoulders of overrun or desolate highways. Her sunshine yellow coating has felt the sting of sandstorms, been doused by myriad rains, and harassed by constant winds attacking her from all directions. Her steel

We're ready to roll once again.
August of 2010

221

frame has worked flawlessly despite all the horrors encountered with her moving parts, parts that could not stand the pressure we placed on them.

One big hill stands between us and Fairbanks, a hill we are going to triumph over like we've conquered all the others. One family, one bike, one vision.

The girls chitchat with Barbara and Laurie as we ride on the wide shoulder that boasts a bicycle lane.

On the left side of the road is a strange looking, carved out mountainside, "Hey Laurie, what is going on with the hillsides to our left?" I ask.

"They used to mine gold here many years ago," she informs us.

"I thought they panned in the creeks and did deep mining. What's up with this?"

"This is called hydraulic mining."

Still not sure what this means I ask, "I know what hydraulic means, but how does it apply here?"

"They used high pressure water and cut the hill sides with the water. It then ran through sluice boxes where the gold was collected."

Cheyenne asks, "What is a sluice box?"

Laurie continues, "It is a long trough like pigs eat from. As the water and dirt travel down it, the heavy gold drops to the bottom of the sluice where crosspieces cause the water to wash over them and the heavier gold to stay. It is kind of like a ladder with a bottom under it. All this hillside damage you see was from those early days of gold mining," Laurie concludes.

A little past the scars of the old mining operations, I inquire about Laurie's bike. "I have a Schwinn touring bike like that at home. Amarins, doesn't it look like it? You rode it until we got Robin's *Wee Ride* seat on the quint."

"It sure does," she responds.

Laurie begins, "I have had this Schwinn La-Tour since I rode the Richardson Highway in 1973. I grew up in Hawaii where my dad worked as a machinist. I was about nineteen and wanted to see the Alaskan wilderness. I popped the question to dad, and he said he wanted to come along. At fifty-four years of age, he bought a bike and we trained in Hawaii. We flew to Anchorage and took a train to Fairbanks. I thought it was downhill to Anchorage." She laughs as she says this. "We rode from Fairbanks to Delta Junction. The rain and climb were so hard that we accepted a ride from two young men in the back of their truck while they pulled their boat. We stopped in Sourdough where we set up camp. Dad found out they were going fishing for salmon and he asked if I could go along. They took me fishing on their boat and sometime early in the morning we stopped on a sandbar and grilled out and ate fresh fish. The next day dad had been talking to some of the campers while I was sleeping. A couple he met gave us their address in Anchorage and told us to stay with them when we got there. We made it to Valdez, took the ferry to Whittier, and then continued riding to Kenai. From there we rode to Anchorage and stayed with the people my dad met in Sourdough. They are still great friends, true Alaskans. When my dad tells people how he flew home to Hawaii alone, he acts as though he was unaware I was going to stay here. When he left, I rode back to Fairbanks alone and have been here ever since. When I heard of your story, it reminded me of mine over twenty-eight years ago."

"What an incredible story," I reply. "Our journeys brought us together."

Meanwhile, Laurie's dad follows us in the old Dodge camper van. We ride past a patch of fireweed on the roadside. "Cheyenne, tell our guests what this flower is about. Puz and Barbara might find out things they didn't know about the plant, since they live in Oregon."

"You mean the fireweek?" she responds.

"Yes."

"We learned that this plant tells us when winter is coming," Cheyenne explains. "It starts with pink blooms at the bottom and when the last one opens at the top and dies, winter will be only four weeks away. It is getting close."

Jasmine adds, "We have seen it almost every day here in Alaska, along the roadside. I like the pinkish color. The flower is beautiful."

Laurie speaks up again, "You girls have learned a lot of things on your journey, haven't you?"

Each girl offers up her precious discoveries along our way, and I find myself looking back. Jasmine learned to keep time and rhythm to the cadence of the pedals. From the mile posts, she began counting by tens and then saying almost any number she saw on the mileage signs or mailboxes. Cheyenne got good at estimating distances. In the barren landscapes of Texas and New Mexico, she was accurate at knowing how far it was to some distant town when she spied the water towers off in the distance. She became quite adept at subtracting distances to know how far it was to the next town. Robin found out how to worm her way into our sleeping bag and snuggle in our tent. Since she's the youngest, we let it slide. They all taught Amarins and me to listen to our environment, to find the natural treasures as seen through a child's eyes—the tadpoles in the water, moss hanging from oak trees, pinecones turned into masterpieces and left behind.

AT THE TOP OF THE hill we somewhat get the view that Amarins has been waiting for. From here, we can see the beginning of town. Laurie tells us it is the University of Alaska that we can see from here. It is located on the outskirts of town. I pull Yeller to a stop to take in the sight. "Girls," I yell toward the back, "This is it. We are entering the final mile of the journey. Are you all ready for this?"

I get a loud "Yeah" in return. On this I say for the last time, "Three, two, one… Go!" It is instinct now as we push on the left pedal and let ourselves roll down the hill. The "Welcome to Fairbanks" sign is on the other side of the highway. With some maneuvering, we make it safely across. I squeeze the brakes at the sign, and we come to a stop.

Amarins helps the girls off and tells them to stay at the bicycle. After handing me the walking stick and letting me secure Yeller to a final standstill, we all walk to the sign together. Cheyenne holds the bottle of apple cider Amarins surprised us with. She'd bought it in a small country store in Nenana. We look at each other, smiles stretching from ear to ear. We hand Laurie our camera and she freezes the moment for us.

I pull out the tarp and unfold it over the tall grass and invite our guest to join us in this moment. We let the bottle of bubbles go round and round. The girls are quiet. I wonder if they perceive the significance of this moment. Do they get it already? This chapter of our lives is complete. When the girls step behind the sign, they officially step into a new chapter of our lives, winter in the interior of Alaska. What adventures will await us here? This journey was only the beginning.

Arrival in Fairbanks, Alaska.
August of 2010

Saying goodbye to James and Owen, on the home stretch from Anchorage to Fairbanks. July of 2010

An Alaskan Wilderness.
July of 2010

Picnic at Savage Rock in sight of Mount McKinley.
July of 2010

The campfire faces of Jasmine, Robin and Cheyenne. August of 2010

Thanks for being on the journey with us!

Jasmine, Robin and Cheyenne have stepped into the next chapter of our lives:
Winter in the Interior of Alaska

More Acknowledgements

ON THE ROAD SUPPORT VIA ALL MEANS
During the Training Rounds
United States:

    Illinois–Atlanta: Ed and Steve

    Kentucky–Berea: Glenda and Alicia, Barbara

    Kentucky–Mount Vernon: Larry Burdette–
       IMAX radio, Bob and Jane

    Kentucky–Renfro Valley: Marty and Fran–
       Renfro Valley KOA

    South Carolina–Greenville: Hal and Tonya

    Tennessee–Johnson City: Sara and Chris

    Virginia–Independence: Garnett and Arville

Mount Vernon, Kentucky to Charleston, South Carolina
United States:

    Florida–Tallahassee: Anita, Michael, Oliver,
       Mamie

    Georgia–Athens: Doug

    Georgia–Hiawassee: Phillips family, Lyle and
       Diane–Spin Lite Cycling

    Kentucky–Berea: Barbara, Glenda, Patricia

    Kentucky–Buckhorn: Raney andTeresa,
       Tracy&Tami, Rick and Shirley

    Kentucky–Lexington: WKYT 27, Philip Gall,
       Pedal the Planet

    Kentucky–Mount Vernon: Mount Vernon
       Police and Fire Department, Regina, Julio,
       Nathan, Erika, Jonathan and Victoria,
       Wendy, Destiny, Brandy, Larry Burdette

    Kentucky–Renfro Valley: Renfro Valley KOA

    Kentucky–Somerset: BP filling station, Peach
       City, Somerset Police Unit, Fitzpatrick and
       Heron families, Burnside State Park

    Kentucky–Whitley City: Visitor Center
       Park, Greg Bird–McGreary County Voice,
       Manager Tanya–Burger King, Peter Ferrara,
       Whitley City Library

    North Carolina–Mt Airy: NC State Trooper
       and family

    North Carolina–Murphy: Larry and Heather

    North Carolina–Peddlers Village Market: Terri

    North Carolina–Raleigh: Harding

    South Carolina–Aiken: Mo and Betty–Aiken
       Bicycle Club, Ray, Pat and Dot, Curt–

    Aiken Bicycle Club, Greg and Mandy–
    Aiken University

South Carolina–Branchville: Ms Arlene

South Carolina–Calhoun Falls: Calhoun Falls
    police officers, Candyman

South Carolina–Carmel: Alex's Snackery

South Carolina–Charleston: George
    McFadden

South Carolina–Greenville: Whit, Steve the
    Sign Guy, Beverly, Stevie Ray, Hal, Tonya,
    Mason, Channel 4

South Carolina–Iva: Jacopys

South Carolina–James Island: Mark–Charles-
    ton Bicycle Company, Manager Brandy–
    Applebees

South Carolina–Ladson: Fraze family

South Carolina–Longcreek: Magley family,
    Two Redneck Chicks

South Carolina–McCormick: Bell family

Tennessee–Coker Creek: Frank Murphy Jr

Tennessee–Exit 62, I-75: Curtis and Kim–
    Dinner Bell

Tennessee–Harriman: Raymond Bowers
    Elementary School

Tennessee–Kingston: Laura, Randi, Bryson,
    Emily

Tennessee–Madisonville: August 5 anniversary
    couple

Tennessee–Sunbright: J.P. Morgan

Tennessee–Tellico Plains: Jerry Owens–Knox-
    ville NBC

Tennessee–Turtletown: Jersey Jim

Tennessee–Wartburg: Jimmy Jones, Pilot
    Mountain Diner

Charleston, South Carolina to Fort Pierce, Florida
United States:

    Florida–Daytona Beach: Ken

    Florida–Flagler Beach: Flagler Fish Company

    Florida–Fort Pierce: Bob and Jen, Wally and
       Betty, Mr and Mrs Brollman, Captain
       Jimmy

    Florida–Jacksonville: Jeff–Champion Cycling,
       Boston Joe

Florida–Marineland: Officer Ryan
Florida–Ormond Beach: Dorothy and Ed, Jim and Carla, Bud
Florida–Ponte Vedra: Luke
Florida–Satellite Beach: Debbie
Florida–Sebastian: Ranger Terry–Sebastian Inlet State Park
Florida–St Augustine: Ryan and Jenny–Turner Classic Weddings
Florida–West Palm Beach: ABC
Florida–Yulee: Angela
Georgia–Hiawassee: Spin Lite Cycling
Georgia–Jekyll Island: Jekyll Island Bicycle Shop
Georgia–Kingsland: Habitat for Humanity Restore
Georgia–Richmond: Richmond Hill KOA
Georgia–St Mary: Mark, Mark and Chuck–Camden Bicycle Club
Georgia–Waverly: Jay–Waverly Minit Mart
Georgia–Woodbine: Stardust Motel, Susan–Camden County Tribune, Beth, Aubrey, Teri, Darlene, Creative Catering and Design
South Carolina–Adams Run: Billy, Jim, Rhett–South Carolina Gas & Oil Company
South Carolina–Charleston: Channel 4, Channel 5, Charleston Bicycle Company
South Carolina–Exit 33, I-95: Bill–Point South KOA
South Carolina–Hardeeville: Miriam, Kerly, Omar, Kerly Jr
South Carolina–Jacksonboro: Donnie
South Carolina–James Island: Manager Brandy–Applebees

Fort Pierce, Florida to Lucedale, Mississippi
United States:
Alabama–Alabama/Mississippi State Line: Escatawpa Campground
Alabama–Fairhope: Glenda–Oak Hollow Farm
Florida–Brandon: Wendy's
Florida–Bruce: Muscogee Tribal Grounds
Florida–Chiefland: Motorcyclist Bill, Ron and Shirley
Florida–Clarksville: Tanya, Amber, Autumn
Florida–Ebro: Ebro Café
Florida–Eugene: Shady Oaks Campground
Florida–Fort Meade: GMC
Florida–Fort Pierce: Wally and Betty, Classic Car Coating, John Hart, Sam and Shirley
Florida–Highlands Hammock: Jack and Joy, Ranger Mike, Ranger Brenda, Ranger Judy
Florida–Highway 66: All About Lawns

Florida–Homosassa Springs: Homosassa Springs Wildlife Park, Gail and Bob
Florida–Okeechobee: Marty Gross, CML Communications, Pilgrim Construction
Florida–Panama City: Kristina–Channel 7
Florida–Santa Rosa Beach: Rita and Ernest
Florida–Tallahassee: Tara–Tallahassee TV, John, Anita, Michael, Oliver, Mamie
Florida–Tampa: Nerissa Prest–Channel 10
Florida–Tarpon Springs: Marty and Fran, Mitch, Joyce and Arnie, Mark
Florida–Wakulla: Primitive Baptist Church, Deshea and Derisha
Florida–West Brandon: La Quinta
Florida–Zolfo Springs: Susan–Pioneer Park Cracker Trail Museum, Pioneer Restaurant
Georgia–Hiawassee: Spin Lite Cycling
Mississippi–Lucedale: Sandy, Kan Kan Boutique, Candice and Billy, Ms Melinda, Pat and Bridget
North Carolina–Raleigh: Harding
South Carolina–Greenville: Hal and Mason
South Carolina–Longcreek: Magley family

Lucedale, Mississippi to Slaton, Texas
United States:
Georgia–Hiawassee: Lyle–Spin Lite Cycling
Kentucky–Mount Vernon: IMAX radio
Louisiana–Jena: Jena Church
Louisiana–Hagewood: Mr Bergeron
Louisiana–Natchitoches: Ms Vicky and Ms Vera, Grayson's Bar-b-que, Chief of Police
Louisiana–Tullos: Chuck's
Louisiana–Winnfield: Mr and Mrs Ferguson, Jerry–Chevrolet Dealership
Mississippi–Brookhaven: Trish–Chevron
Mississippi–Bude: First Baptist Church, Brad Moak, Dr Larkin
Mississippi–Hattiesburg: Dan's Truck Stop
Mississippi–Jackson: Barbara
Mississippi–Monticello: Atwood Waterpark, Pam and Bill, Bo, Lawrence County
Mississippi–Natchez: Hampton Inn, Natchez Democrat, Janelle Williams, Sally–Natchez Visitor Center, Natchez Coffee Company, Cock-of-the-Walk, Natchez Police Department, Becky, Mayor of Natchez
Mississippi–Prentiss: Officer Steven
Oklahoma–Weatherford: Kay and Wesley
Texas–Abilene: Abilene Newspaper, Howard
Texas–Albany: City Park, Hubbard House Café
Texas–Anson: Greg, Coffee Bean Café

Texas–Centerville: Sondra–Yellow Rose of
Texas Ranch
Texas–Clifton: City Park, Mayor Fred
Texas–Crockett: Fire Department, Fire Chief,
Christian and Dusty Cockerell, EMT crew
Texas–Dallas: REI Dallas
Texas–DeLeon: Linda and Mike Flora,
Savannah, Ray
Texas–Dublin: Dublin High School
Texas–Eastland: McDonald's
Texas–Etoille: Spencer family
Texas–Flo: Flo Community Center, Macy
Texas–Groesbeck: RV Park, Exxon Filling
Station, Mary's Breakfast and Burger Barn,
Mary and Willy
Texas–Hico: Willemina
Texas–Iredell: Iredell Café, Rancher Mike
Texas–Justiceburg: Burnham Country Store
and Grill
Texas–Mart: Lynd Auto Parts
Texas–Meridian: Bosque County News, Cactus
Grill
Texas–Milam: Milam Settlers Park, Sandra and
Bill–Sandra's Hamburgers
Texas–Roby: First Baptist Church, Bob
Texas–Slaton: Altman family, Slatonite
Texas–Snyder: Jeff and Michele, Kenny
Texas–Speegleville: Ashraf
Texas–Spicewood: Michael and Amanda
Cromer
Texas–Waco: Larry–Bicycles Outback

Slaton, Texas to San Diego, California
Mexico: Rosarito: Annie and Caitlyn
Netherlands:Nieuwegein: Wâtte
United States:
Arizona–Bouse: Rhode Island, Missouri, New
York
Arizona–Buckeye: Officer Kelly
Arizona–Cactus Forest: Rancho Sonora,
Officer Hansen
Arizona–Catalina: Wishing Well
Arizona–Parker: Early Bird Café
Arizona–Phoenix: Gila River Indian Reser-
vation, Carol, Jean and Chuck Magley,
Audrey, Gill and Lily
Arizona–Salome: Shefflers Inn
Arizona–Wintersburg: Karrilee, Sydney, Riley
California–Encinitas: Manager Pam–McDon-
ald's, Kevin, Melissa, Kai, Mae
California–Escondido: Ray and Rosemary
California–Hemet: Joe and Ed–Boy Scouts
California–Malibu: Don and Scott
California–Palm Springs: David and Leanne,
Javier

California–San Diego: James–San Diego Zoo,
Todd, Pat and George, Mr Mandaric
California–San Jacinto: Rex family

California–Temecula: John, Rosa, Anna, David
and Cathie, Big Boy's
California–Twentynine Palms: Pete's, Twenty-
nine Palms Police
California–Valle Vista: Ed and Chris
California–Yucca Valley: Dennis and Tami,
Bandit and Punky, Carl and Vivian
Georgia–Atlanta: Fred
Georgia–Hiawassee: Lyle–Spin Lite Cycling
New Mexico–Albuquerque: Jim, Kevin Bobb,
Kevin, Mark, Joe, Kay, Paul, Dave, Steve
and Jennifer
New Mexico–Bernardo: Howard and Heidi
New Mexico–Clovis: Amy and Travis, Scott,
Kim, Isaiah, Madelin
New Mexico–Encino: Fire Station, Mayor
Gordo and Martha
New Mexico–Fort Sumner: Missy and Gary,
Rodeo Grill
New Mexico–Melrose: Judy and Ron, Jamee,
Andrea
New Mexico–Mountainair: Turner Inn, Ruth
and Kevin–Turner Inn
New Mexico–Santa Fe: Fletcher, Rhonda,
Alicia
New Mexico–Santa Rosa: Salado Canyon
Guest Ranch, Jon and Suzanne
New Mexico–Socorro: Patrick and Catherine
New Mexico–Taiban: Post master lady
New Mexico–Texico: Chauntal and Steve, A
Me D's, Fire Station, Josh, Zach, Nick, Fire
Chief Lewis, Hal and Gloria
New Mexico–Vaughn: Peggy, Penny's Diner,
Desert Motel
Oregon–Eugene: Burley
South Carolina–Duncan: Steve and Beverly
Texas–Amherst: Kees and Piertsje–5 Star Dairy
Texas–Littlefield: Howell family
Texas–Lubbock: Christy and Jon Moreland,
Tech Café, News Channel 11, Kenneth
Texas–Muleshoe: Muleshoe Rotary Club,
Channel 6, George
Texas–Sudan: Church of Christ, Mrs Kerr,
Terry, Foodjet, Kendel

San Diego, California to Crescent City,
California
United States:
California–Aptos: Kathleen, Mary
California–Cambria: Alan, Nora, Cambria
Bicycle Outfitters, Mike and Kathy,

Cambria Fire Department, Linn's Bakery

California–Camp Pendleton: Jeff, Erin, George, Audrey

California–Carmel: Bob and Heather

California–Carpenteria: Holiday Inn Express

California–Cayucos: Brown Butter Cookie Company

California–Cloverdale: Sher and Steve, Vintage Towers

California–Corte Madera: David and Kia

California–Costanoa KOA: Jacob and Greta, Mike and Ester, Alexis

California–Crescent City: Village Camper Inn, Officer Depee, Fishermans Restaurant

California–Elephant Seal Beach: Milton

California–Encinitas: Kevin, Melissa, Kai, Mae, Victoria, Sullivan

California–Fortuna: Ambrosini Elementary School

California–Goleta: Motel 6, Chris

California–Guadelupe: Guadelupe K–9 Unit with Atza

California–Half Moon Bay: Len

California–Healdsburg: Brad and Trinidad

California–Hopland: Solar Living Institute, Bluebird Café

California–Huntington Beach: Jim

California–Klamath: Yurok Tribal Police

California–Larksfield: George–Big Boys Buns and Burgers

California–Laytonville: Kosta and Rhonda, Shady Nook Snack Bar, Josh, Uncle Ros

California–Leggett: Drive Thru Tree, Marshall, John, Sean

California–Lompoc: Jim

California–Long Beach: Robert and Carrie

California–Los Osos: Pat, Deanne

California–Malibu: Eric and Christy, Spruzzo, Emmett Finch

California–Marina: REI, Brian, Tony

California–Mendocino: Cally–Little River Inn

California–Monterey: Melanie, Jon, Noah, Hannah, Devian Gilbert–Asana Cycles, Kate Spencer, Velo Club Monterey, Dennis

California–Novato: Troy, Novato Middle School

California–Oceanside: Bob and Vicky, James

California–Pepperwood: John and Marge, Ms Lois

California–Petaluma: Scott and Suzan, Carolyn and Tom, Petaluma Wheelmen, Pizzicato Pizza, Manager Jen–Club One,

Joe, Press Democrat, Argus–Courier, Maloneyville, Grant Elementary School, Bill Harrison and Bill Harrison, Papa John and Jean, Petaluma Pete, Quintessence, Greg and Yuri–Bike Monkeys, Art Ibleto–Pasta King, Tiffani, Michel

California–Redondo: Mark

California–Salinas: Gwen and Dave

California–San Diego: Todd, Doug–Channel 8

California–San Francisco: NBC, Derek, Jim, Tony, Golden Gate Police Department, Jun

California–San Francisco Bay: Channel 11, Mike Sugarman–CBS5

California–Santa Maria: Suzanne

California–Santa Rosa: Dianne and Alex–Safari West, KZST Radio, Molly–Safari West

California–Sebastopol: Elizabeth

California–Torrance: John, Yumi, Shane, Nanami, Thomas Kirk

California–Ukiah: Daily Journal, Schat's Bakery

California–Ventura: Steve, Morna, Alec, Harry, Byron Cherry, Blooms, Mr Biker

California–Westhaven: Mario and Adrian

California–Willits: Willits KOA, Tom and Colleen

Florida–Melbourne: Gig and family

Washington–Spokane: Theresa and Carl

Crescent City, California to Port Angeles, Washington

United States:

California–Crescent City: Nancy

Georgia–Hiawassee: Lyle–Spin Lite Cycling

Oregon–Astoria: Scott and son, Fort George Brewery, Vern and friends

Oregon–Brookings: Wild Rivers Motorlodge, Officer Larry and family, Wild River Pizza Company

Oregon–Cambria: Mike and Kathy

Oregon–Canby: Church of Nazarene, Don&wife, Jilly, Scott

Oregon–Coos Bay: Bill and Barb, Gib's RV Superstore, Allen, Heather, Grace, Annie

Oregon–Coos Bay/North Bend: KCBY

Oregon–Deer Island: Tom and Margie

Oregon–Elkton: Elkton RV Park, Tomasilo's, Joan and Jeff, Arlene's Café

Oregon–Eugene: Burley, Randi–Register Guard

Oregon–Gladstone: Shari's

Oregon–Gold Beach: Karen and Scott–Indian Creek Resort, Double D's Café
Oregon–Halsey: Julie, Delaney, Jaden
Oregon–Independence: Andy's Café
Oregon–Junction City: Elaine, Tom, Greta, Sophie, Meggie
Oregon–Langlois: West Coast Game Park
Oregon–Lorane: Lorena's Café
Oregon–North Bend: Moe's Bicycle Store, Mom's Kitchen, Dave
Oregon–Port Orford: Ernie and Holly
Oregon–Portland: Angela, Craig, Libby, Ellie, Clementine, Carolyn, KEEN Footwear, Fox News Channel, Liza–KPFF, Peg, Beth and Joe, Jody, Pretty Dress Ride Group
Oregon–Salem: Josh, Cedar, Ainsley, Britta, Luca
Oregon–Twin Oaks: Twin Oaks Elementary School, Principal Soberman
Oregon–Winchester Bay: Ms Edith
South Carolina–Duncan: Steve and Beverly
Washington–Amanda Park: Lake Quinault Inn, JJ's
Washington–Artic: Armenian Couple
Washington–Bear Creek Campground: Kristal
Washington–Cape Disappointment: Eddie
Washington–Forks: Pizzaria customers
Washington–Humptulips: Promised Land Campground, Josh and Jeremy
Washington–Kalaloch: Chris and Debbie
Washington–Mt Rainier: Ellen
Washington–Port Angeles: Quality Inn, Steve and Mirja, Lynn, Bella Italiano Restaurant
Washington–Sequim: Mr&Mrs Cockerell
Washington–Willapa: Ranger Marianne–Willapa Wildlife Refuge Center

Port Angeles, Washington to Fairbanks, Alaska
Canada:
British Columbia–Brentwood: Earl and Anne
British Columbia–Campbell River: Niels, Kelly, Jarred
British Columbia–Canada One: Sue's Luncheon
British Columbia–Esquimalt–Victoria: Renaat and Krista
British Columbia–Fernwood–Victoria: Esther, Alberto, Soledad, Paloma
British Columbia–Gabriola Island: Paul, Michelle, Thea, Rosie, Slow Rise Bakery, Brent G Hair and Spa, April, Brent, Micah
British Columbia–Ladysmith: Bruce and Mike
British Columbia–Mill Bay: Ken and Susan, Irmgard and Ron

British Columbia–Nanaimo: Ben, Charlene, Noah, A–channel, SHAW news, Frederic and Faith, Uplands Bakery, Homeschool group
British Columbia–Qualicum Beach: John&wife, Dan and Richard
British Columbia–Rathtrevor: Gary and Shaula, Marcella
British Columbia–Royston: Sharon and Sig
British Columbia–Sayward Junction
British Columbia–Swanigan Lake: Paul, Lynne, Angela
British Columbia–Vancouver: Greta
British Columbia–Victoria: CHEK, WannaWaffle, Richard&wife, Bike to Work week, Mike–Fernwood Inn, A–news, Margaret
British Columbia–Woss: Kiwasa Café
Yukon Territory–Whitehorse: Lexi
Germany: Rudy
Netherlands–Friesland:Pake en Beppe
United States:
Alaska–Anchorage: Erin, James, Owen, Salmon Berry Tours, Anchorage Zoo
Alaska–Anderson: Allen and Erika, Brad
Alaska–Byers Creek: Byers Creek Lodge
Alaska–Denali National Park: Chelsea and Jacob, Abby, Park Rangers
Alaska–Denali town: Denali Raft Adventures
Alaska–Ester: Ester Fire Department, Tom and family–Calypso Farms, David and Norma Runfola, Ester Community Park
Alaska–Fairbanks: Bob and Melissa, Casey–Hampton Inn, Laurie, Puz, Barbara, Mrs Lou Williams, Joe Williams
Alaska–Healy: David and Martha
Alaska–Honolulu Creek: Ms Honolulu and family
Alaska–Inside Passage: GiGi and PaPa
Alaska–Juneau: Donna's Restaurant, Ms Mary, James, Anji, Macon, Max, Nora, George
Alaska–Mile 224: Creekside café
Alaska–Nenana: Kristi's Cuisine
Alaska–North Pole: Cindy Webb
Alaska–Palmer: Homestead RV Park
Alaska–Talkeetna: Karen and Mike, Rahla, Paul–Talkeetna Air Taxi
Alaska–Trapper Creek: Trapper Creek Inn and RV Park, Bob, Jennie, Jason
Alaska–Wasilla: Mat-Su Dental Lab, Roger and

Mason, Loraine and Casey–Ma-Su Visitor Center, Metro Café, Laurie and Fred, Duane and family
Alaska–Willow: Willow Community Center, Rhodi–Big Susitna B&B
Alaska–Yakutat: Geoff and Rebecca
Colorado–Boulder: Colorado Couple
Indiana: Marlin and cousin
Michigan–Holland: Bob and Lois
Washington–Bellingham: Gary, Stacy, Naomi, Mackinzy
Washington–Port Angeles: Zane
Washington–Seattle: Auggie
Washington–Walla Walla: Musick family

TANGIBLE GIFTS
China: Wu Yinlong
India: Uttar Pradesh–Lucknow: Online Learning Solutions
United Kingdom: Avon–Bristol: Christopher Speller
United Kingdom: Bristol–Montpelier: Christopher Duncan
United Kingdom: Kent–Broadstairs: T.M. Staynes
United Kingdom: Leicestershire–Leicester: David Gray
United Kingdom: Swansea–Swansea: Loca Records
United States:
    District of Columbia–Washington: Eileen McCarthy
    Alabama–Fairhope: Sally Wall
    Alaska–Anderson: Allen Miller
    Arizona–Phoenix: Carol Harris, Chad Kurtzman, Michael Spandau
    Arizona–Pinedale: Terri Brewer
    Arizona–Prescott Valley: Thomas Swinford
    California–Alamo: Judy Flick
    California–Albany: Linda H. Rugg
    California–Aptos: Julie Ales
    California–Banning: Todd Partridge
    California–Burbank: Stella Rose
    California–Carlsbad: Eugene Schwartz, Gary Seiler, Kelly Salmon, Tim Griffin
    California–Carmel: Deborah Warcken
    California–Cloverdale: R M Cox
    California–Corte Madera: Kiran Macpherson
    California–Cotati: Harry Boatright
    California–Crescent City: Craig P Dauber, Grant Werschkul, Linda Loughridge, Mandy Duval
    California–Encinitas: Kevin McClave
    California–Fremont: Stuart Rohnstock
    California–Glen Ellen: Julie Skinner

California–Inglewood: Pan Zhuo
California–Los Angeles: Joan Cathey
California–Malibu: Christine Orloff
California–Mill Valley: Keith Buckley
California–Monterey: Dennis & Martha Renault, Maria Megnin, Steve Anderson, Velo Club Monterey, Inc
California–Moreno Valley: Javier Huizar
California–Occidental: John Michael Bohm
California–Oceanside: Kristen Sleboda
California–Orange: Michele Ryan
California–Oroville: LS Wright
California–Pacifica: EJ Service
California–Petaluma: Christine Ruzick, John Nelson, Lenie Metro, Ryan Schmidt, Scott Andrews, Sharon Terrel, Utility Management Services
California–Rohnert Park
California–Roseville: David Tanforan
California–Salinas: Gwen Drechsler, Terrance Ryan
California–San Francisco: John Bowers, Patricia and Duane Pellerro, Sam Christian
California–San Jose: Alan Salazar, Mary Paquet, Michael & Ester Lyddane, William Reisinger
California–San Rafael: Andy Phelps
California–Santa Rosa: Doug Johnson, Eleanor Guerin, Geoffrey Larkin, Lynn Heyer, Lynn Ravazzini, Michael McGuire, Nelson Pereira, Robert Brown, Ronnie Roche, Virginia Hughes
California–Sebastopol: Alici Petersen, Ellia O'Donnell, Gordon Ghirann
California–Solana Beach: Ruth Voorhies
California–Sonoma: Don Kreutzberger, Keith Davidson
California–Sunnyvale: Steve Lemke
California–Ukiah: Steven Lincoln
California–Woodland Hills: Alan Levy
Colorado–Arvada: Ted Hibbs
Colorado–Pagosa Springs: Paul and Kathy Henry
Colorado–Palmer Lake: Kathi Cash
Connecticut–Waterbury: Donald Surprise
Florida–Eustis: Final Embrace
Florida–Fort Pierce: Mr. & Mrs. Johannes Brolmann
Florida–Fort Walton Beach: Sarah Jones
Florida–Gainesville: Joe Haldeman
Florida–Melbourne: Gregory Muro, Jan and Anna Koper, Jan Koper, Jimmy Dean and Karen J. Terry
Florida–Miami: Rita Horton

Florida–Tallahassee: John and Joann Malloy
Florida–Vero Beach: Sharon Brennan
Georgia–Decatur: Daniel Magee
Georgia–Villa Rica: Desi Ashby
Idaho–Boise: Keri Barbero
Illinois–Yorkville: Christine Hardersen
Kentucky–Bardstowns: Lee Ladouceur
Kentucky–Berea: Barbara Prairie, Dale Van-Winkle, Granny Glenda Productions, Laura Eiselt, Sarah Hawker, Thomas and Joy Frazier, William Stolte
Kentucky–Brodhead: Frank Bradley, James Harris
Kentucky–Buckhorn: Raney and Teresa Gay
Kentucky–Livingston: Donnie Statum
Kentucky–Louisville: Mary and Robert Barnes, Misty Borders, Norah Kute, Teri Becker
Kentucky–Mount Vernon: Bob and Jane Larkey, Ron Cooper, Sarah and R. Lee Bivins, Tanner and Jenna
Kentucky–Radcliff: Gene Raymond Wilson
Kentucky–Somerset: Jim Thompson Autos, Inc
Maryland–Deal Island: Timothy Dale
Maryland–Rockville: Dennis Freezer
Massachusetts–Brookline: Katherine Edwards
Michigan–Clinton Township: Dave Bainbridge
Missouri–Columbia: Rachel Ruhlen
Missouri–New London: Harris
Missouri–St Louis: Tapei Cheng
Nebraska–Lincoln: Lee Todd
New Jersey–Glassboro: Robert Hahn
New Mexico–Albuquerque: J. Richard Sena, Michael Lucero
New Mexico–Clovis: Scott Falkner
New Mexico–Los Alamos: Joseph Tesmer
New Mexico–Sandia Park: Jim Devenport
New York–Yonkers: Jeanette Catala
North Carolina–Salisbury: James Walker, Kristen Isaacs
North Carolina–Wilmington: Thomas Clarke
North Carolina–Winston-Salem: Precision Part Systems
Ohio–Cincinnati: Adrienne Cruise
Ohio–Columbus: Mimi Carol Davis, Vicki Hawthorne
Ohio–Gahanna: Geiger Lee
Ohio–New Paris: Heather Norton
Oregon–Brookings: Barbara Edmiston
Oregon–Coos Bay: Joan Glasgow
Oregon–Eugene: Alpha Schram, Kurt Jensen
Oregon–Keizer: John Sherwood
Oregon–Portland: Ben Salzberg
Oregon–Salem: Jacqueline Allen

South Carolina–Columbia: Stan Gomberg
South Carolina–Duncan: Beverly Swain
South Carolina–Mount Pleasant: Patricia Bennett
Tennessee–Madisonville: Shelby Diann Allison
Tennessee–Signal Mountain: Cori Hagan
Texas–Austin: Mark Mallett
Texas–Etoile: John Spencer III
Texas–Houston: Herlaina Fowler
Virginia–Alexandria: Michael Anderson
Virginia–Charlottesville: Scott and Karen Ransom
Virginia–Independence: Garnett Sturgill
Washington–Duvall: Sick Bike Parts LLC
Washington–Ilwaco: Foxglove Enterprises
Washington–Sequim: Paula Ice
Washington–South Bend: Linda Krume
Washington–Walla Walla: Bill and Becky Musick
Washington–Wenatchee: Joshua Tarr
West Virginia–Hinton: Susan Rogers

MORAL SUPPORT VIA OUR WEBSITE: WWW.PEDOUINS.ORG
Afghanistan: Blaine, Ginetta Harris
Albania: Erling
Algeria: John
Argentina: Diego, Ignacio, Sebastian Alvarez
Armenia: Ron Jackson
Autralia–Canberra: Antonia
Australia–Western Australia: Michelle
Australia: Alistair, Gary, Lucy, Zak
Belgium: Mario and Mieke
Bhutan: Lotay
Canada: British Columbia–Courtenay: Jo, Sheila
Canada: British Columbia–Duncan: Bryn
Canada: British Columbia–Gabriola: April
Canada: British Columbia–Nanaimo: Brenda, Brianna, De and Darren Rinaldi, Kamla, Mary, Mark, Kait
Canada: British Columbia–Qualicum Bay: Cat
Canada: British Columbia–Vancouver Island: Scott
Canada: British Columbia–Victoria: Renaat and Krista, Jessica
Canada: British Columbia: Ben, Bonny Jones, Cheryl Morch, Dave Donald, Don, Ian, Jonathan Bartlett, Mark, Tarah and Chris Mc Pherson
Canada: Ontario–Ottawa: Caroline
Canada: Saskatchewan–Regina: Jennifer
Canada: Angela Rafuse-Tahir, Annie, Beverley and Gary Munro, Bruce, Carol, Carolyn, Chris, Chris Gerow, Dana, Dara, Darrin

Grafton, David, Debbie, Diane, Doug, Doug and Annlee Grimson, Dustin, Erling, Faith, Florian, Rebekka, Chan, Frankie, Frederic, Gaby, Gary, Heidi, Hugh, Ingrid, Jacques Gobeil, James, Jawn, Jeff Posted, Jennifer, Jf Tousi, Jim, Jim and Marian, Joel, John, John and Marie, John South, Joho, Jonathan, Jonathan Marcotte, Ken and Eunice Gaglardi, Kimberly Plumley, Lorin, Nelson, Paloma Callo, Papa and GG, Paul, Paul MacEwen, Paul Rudan, Rich, Richard and Jacque Blache, Rick and Tanya McFerrin, Ron Richings, Sandra, Ruth, and Carl, Shaula, Shawn, Terry, Todd, Tony, Tracey, Tracy Waters, Tristan, Wendy, Wes, Winston and Ann

China–Hong Kong: David

China–Tianjin: May

China–Shenzhen: Sharon

Costa Rica: San Jose–Coronado: Max

Cuba: Kevin

Denmark: Hjorring: John

Ecuador: Ernesto and Maria, Isabel and Mateo

France–Paris: Rob

France: Wally

Germany: Julia Roder, Ruediger Fessel, Veronique Goelz

Hungary: Reku Papa

India: Karnataka–Bangalore: Gaurav, Yogesh

India: Kerala–Trivandrum: Nitin Rajan

India: Madhav

Ireland: Limerick–Cappamore: Ineke

Ireland: Munster–Limerick: Simon

Ireland: Darryl Collins

Israel: Palestine: Saif

Israel: John Dorr, Khaled Zarura, Khalid

Italy: George

Japan: Tom, Will, Yoshikatsu

Kenya: Rift Valley–Nanyuki: Jeff Pk

Kyrgyzstan: Cho Hee-song

Malaysia: Frank Shaw

Mexico: Colima–Colima: Ale and Andres Furet

Mexico: Annie

Nepal: Kathmandu: Niroj

Netherlands–Boer: Magdalena en Peter

Netherlands–Breda: Irene

Netherlands–Delft: Claudia

Netherlands–Leeuwarden: Pieter en Ieke Wijbenga, Tineke

Netherlands–Nieuwegein: Tanja en Wâtte

Netherlands–Surhuisterveen: Heit en Mem

Netherlands–Veenwoudsterwal: Fred en Jifke

Netherlands: Afina, Albert, Roderick en Saskia, Andre Bloemendaal, Annamarie, Dries

and Liz, Erwin, Hiske Tijseling, Jan, Jan and Marian, Jan en Alie Tijseling, Kirsten, Maaike and Sybren Sytsma, Sean Cody, Tante Rinnie en Omke Meine, Timo de Boer

Phillipines: Leyte–Tacloban City: Larry and Bobbie

Poland: Anna and Krzysztof

Portugal: Rui Oliveira

San Juan–San Juan: Ivana

Slovenia: Peter

South Africa: Jean-Pierre

South Korea–Seoul: Harry

South Korea: Ka-Eul

Spain: Sol

Turkey: Deniz Enul

U.S. Minor Outlying Islands: Leo and Molly McGinnis

Ukraine: Victor

United Arab Emirates: Iftakhar

United Kingdom–Derbys–Ilkeston: Anne

United Kingdom–London: Brian Lavery

United Kingdom: Camilla, Clare, James Proud, Jim, Jonathan, T. Michael

United States:

Alabama–Tuscaloosa: Bryan Martin

Alabama: Howard and Helena

Alaska–Anchorage: Donna, Gail, Matt, Amy, and Emma, Michael Johnson, Raenette

Alaska–Denali National Park: Jennifer

Alaska–Eagle River: Beth

Alaska–Fairbanks: Fred, Jane, Katrina, Mercedes

Alaska–Girdwood: Misty

Alaska–Juneau: Anji

Alaska–Ketchikan: Mary

Alaska–North Pole: Jeff, Julie, Katie Keener, Mary Lou, Russell Robinson

Alaska–Soldotna: Tasha

Alaska–Talkeetna: Denise

Alaska–Trapper Creek: Robert

Alaska–Wasilla: Duane, Laurel

Alaska: Allen, Cindy, Ellie Mason, Gay, Jesse L, Johnna Underwood, Magali, Martha, Ray, Kary, Stephen, and McKinley, Richard, Trapper Creek Inn, Claudi

Arizona–Flagstaff: Janyel Pitman

Arizona–Green Valley: Robert

Arizona–Phoenix: Carol, Mary, Chuck and Jean Magley

Arizona–Pinedale: Kent and Cherylee Brewer

Arizona: Alison, Charles, Dan, Dave Boskee, Thomas, Vera

California–Arroyo Grande: Sean

California–Camarillo and Seaside: Terry Schuller

California–Cardiff by the Sea: Patrick

California–Carlsbad: Kelly

California–Cloverdale: Terry, Vintage Towers Bed and Breakfast Inn

California–Corte Madera: David

California–Cotati: Reshma

California–Crescent City: Larry, Lu Ella, Monica

California–Danville: Lisa

California–Del Mar: Connie

California–El Portal: Karen and Paul

California–El Segundo: Scott

California–Encinitas: Michelle

California–Escondido: Pam

California–Forest Knolls: Doug

California–Fort Bragg: Marieke

California–Fulton: Nancy

California–Glen Ellen: Julie

California–Hemet: Bill, Jacqueline C., Jess and Donna Freeland

California–Huntington Beach: Carl and Joyce, Janet

California–Kelseyville: Cody

California–Lafayette: Len

California–Lake Arrowhead: Leslie

California–Los Angeles: Heather Budman

California–Malibu: Amy and Tim Webb, Eric

California–Marina: Ben

California–Monterey: D. Roth, Toni Schulman

California–Novato: Troy

California–Oceanside: Ed, Patti

California–Pacific Grove: Lacey

California–Pacifica: Mike Romano

California–Palm Springs: Javier

California–Palo Alto: Brian Koss

California–Paradise: Nicholas and Kirsten-Grace

California–Parker Dam: Fran

California–Petaluma: Carlin, Carolyn, Cheyenne, Chris, Emily, Jordan, Molly, Papa John, Ricky, Sara

California–Riverside: Nancy

California–Rohnert Park: Nicole

California–Salinas: Audrey, Dannie, Gwen, Hallie Pacheco

California–San Diego: Christa

California–San Francisco: Denise, Jim, Matt

California–San Jose: Alan, Gino

California–Santa Rosa: Cassie, Celosia, Denise, Donavan, Laura, Mario, Michael, Michelle, Steve, Thea, Nelson

California–Seaside: Janet and Jack

California–Sebastopol: Chandra, Elizabeth

California–Simi Valley: Chewy

California–Sonoma: Andy, Sanghee Davidson, Michell

California–Summerland: Christina Welch

California–Three Rivers: Linda and Tony

California–Ukiah: Paul

California–Vacaville: Linda Patrick

California–Ventura: Steve

California–Vista: Randy and Geoff

California–Watsonville: Tasha

California–Willits: Charles

California–Windsor: Jesse and Mommy, Randy, Kathy and Mary, Sandi

California–Yucca Valley: Ann, Angie, Anni, Arlene, Ashok Mukherji, Bob Padecky, Bonni, Bruce, Byron Cherry, Cally, Chris, Cindy, Colleen, Coy Duke, Derek, Diane, Greg, Gretta, Jeanie, Jeff, Jennifer, Jim, Joe and Shoshana, Joey, John, John and Gail Dammuller, Jon Curtis, Karla, Kathleen, Lauren, Lisa, Lloyd and Joan Martin, Louis, Mike, Pandoria (Pam), Robert, Russell, Scott, Sher and Steve Tice, Susan, Suzanne, Tammy and John, Tim, Tom and Karen, Victoria

Colorado–Aurora: Laura, Caitlin and Cara, Steve

Colorado–Canon City: Leah

Colorado–Longmont: Denise

Colorado–Thornton: Michael Mullins

Connecticut–Lakeville: JoAnn

Connecticut: Robert

Florida–Bell: Sherry

Florida–Blountstown: Alyssa and Destiny, LaTosha, Paul and Annalyn

Florida–Boca Raton: Joe

Florida–Bowling Green: Ron and Lori

Florida–Cocoa Beach: Annetta Gross

Florida–Crystal Beach: Arnie, Joyce, Bill

Florida–Fort Pierce: Wally and Betty, Jonathan Hart

Florida–Hutchinson Island: Wally

Florida–Indian Harbour Beach: Brianna

Florida–Jacksonville: Fernando and Josie, Jasmine

Florida–Jacksonville Beach: Gary and Luann

Florida–Lake Placid: Jim, Ranger Brenda, Tiffani

Florida–Lakeland: Jordan, Liz

Florida–Melbourne: Chrissy, Jan and Anna Koper, Noni, Robin and the Gang

Florida–Melbourne Beach: Eileen and Gary, Wiley T.

Florida–Niceville: Adrian and Ashlee Bears

Florida–Ocala: Thomas
Florida–Okeechobee: Jackie
Florida–Palm Bay: Becky
Florida–Palmetto: Kris
Florida–Pensacola: Mae
Florida–Ponte Vedra Beach: Luke
Florida–Port Saint Lucie: Gail, Michele,
    Nancy, Rebekah
Florida–Rockledge: Jeri
Florida–Santa Rosa Beach: Judi Rutland,
    Murray
Florida–Satellite Beach: Mary
Florida–Sebring: RoseMarie, Tully
Florida–Stuart: Janet Porter
Florida–Titusville: Caleigh, Imperial Estates
    Elementary School, Melanie, Shawna
Florida–Valkaria: Wally
Florida–Vero Beach: Katie Lee, Lauren
Florida: Angela Mercer, Brenda Janus,
    Deborah Orr, Faye, Glenn, Kelly, Linda Vil-
    larreal Zehr, Sarah, Lisa
Georgia–Adairsville: Carson
Georgia–Athens: Doug
Georgia–Atlanta: Fred
Georgia–Ellijay: Ashton
Georgia–Ft Stewart: Brennan
Georgia–Hazlehurst: Hannah
Georgia–Jekyll Island: Alex
Georgia–Woodbine: Donna
Georgia: Barbara, Christopher, Donna
Hawaii: Janet
Illinois–Chicago: Brad, Patrick, Stephy
Illinois–Libertyville: Brett Lichty
Indiana: Alexis, Betty J.
Iowa–Dubuque: Jenny
Kentucky–Bedford: Hannah
Kentucky–Berea: Barbara, Bayla, Geoffrey,
    Glenda, Jenna, Maureen, Patricia, Ralph,
    Sara, Tanner, Tom and Joy
Kentucky–Brodhead: Mrs. Jennifer Adkisson's
    First Grade Class
Kentucky–Buckhorn: Tammy
Kentucky–Clay City: Lucille
Kentucky–Corbin: Karen
Kentucky–Covington: Cara
Kentucky–Elkton: Kyla
Kentucky–Hawesville: Kim
Kentucky–Hindman: Julia
Kentucky–Jackson: Caleb, Morgan, Johnathan
Kentucky–Lewisburg: Karyn, Miranda
Kentucky–Lexington: Cathy
Kentucky–London: Joyce
Kentucky–Louisville: Asher, Beth, Bob, John,
    Linda, Misty, Teri, William

Kentucky–Morehead: Chrissy
Kentucky–Mount Vernon: Chandler and
    Mommy, Noah, Tim Roberts, Delores, Lee
    and Sarah, Ms. Darlena
Kentucky–Mt. Washington: Pattie
Kentucky–Nancy: Cynthia
Kentucky–Oneida: Darrell Glenn
Kentucky–Pine Knot: Kemen
Kentucky–Radcliff: Gene R. Wilson
Kentucky–Renfro Valley: Marty Brooker,
    Renfro Valley KOA
Kentucky–Russellville: Alyssa, David, Megann,
    Shannon
Kentucky–Somerset: Caleb, Jordyn, Justin,
    Kendra, Patrick, Ross
Kentucky–Tateville: Evelyn
Kentucky–West Liberty: Jacen, Jordan
Kentucky–Whitley City: Raylee, Nikki,
    Tammy and Rusty
Kentucky–Winchester: Joy, Susan
Kentucky: Bob, Carla, Joe, Lee, Paula, Teresa
    Gay, Teresa & Raney and family
Kentucky and Florida–Louisville and Destin:
    Dee Ann and Sven Ekman
Louisiana–Brusly: Taylor, Melissa, Preston
Louisiana–Gonzales: Olivia, Lance
Louisiana–Vidalia: Cappy
Louisiana–Waterproof: Mariah
Louisiana: Vee, Judith
Maryland–Baltimore: Emma
Massachusetts–Boston: Victoria Merriman
Michigan–Clinton Twp: David
Michigan–Farmington Hills: Nicole
Michigan–Lansing: Katherine, Meghan
Michigan–Novi: Josh
Michigan–Parma: Gabe
Michigan–Riverview: Brooke, Rob and Rhyse
Minnesota–Saint Peter: Halla
Mississippi–Brookhaven: Judy
Mississippi–Bude: Ty
Mississippi–Lucedale: Pat
Mississippi–Meadville: Willie
Mississippi–Monticello: Susan
Mississippi–Natchez: Elisha, Janelle
Mississippi–New Augusta: Cornelia
Mississippi–Prentiss: Darrick and Tammy
    Linton, Missy
Mississippi: Billy and Candice Mitchell,
    Brenda and Andrea, Weeds and Things
Missouri: Kelly
Nevada: Robin
New Jersey–Glassboro: Robert
New Jersey–Hillsborough: Leo
New Jersey–Seaside Heights: James Gillen

New Jersey: Ruth
New Mexico–Albuquerque: Havah, Kevin,
 Cindy and Spencer
New Mexico–Clovis: Earl
New Mexico–Guadelupe County: Jonathan
New Mexico–Melrose: Andrea Bako
New Mexico–Santa Fe: Fletcher, Rhonda,
 Alicia, Laura
New Mexico–Socorro: Ephraim, Wes
New Mexico: Chauntal, Gina, Keith, Liz,
 Suzanne
New York–Lansing: Wendy
New York–Yorktown Heights: Bryan M.
North Carolina–Cramerton: Sherry
North Carolina–Hayesville: Candice and
 Weymon
North Carolina–Laurel Springs: Pam
North Carolina–Raleigh: Dianna
North Carolina–Salisbury: Kristen
North Carolina: Mr. and Mrs. Brad
North Dakota–Fargo: Vanessa
Ohio–Bladensburg: Kevin and Kris, Kris,
 Kristine
Ohio–Cincinnati: Adrienne C, Steve and
 Grace
Ohio–Eastlake: Connor
Ohio–Greenville: Alan and Betty
Ohio–Reynoldsburg: Brittany
Ohio–Troy: Tim
Ohio: Bill
Oregon–Astoria: Jeannette
Oregon–Brookings: Barbara
Oregon–Canby: Pastor Chuck Dye
Oregon–Clatskanie: Kris Lillich
Oregon–Coos Bay: Joan
Oregon–Eugene: Darin, Geno, Juli, Larry
Oregon–Gold Beach: Becky
Oregon–Government Camp: Sara
Oregon–Hillsboro: Kim
Oregon–Mt Hood: Mary
Oregon–Newberg: Maxine
Oregon–Oregon City: Shaun
Oregon–Portland: Kristie, Mr. G's 8th grade
 Class, Carolyn, Duane
Oregon–Redmond: Jessica
Oregon–Rogue River: Julee
Oregon–Salem: Bobbi, Josh and Cedar
 McMurrin, Trudy
Oregon: Aaron and Laura Beese, Adam, Alan,
 Alpha, Angela, Dave, Edith, Geri, Jane,
 Jane and John, John and Belladona, Larry,
 Principal at Twin Oaks Elementary, Sarah,
 Tom and Margie, Wayne

Pennsylvania–Bethlehem: Marie
Pennsylvania–Downingtown: Mike
Pennsylvania–Gouldsboro: Joe-Lee A Maitin
Pennsylvania–Harrisburg: Bob and Eileen
Pennsylvania–Reading: Sharon
Pennsylvania–Scranton: Jen
Pennsylvania–Sunbury: Cheyenne
South Carolina–Anderson: Allen, Whit
 Landreth
South Carolina–Charleston: Ivey Dunaway
 Lynn
South Carolina–Little Mountain: Michael and
 Marcie
South Carolina–Longcreek: Howard, Katie,
 Martha, Mary Eunice, Sarah, Scott, Polly
South Carolina–McCormick: Albert, Allisa,
 Destiny
South Carolina–Rock Hill: Mae
South Carolina–Westminster: Amanda
South Carolina: Ann Widener, Bill and
 Barbara Olendorf, Margaret
Tennessee–Brentwood: Carol
Tennessee–Cleveland: Jonathon
Tennessee–Harriman: Chris
Tennessee–Kingston: John
Tennessee–Knoxville: Tammy
Tennessee–Louisville: Isaac
Tennessee–Mount Juliet: Lee Ann
Tennessee–Rockwood: Alyssa
Tennessee–Sweetwater: Craig and Callie
Tennessee–Tazewell: Dave, Eva
Tennessee–Tellico Plains: Margaret, Marjorie
Tennessee: Lee
Texas–Abilene: Pamela
Texas–Houston: Jimmy
Texas–Iredell: Mark
Texas–Lubbock: Christy Moreland, Lariesha/
 Jerry, Tiffany
Texas–Lufkin: Butch, Gloria
Texas–Mansfield: Austin
Texas–Sudan: Norma Burnett, Pat and Patsy
 Kent
Texas: Elaine, Reuben, Stephanie
Utah–West Valley City: Criss
Vermont–Burlington: Carmen
Virginia–Chantilly: Brooke
Virginia–Falls Church: Eric Rice-Johnston
Virginia–Norfolk: Gnome
Washington–Bellingham: Linda
Washington–Forks: Annhelica, Caitlynn
Washington–Newcastle: Alison
Washington–Olympia: Seth
Washington–Richland: Johanna

Washington–Seattle: Augustin, Mark
Washington–Sequim: Myrna, Steve and Stephanie Vieira
Washington–Vancouver: Erika
Washington–Woodinville: Brad, Esther
Washington: Auky, Charlotte C Valbert, Joseph, Kathryn, Kimberly, Natalie, Steve, Tim
West Virginia–Hinton: Susan Rogers
West Virginia: Wilma
Wisconsin: Zac
United States: David (Claremont), Aaron Brattstrom, Alastair Humphreys, Alexa, Alice, Alisha, Allie, Amanda Cannon, Amanda Osad, Amber, Amber Topham, Amos, Amy, Amy, Elliott, Miles and Clara, Andrea, Andrew, Andrew and Tracyann George, Andrew Spencer, Angel Hess, Angela Pless, Anita, Ann, Ann and Bill, Ann Ralston, Anne, Anneclaire, Anni, Annie, Anthony, Anthony Cooper, April, Armando Varela, Ashleigh, Ashley, Autumn, Ayesha Faines, Azenith Smith, Barbara, Becca, Ben Garrett, Benjamin J. Comin, Bert, Betsy, Beverly A. Maizland, Biking Viking, Bill (motorcyclist), Bill Eastman, Bill Harrison, Bill Leslie, Bill S, Bill Stolte, Blake, Blisseth, Bob and Jane, Bob DeCamp, Bob Martin, Bob Mitchell, Bobbie and Mike, Bobby Bishop, Brad, Brad and Becky Cleghorn, Brad and Donna Shepherd, Braeden, Brandy DeLuca, Brenda, Brett, Brett Roncelli, Brian, Brian Pangburn, Brittany, Bronson, Brooks, Bruce, Bruce Harrison, Bryan and Kathy, Buck, Buzz, Cady, Cammy Wesson-Cohen, Carl, Carol and Jim Janakes, Carolyn Calhoun, Carrie, Carrie Williams, Carye, Cassady, Cassandra, Cassidy, Cat, Catharine, Catherine, Cedie, Ceirinan, Celeste, Chad, Charis, Charles Korn, Charley, Charlie, Chaz, Chelsea Bond, Cheri La Rue, Cheryl, Chris, Chris, Carolyn, Cole, Christian and Caylee Casper, Christa, Christie and Tim, Christine, Christy, Chuck, Chuck Fulton, Cindy Webb, Clint, Collene, Corey Stout, Craig, Cricket, Crystal Ogletree, Dale, Dale and Nancy, Dan, Dan and Deb Bainbridge, Dan T, Dana, Daniel Anggrianto, Danielle Greenspoon-Lebbink, Danny, Darlene, Darrick Linton, Dave, Dave Runfola, Dave Swinford, David, David and Gina Lawless, David and Leanne

Cooper, David Phillips, David Tanforan, David Waller, Debbie, Debbie Abrams, Debbie Bennett, Deborah, Debra, Debra Burdick–Hinton, Delores, Dennis, Dennis Magley, Diana, Diane, DJ, Donna, Donna, Donna Marchlewski, Donna Martin, Dori, Dorothy, Dorrie Williams, Doug, Douglas (Doug), Dr Brolmann, Dru, Duke Smith, Dustin, Dusty, Ed, Ed Tunison, Eddy, Edna, Edward (Eddy), Elaine Pflugh, Eleanor, Elijah, Elizabeth, Ellen, Elliott, Elmer, Emily Lee, Emma, Ericka Sexton, Erin, Erin and Jerel, Erin Axelrod, Ernest Orosco, Ernie and Holly, Finn, Fletch, Fletcher and Alicia, Frank, Frannie, Fred, Gabriel, Gail B. Mitchell, Gar, Garren, Garvin, Gary, Gary and Audrey Seiler, Gary and Cathy, Gary and Diane, Gary and Karen, Gary and Shirley, Gary Walker, Gene, Geoff, Georganne, George, George and Linda, Geri, Gerry, Gerry Fox, Giovanni, Grant, Greg, Greg Coates, Greg Hughes, Greg Wilson, Gretchen, Gus, Hailey, Hal, Hal and Veronica Howard, Hans Henning and Patricia Boerst, Harold, Harry, Hayden, Heather, Heather Ford, Heidi, Holly, Holly Sowden, Ian Schwartz, Iris, Izzy, J.A. Tisdall, Jane, Jack, Jacob Stone, Jack and Phyllis, Jacqueline Winter, Jacqui Brumley, Jake (Mount Vernon), Jaki Oliphant, James, Jamie, Jamie Chatman, Jamie Moore, Jan, Janelle, Jason, Jay, Jean, Jeff, Jeff Brady, Jeff Richardson, Jeff Spahn, Jeffrey, Jeffrey M Tuttle, Jeni, Jennefer, Jennifer (Bristol), Jenny Raye Beach, Jerry, Jerry and Brenda Rice, Jerry Olinger, Jersey Jim, Jesse Walters, Jesse, Noah and Anna, Jessica, Jessica Oliver, Jessie, Jim, Jim (Lake Forest), Jim and Carol, Jim and Susan, Jim and Valarie Fairchild, Jim Whitford, Jim+Amy Sullivan, Jimmy, Jo, Joan, JoAnn, Joanne, Joe, Joe (Boston Joe), Joe Tatosky, Joeanne, Joe Nancy Carlson, Joette Marley, Joey, John, John and Linda Houston, John Sherwood, John Spencer, John Vogel, Jolynn McClary, Jon, Jonathan, Jonathan Bowen, Jonathan Glass, Joseph, Joy and Tom, Joyce, JP, Judi, Judy, Judy and Bob De Boer, Judy Starkey-Saylor, Julia, Julie, Julie and Erica Ales, Julie Dickey, Julio Carrillo, June, Justeena, Justin, Justin Christopher, Justin Tooke, Kaaren Westlund, Karalyn, Karen, Karin,

Kassie, Kate, Katelynn (Mount Vernon), Kathleen, Kathryn, Kathy, Kathy Abney, Kathy Jackson, Kathy Means, Katie Chan, Katie Doyle, Kay, Kay Wesley Weast, Kayla, Keith, Keith and Kay Euhus, Kelley, Kelly, Ken, Ken and Sharon–Ann, Ken Henjum, Kenneth, Kenneth C., Kerri, Kevin, Kevin Bobb, Kevin Brinkley, Kevin Holder, Kim, Kimber, Kimberly, Kit, Kris, Kristin, Kristy, Kurt, Kylie, Larry, Larry Burdette, Larry Depee (CHP Officer), Larry Thornton, Laura, Lauren, Lauren Tibbitts, Lauri, Laurie, Laurie Klein, Lea, Leara Harvey, Lee, Lee Ann Bowman, Leo, Leona, Leslie, Leslie (Naples), Leslie Ann Paris, Lilian, Liliana, Lillian and Lute Wheeler, Linda, Linda Robertson, Lindy, Lisa, Lisa Molnar, Lisa Shivel, Lisa Tuomi, Liz Victor, Liza, Lloyd, Lloyd Kreider, Lois, Lori, Louise, Luella, Lyle and Diane, Lynn, Maggie, Makenna Williams, Maloneyville, Margie, Margo, Mari Lynch Dehmler, Mariela, Marjorie, Mark, Marlin, Martha, Martha Frazier Krempel, Martha Gamble, Martin, Marty, Marty and Jerry, Marty and Joan, Mary, Mary Ann, Mary Beth Smetzer, Mary Stuart, Mason, Matt, Matt and Renee, Matt Clarke, Matt Wall, Matthew, Max, Maya, McKinley, Melanie, Melba, Melinda, Melissa, Melissa and Jose, Melissa Hartigan, Melissa Littrell, Merlin, Mia, Michael, Michael and Eve, Michelle, Mike, Mike and Daphne, Mike and Ester, Mike and Karen Sears, Mike and Kathy, Mike Lucero, Mike Phillips, Mikio, Mikl, Miles and Marti, Milton, Mindi, Mischa, Missy, Missy Smith, Mo Mims, Monte, Monty, Morna, Moshe, Moss, Mrs. Wayne Hunter, Myranda, Myrna Jensen, Nancy, Naomi, Natalie, Neal, Neil Pallaver, Nelson, Nicholaus Slone, Nick, Nicole, Olivia, Page, Pam, Pat, Pat Barella, Pat Fast, Patrick, Patsy Hopkins, Patty, Paul, Paul (Dewey) and Robin, Paul and Joyce Noble, Paul Andrews, Paul Brown, Paul Gracey, Paula Ice, Peaches Hahn, Peg, Peggy, Petaluma Bob, Pete, Phil, Phyllis, Piet, Polly, Pottercraft, Rachel, Ralph, Ramon, Ramona, Randy, Randy Dolen, Randy Raybon, Ranger Mike, Ray, Ray DePouli, Raylene, Reade, Rebecca, Renee, Rev Johannes Myors, Rich, Richard, Rick and Finn, Rita, Rita and Joe, Ritch, Rob, Rob and Carrie Hertzberg (Tustin), Robert, Robin, Robin and Dewey, Rocky, Ron, Ron Herzberger, Ron Martin, Rose Johnson, Rowan, Russell, Ruth, Ryan, Sally, Sally Wall, Sandra Miller, Sandy, Sara Timberlake, Sarah Kass, Sarah Mattingly, Scott, Scott and Christiane, Sean, Sequoyah, Serena, Seth (Mount Vernon), Shalane, Shane, Shannon, Sharon, Shaun T. Cox, Shawna Cherry, Sheilia, Sherry Kennard, Shirley, Simona, Skip, Sofiya, Sondra, Spike, Staci, Stacy, Stephen, Stephy, Steve, Steve and Cyndi, Steve and Linda Kramer, Steve Vise, Steven, Stuart, Sue, Sue and Barry, Susan, Susan (Woodland Hills), Susanne Menke, Suzie, T and K, Tad, Talora Gay, Tammy, Tapia, Tara, Tarpon Tom, Ted, Teresa, Teresa Powell, Terri And Pete, Terry, Terry (Theresa), Tess, Thea Daniels, Thomas, Ti, Tim, Tim Campbell, Tim Rooney, Tim, Andrea, Marley and Lilliana, Timmy Eaton, Timothy, Toby Osborn, Todd, Todd (USMC), Tom, Tom and Linda, Tony, Tony Farao, Traci, Tracy, Tracy Spain, Travis, Trina, Troy, Troy Simpson, Uni, Valeska, Vera Baker, Vern Hall, Vicki, Vickie, Vickie Deeson, Vickie McCorkel, Vicky, Victor, Victoria Thompson, Vivian, Vivian Downs, Wade, Wade and Juanita, Wally, Wanda (Everywhere), Wanda, Waneta, Wayne, Wayne Johnson, WD, Wendy, Wes, Wil, Zak Lynch

Venezuela: Merida–Merida: Libny

Other: Ainsley, Al, Anton, Ash, Azul, Bonnie, Bonnie Ball, Bryan and Tiffany, Carolyn Casper, Chris (Bristol), Cliff, Craig Koch, Dan Simpson, Deborah Bainbridge, Doug Kolk, Felicia, Frally, Gee, George (The World), Jackie Hall, Jeff Stepp, Jeff Zeller, Jennie, Joe Barnett, Josh, Kacee, Kaitlyne , Kay Sobotka, Kit Sanders, Mace and Heather, Misty, Nynke, Phil, Rupert (Brighton), Shawna, Tamara, Tanja Smith, Tereza, Toby

Our thanks to our Facebook friends.

Our thanks to all of you who are not named above, but have been a part in our journey nonetheless. Any forgetfulness has been by mistake.

GRAPHS AND CHARTS

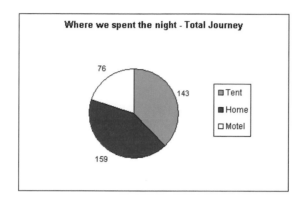

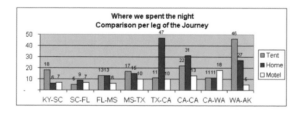

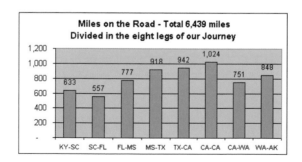

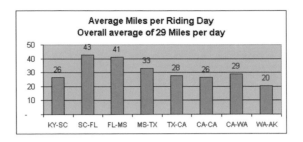

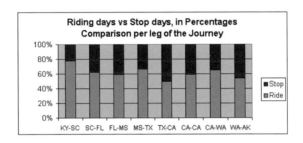